DAVID BOWIE

A ROCK 'N' ROLL ODYSSEY

PROTEUS BOOKS is an imprint of The Proteus Publishing Group

United States
PROTEUS PUBLISHING COMPANY, INC.
9, West 57th Street, Suite 4503
New York, NY 10019

distributed by:
CHERRY LANE BOOKS COMPANY, INC.
P. O. Box 430
Port Chester, NY 10573

United Kingdom
PROTEUS BOOKS LIMITED
Bremar House, Sale Place
London W2 1PT

ISBN 0 86276 221 9 (paperback)
ISBN 0 86276 222 7 (hardback)

First published in U.S. 1984
First published in U.K. 1984

Photocredits: Ace Photo Agency, Cyrus Andrews, Aquarius Literary Agency, Ian Dickson, Keystone Press Agency, Rex Features, Frank Spooner Pictures, Syndication International

Editor: Mike Brecher

Designed by: Adrian Hodgkins
Typeset by: Communitype Ltd
Printed in Great Britain
by The Chanctonbury Press

DAVID BOWIE
A ROCK 'N' ROLL ODYSSEY

KATE LYNCH

PROTEUS BOOKS
London/New York

DEDICATION

To Sonja, of course.

ACKNOWLEDGEMENTS

To the authors of the forthcoming book, *What It Means To Be A David Bowie Fan*, Natalie ('Rationalizing Lust'), Mat-Boy ('Love-Hate and the Great Snub'), Norman 'The Professor' ('I Like Pop Music') and to Chuck ('David and the Dream'). Also to Bob Sheehan, The Guys at Golden Disc, the staffs of Sounds and Freebeing, Barbara Jeff and Maggie of RCA publicity, Madeline Morel, the Mikes at Proteus, not to mention Phyllis, Diane, and Diana Clapton for *Lou Reed*. In this category there is special indebtedness to other writers on the same subject, especially to Chris Charlesworth for direct assistance, and to Charles Shaar Murray for attitude, Miles of the Black Book for the fan's-eye view and to George Tremlett for some much needed background. Likewise to several periodical writers, particularly Michael Watts, Timothy White, Tim Ferris, Cameron Crowe, Greg Mendelsohn, David Thomas, Kurt Loder and Rex Reed. There are others, so please see footnotes. Big thanks to Tim for good eyes and nimble fingers and to S.M. for what it takes. Thanks also to David Bowie for getting me around to reading, hearing and seeing certain things, and without whom this would be a rather absurd piece of fiction.

Finally to the clans Lynch, Mereu and Williams, plus friends, without whom....

INTRODUCTION

I've already said quite a lot about David Bowie in the pages that follow, but I'm quite aware that I haven't said it all. That would be impossible anyway, because Bowie can be approached and analyzed from so many angles (though he's not alone in that). Bowie put this dilemma in perspective with the comment that 'There is no definitive David Bowie.' By the same token, no definitive account is possible. You may find a sense of history somewhat lacking, and you'll have to look elsewhere for the sensational details of his life. This should become ever easier since people that were close to Bowie in the past have now begun to publish books, thereby giving more of an "insider's perspective". What I have done in general is to try to be fair, and fairly objective, and I've usually refrained from passing judgement, since the total picture of Bowie is warped when any one aspect or action is overly emphasised. He is also perpetually progressing, and I wouldn't take that away from him. Instead, I'd like to present a list of some of the words that others have used to describe Bowie, with the purpose of illustrating why I sometimes reacted ambivalently to such a contradictory and multifaceted subject.

ONE

'I am a D.J./I am what I play' ..

'D.J.' — *Lodger*

David Bowie made his first public appearance with a minimum of fanfare. The date was January 8, 1947 and he played the squawking infant David Robert Jones to an intimate audience at 40, Stansfield Road in Brixton, South London. We can only guess that he was born at night, (his birth certificate gives no time) with the moon just one day past full, though obscured by fog and mist as the weather was 'cold, becoming milder.' The news of David Jones' birth wasn't carried by any of the major papers of the day, which instead were full of stories which remind one that a war had recently ended. There were fuel and sugar shortages, executions of war criminals, shortages of ball bearings in Newcastle, an announcement of the first batch of imported Rolex watches available in seven years and classified ads specifying 'No Coupons accepted.' The film listings featured some classics enjoying their first runs. Carl Dreyer's *Day Of Wrath* and Carne's *Les Enfants du Paradis* were at the Academy and the Rialto.

There was another film showing that day which did not make a lasting impression, but which signaled a cultural trend that laid the foundations upon which rock music (and rock stardom) were built. The film was *Janie Gets Married* and the reviewer made these observations about it:

> The teenage in America has established itself as a phenomenon
> of immense importance. Films are made, fashions created,
> magazines written for it, and it surrounds itself, if the cinema is
> to be believed, with a multitude of taboos and fetishes which
> would do credit to a backward African tribe. [1]

An American who shared David Jones' birthday (though twelve years his senior), was an early teen idol and the first real rock star. In several ways David Jones would follow in the footsteps of his predecessor, Elvis Presley. Bowie was also to go beyond Presley, but there is ample basis for comparison, starting with their 'humble' beginnings.

David Bowie has always been one to alter a story for the desired effect, and this tendency to rewrite his own history extends back to his earliest years. He was to change his birthdate when it suited him, but since he will always admit to hailing from Brixton, it can be assumed

1

that he's proud of that fact, especially since he's left it so far behind. In fact, Bowie (Jones) was born into rather poor circumstances, but through the efforts of his parents his situation was never as grim as that of those around him.

At the time of David's birth, his parents were not married, since Mr. Jones had yet to be divorced from his first wife. David's father, Hayward Stenton Jones had married Hilda Louise Sullivan in 1933, and they had a daughter named Annette. Their marriage began to disintegrate during the war, and though it's not clear just when Mr. Jones met Margaret Mary Burns, their ensuing relationship might have contributed to the demise of the marriage. David's mother is still alive, but refuses to speak to anyone about herself or her son, and since David's father is dead, all we know about her are David's claims that she was an usherette in a cinema when she met Mr. Jones, and that she had a son, Terry, who was seven years older than David. Margaret Burns and Hayward Jones began living together in Brixton shortly after Mr. Jones' return from service in North Africa, and David's birth soon followed. In July 1947, Hilda Sullivan finally filed for divorce (on the grounds of adultery) and the decree became final on August 11, 1947. Thus free, Hayward Jones and Margaret Burns were married on September 12, 1947, giving David a new step-brother Terry, in addition to his half-sister Annette.

Annette and Hilda Sullivan hardly seem to figure in David's early life. He has occasionally mentioned that he has a sister, Annette, who married and moved to Egypt and that is the last that anyone ever heard of her. They apparently weren't close and hardly saw each other. As regards his mother, David has recently claimed that he feels closer to her with age, though for many years they had no relationship at all. It seems that she barely figured in Bowie's own perceptions of his childhood, and since she will not speak to anyone about her son, David's is the only point of view we have. This is also the case with her son Terry, who may or may not be alive, and if he is living is presumably still in a mental institution. David's father died in 1969 and thus his story is also lost.

The day to day life in Brixton also seems to have had some impact on David. Brixton has been compared to Harlem or the South Bronx and at that time it was composed primarily of working-class Irish and Jamaican families, many left homeless by the bombing of London. It was a lively, noisy place, and studies done on the kids just a couple of years older than David who had grown up beneath the air raids, discovered that they had grown used to the noise of the bombs and felt uncomfortable with the silence that came with the end of the war. Poverty and deprivation were commonplace at the time ('No coupons accepted') and although David claimed that he never went hungry, he saw hunger all around him. He's also mentioned that his creative instincts were encouraged, although he doesn't specify by whom. Presumably it was by his father. David's mother was picking up on another aspect of David that to many is at least as important as his creativity. As she put it to one of David's early managers: 'You know, he was always the prettiest boy in the street...

the sort of boy that all the neighbors loved.' He must have been a charmer even at an early age, and such a positive response could only have been encouraging.

In a conversation with Mick Rock, the subject of Bowie's various voices came up, how he'll switch from a 'proper' English into a broad London-not-quite-Cockney accent. As Bowie explained:

> It's all part of me general schitzophrenics. I usually do it when I'm excited, or want to emphasize things. I am real London remember. Born in Brixton in 'ouseful of blacks. I loved my childhood. [2]

Bowie also had occasion to return to Brixton as a teenager, as it was home to a lively music scene, though when he returned in 1977 to see the house that he was born in, he was too intimidated to ask to look inside. Brixton was grimmer than ever and the racial tensions were palpable.

By most accounts, David Jones only lived in Brixton until he was eight years old (Bowie occasionally says he was eleven or twelve), at which time he and his brother Terry were sent to Yorkshire. They lived there for two years with their father's brother in his ancient farmhouse near Doncaster — Mr. Jones' home town. Although life in the country must have held a certain fascination for two boys from the city, it seems that a two week visit rather than a two year stay would have been more to their liking. The pleasures of hidden rooms in the farmhouse, the open countryside and the glories of cattle soon wore thin, and they were both quite happy to return to London. In the meantime their parents had moved into a new home at 4, Plaistow Grove in suburban Bromley. It was a small terraced Edwardian home where David lived on and off until his father's death. Later, Bowie talked to journalist Patrick Salvo about this period of his middle youth and attendant moves:

> I've seen pretty well the best of both, from the terrible slum area of Brixton, with a pretty heavy Black population, to right up in the country on the farms. I've been a child through both, so that both halves of it really influenced me and produced a schizoid attitude in life. I think that's what confused me. [3]

Bowie later denied being 'schizoid' and also talked about his exposure to different classes as enlightening.

Bowie is rather forthright in describing himself as a manipulator of both the media and the truth, so it's appropriate that he refers to stories he'd heard (and retold) as his 'family mythology', which later became part of the larger 'Bowie mythology'. Like most myths, these are prone to revision, but what follows is the 'standard version' of his father's background:

> His father died and left him with a lot of money, so he put it

into a travelling theatre troupe, which lost most of the money. What was left he put into a London club for wrestlers in Soho, a nightclub that was gangster and wrestler oriented. I don't know *how* he got involved in that! Then he went into the army and when he came out he started working as a P.R. man for a charity organization (Dr. Barnardo's Children's Home), and he stayed there for the rest of his life. 4

By most accounts, David and his father were quite close, especially around the time David began his recording career. His father offered support, while not quite understanding just what David was going through. Whether it's due to an ambivalent attitude, or the fact that David felt flippant talking to Rex Reed, (knowing that Reed would eat it up) this was how he described his father — from the back of a limo during a wild night-time drive through New Mexico:

My father was a gambler and a drinker and a layabout for most of his life. I have one brother and one sister that I know about. We're all illegitimate. After I was born, they made it legal and my father went straight.

Mr. Jones remained at his straight job for the rest of his life, moving from P.R. officer to executive at Dr. Barnardo's.

Although this phase was as boring as his earlier days were sensational, some of David's actions point to a sympathy with his father and with the Children's Home. Angie Bowie tells of David gathering Christmas toys for the home, and mentions that they thought of adopting children out of David's sympathy with their plight. And perhaps David's early awareness of the art of public relations is in some way attributable to his father.

So life in Bromley found Mr. Jones working at Dr. Barnardo's, with David attending Bromley Technical High School, and brother Terry at home for part of the time. The accounts of Terry's role in David's life vary as much as those of his father. At one moment Bowie recalls being raised as an only child, with occasional 'lightweight' appearances put in by his older brother and sister. But more frequently, he attributes his budding musical interest to Terry. David mentioned this influence to George Tremlett:

It was Terry who really started everything for me. He was into all these different beat writers, and listening to jazz musicians like John Coltrane and Eric Dolphy... while I was still at school, he would go up to town every Saturday evening to listen to jazz in the different clubs, and this was all happening to him when I was at a very impressionable age... he was growing his hair long and rebelling in his own way, later travelling twice around the world as a merchant seaman, while I was still dressed up in a school uniform everyday... it all had a big impact on me. 5

Terry's musical tastes and lifestyle were having a major impact on David; his influence didn't end there. In the aforementioned interview with Rex Reed, David spoke generally about his childhood, linking his perceptions of it to his brother's condition:

> I was really out of place as a child. I've literally wiped that whole period out of my life. It's like a nightmare. One reason I've never been in analysis is that I've always been afraid of what I'd find out. My brother is in a psychiatric hospital and madness has always run through our family. I have a terrible fear it's genetic.

Terry's hospitalization didn't come until a little later, and for whatever reasons, David refuses to go into detail about his childhood, though his musical influences are more apparent and less subject to secrecy. The cool jazz that Terry introduced to David had a direct influence on him up to the formation of his first 'progressive blues' group, and 1983 found David returning to those same roots as an inspiration for his *Let's Dance* album. Terry also gave David a copy of Jack Kerouac's *On The Road*, which was admittedly a major influence. David claims that *On The Road* helped him decide on the saxophone as his instrument (painting had been his first artistic love), since the sax plays a major role in that book, serving as the soul voice of the 'beat generation'.

David obtained his first instrument at the age of twelve and, as usual, there are several accounts of this mythical moment. Some biographers state simply that 'he purchased' his first saxophone. Elsewhere, it has been described as a plastic saxophone which he either 'scraped a few pounds together' to buy, or which was a gift from his father. The stories as to why he became so obsessed point either to *On The Road*, Little Richard and/or King Curtis, who played with Little Richard and other early rockers. In fact, all of these influences probably reinforced each other. David claimed that after reading Kerouac he wanted to be just like Sal Paradise and Dean Moriority and that he almost made it, 'as much as one can within the confines of Bromley'. Another version of this story is taken from a biography issued in conjunction with David's (still Jones) first release, which states that he received a Little Richard demo via his father's secretary (who used to work in the music biz) and that he was 'knocked out', knew that music was it, and somehow got the sax. Some people claim that he still has his original instrument, be it plastic or gold.

David Jones' twelfth year was obviously a significant one; his current recollections still acknowledge it as a turning point. Speaking with David Thomas about his son Zowie, who was eleven at the time of the interview, Bowie was asked Bowie whether he had any inkling as a kid of what lay ahead, whether he had any burning ambition or feelings of being different from his friends. The thirty-six year-old, commenting on his younger self replied:

> I had every inkling. I knew from when I was about my son's age now exactly what would be happening to me, that I was going to do something very important. I didn't quite know what. At the time, I thought I was going to be a great painter, but that changed in my teens... But I really thought it was my task to do something important, and make a statement about something or another. [6]

In another interview, (this one in 1973), Bowie spoke about this period of time, saying that, 'As for my inspiration, I haven't changed my views much since I was about twelve really. I've just got a twelve year-old mentality.'

Though his consciousness has gone somewhat beyond that point, it was a decisive time for Bowie. While most kids dream of greatness and fame, he seems to have realized that he could actually achieve it, and at least had an idea of his path, as evidenced by his choice to pursue music. His consciousness of himself as an actor was probably also formulated at that point, and he became aware of his image and began to manipulate it.

Bowie was also realizing that the meek inherit nothing, and he showed an early streak of boldness in relation to his new found loves of music in general, and the saxophone in particular. David looked up the number of sax player Ronnie Ross, whom he called 'his idol' (forgetting King Curtis for the moment) and asked if Ross would give him lessons. Ross agreed and they met; David played a few bars and Ross supposedly commented: 'Right now we can start working on you, that was bloody awful!'

Evidently the lessons paid off, and by the age of fourteen, David was playing with a group of friends from Bromley Technical called George and the Dragons, whose only known appearance was at the school Christmas Pageant in 1962. Sharing the bill with them was a group called the Little Ravens featuring guitarist Peter Frampton, whose father, a master at the school and David's art teacher, had arranged the show. By most accounts, the result of this premature battle of the stars was that David stole the show. Frampton recalls the event:

> David had already become quite a hero at school, because he would bring his saxophone to school and it was generally known that he had already spent three years learning how to play it. [7]

So at the performance, David's group got top billing (even over the lost property lady singing *There's A Hole In My Bucket*) and with David playing saxophone 'the kids all stamped and cheered — he was sensational... and in the evening at the parents show, he brought the house down... no-one there had ever heard anything like it.' While

David must have been the embodiment of cool, soloing on his sax, the fact was that with so called 'trad' jazz (watered down versions of older jazz styles) enjoying its heyday, the more modern approach of the Dragons must have been a refreshing surprise.

By his own admission, around the age of fourteen, all that David thought about was sex. This may have been the basis for a scrap with friend and fellow musician George (of George and the Dragons?) Underwood, which took place around the time of the Pageant appearance. The story goes that David made a pass at Underwood's girlfriend, prompting Underwood to punch Bowie in the face, nearly causing David the loss of sight in both eyes. During a two month hospital stay, his right eye was saved, but the iris of his left eye was left permanently paralyzed in a dilated state. In Bowie's words, it's 'dodgy', causing occasional problems in the way of headaches and depth perception. The damage gave him a grey left eye (the other is blue) creating one of Bowie's more distinctive facial characteristics. Despite this incident, Bowie's friendship with the man who redesigned his face has remained excellent. Underwood subsequently designed two of Bowie's album jackets, and David claims that of all the people he knew at that point in his life, Underwood was the only one that he thought might eventually be more important than himself. He even went on to say that Underwood probably is more important but just hasn't been recognized as such.

It was while David was hospitalized that he received another blow. His brother Terry had just returned from his stint in the merchant navy (some say the R.A.F.), when he was quickly committed to an institution for an undisclosed 'mental illness'. David painted a rather surreal picture of the ensuing relationship with his brother:

> We go every fortnight and we take a hamper of sandwiches and apples, new shirts and fresh stuff. Take his laundry. And he's always very happy to see us but he never has anything to say. Just lies there on the lawn all day, looking at the sky.

Bowie's attitude to his brother's insanity has varied. Occasionally he makes light of it, saying his whole family is 'nuts', while at other times he takes it as a warning. Disparaging remarks aside, it seems that the brothers were quite close, and that Terry did indeed have a major influence on David.

During this chaotic period of his life, Bowie was also cultivating a couple of friendships that were to last for years. David was friendly with both George Underwood and Geoff McCormack from high school or earlier.

Like Underwood, McCormack remained an important figure in David's life. He made his stage presence and singing felt during the Ziggy Stardust tour, and was credited as 'Mac Cormack' for back-up vocals on *Aladdin Sane* as well as singing and touring with the Diamond Dogs Revue. This hints at a certain loyalty in Bowie (and his respect for those who can punch him out), as well as the fact that his friendships are usually with other artists, a trend which continues to this day. McCormack in particular shared David's interest in music, and Bowie attributes the nature of his music collection to his relationship with Geoff:

> A friend of mine, Jeff (sic) McCormack, who ended up as
> Warren Peace in the Diamond Dogs band, had the big ska
> record collection, and it just wasn't worth competing with him,
> so I went straight into buying Chuck Berry, Little Richard and
> the blues stuff. [8]

They were also listening to a lot of live music, all of which had an effect on Bowie's sensibility.

Along with each musical style there was a specific social scene. Of all the scenes, Bowie became particularly enamoured of the early Mods (short for modernists) who, as he put it, were into dandy fashion, theatrical make-up, pills, trains, and James Brown. The whole sense of style appealed to David, who typically went into it all the way. As he put it:

> I dressed the archetype; mohair suits, two-tone shoes, the shoes
> were highpointers; Billy Eckstine shirts with big roll collars...

He was obviously a dedicated follower of fashion long before he became a leader.

During his last couple of years in high school, David was gravitating back to Brixton for the ska and bluebeat clubs. Plus it was one of the few places to hear James Brown records. Later he began to frequent The Marquee, The Scene, and Eel Pie Island in Twickenham, where Bowie says he got friendly with the owners and they let him 'creep in and watch what was happening'. In the meantime, he was playing with several bands, mostly in a jazz vein. They included The Konrads and The Buzz, as well as The Hooker Bros., who later became known as The King Bees. All the musical activity took time away from school which probably wasn't too interesting for him anyway, and he left Bromley Tech at the age of sixteen with O-level passes in only two subjects: art and woodwork. (He was also quite a good runner but there were no O-levels in track...) This is the art school that Bowie often mentions, though he did study art many years later in Berlin. From that time on, Bowie has been essentially self-educated with a method that hasn't changed much since his teens. He immerses himself in his chosen subject, emphasizing both 'hands on' experience and formal background by way of books, records, films or whatever is necessary to satisfy his curiosity.

There were a couple of other subjects which aroused the young David's interest: sex and religion. On the subject of sex, Bowie is prone to sensationalism, so that one of the few recorded 'insights' thereon also occurs in the context of one of Bowie's most outrageously inflammatory interviews ever. Speaking to Cameron Crowe for Playboy magazine, this is the picture Bowie paints:

> When I was fourteen sex suddenly became all important to me. It didn't really matter who or what it was with, as long as it was a sexual experience. So it was some very pretty boy in class in some school or another that I took home and neatly fucked on my bed upstairs. And that was it. My first thought was, "Well, if I ever get sent to prison, I'll know how to keep happy." [9]

The issue of Bowie's sexuality has already received enough attention, and though he knows the value of shocking statements, it seems likely that he had some homosexual experiences when he was fairly young; so do many people, but few have gotten as much mileage (or grief) out of them as Bowie.

On the other side of what seems to have always been a rather extreme nature, Bowie was developing an interest in religion and philosophy, especially in Tibetan Buddhism. He talked about writing a paper on the subject in high school, and he was fascinated with the esthetic lives of the lamas, speaking in amazement about how they bury themselves inside mountains and go for days without food. Not stopping there, he also made himself familiar with Nietzsche, astrology and other arcana. He seemed to have an intuitive grasp of myth, ritual and symbolism and later he would refine his ideas and put them to use. And while he may not have known at the time where all this would lead, he seemed to have quite a sense of his own destiny from approximately the age of twelve, and he must have felt it to be an expansive, inclusive fate that he possessed. Presumably the qualities Bowie would later display were developed during these early years. These qualities would include a strong will, self-confidence and determination, the capability for self-discipline and hard work balanced with restlessness, impatience and imagination, with a veneer of charm over all of this. By the age of seventeen, when he made his first professional recording, Bowie was displaying the manner that almost everyone who meets him is compelled to mention. Some have called it 'expertly charming', implying something learned, and for lack of details, the picture emerges of Bowie's growing realization of his own powers and abilities, his efforts towards honing them, and becoming the person he wanted to be, (and felt he needed to be). To borrow a phrase from another writer, Bowie had the usual nine thousand influences, but one thing that separates him is that many were sought out. He seems to have been attuned to several facets of the world around him (he says he has 'antennae'), and by the end of high school he was getting farther and farther from the small world of Bromley. By the time that he graduated from Bromley Tech, he was still undecided about what he wanted to do, but music soon came to the fore.

The reason was that a near revolution was about to take place in music, with David living almost on the front line. In 1963, (the year David graduated from Bromley) The Beatles, The Stones and The Kinks exploded onto the scene, immediately opening doors and expanding possibilities. David was caught up in the general excitement and described his situation rather matter-of-factly, saying, 'I had the usual desire to break ties with home and parents, the general anger of youth.' Although he was actually quite slow to break those ties, he did set off in his own direction, psychologically at least, leaving mom, pop and the family dog behind. Like Presley, he was to have a record out within a year of leaving school, though for David it took several more years before one could say, 'the rest is history'.

TWO

'Put on your red shoes/And dance the blues' ..

'Let's Dance' — *Let's Dance*

Compared to groups like The Who, The Stones, The Beatles and The Kinks (and the stellar individuals therein), success took a while to catch up with David Jones. It wasn't because he wasn't trying, or that he didn't also have his fair share of luck. While he was drawing from the same sets of influences at that time, (Lennon called the blues a "chair" and they were all sitting in it at times) and in some cases directly from the music of his compatriots, it took Bowie a bit longer to develop his style and strategy — at least to the point of his first hit. What followed in the way of early experience and lessons in the music business, in combination with his temperament, may have compelled Bowie to acquire a resilience that most of the above mentioned groups lacked. While these others (excluding The Beatles) generally got by for years on variations of their earliest successes, Bowie was scrambling and trying his hand at several styles and images. Who knows what would have happened if The King Bees had hit?

In fact, the relation to a group (or lack of one) seems to have been a source of some confusion and distress for David Jones. The time is 1963-64 and the thing is GROUPS, so Bowie tries working along those lines for the next two years with almost no success. Was he going to take Paul Anka as a precedent? Of course, there were others too: the likes of Elvis, James Brown, Chuck Berry and Bob Dylan, who probably gave Bowie/Jones some consolation as the realization dawned that going solo was the route for him. And since collaboration would also count for a lot, this period of his early recording for Vocalion (Decca), Parlophone (EMI) and eventually Pye and Deram, was crucial in the development of contacts, as well as in ideas and expertise.

What went down in music, and in England in particular, at the time that Bowie was finishing high school, was the advent of the Big Beat and The Beatles were its prophets. David Jones was on the right side of the Atlantic to pick up on the message, and in the right field (there was no British invasion in painting, though fashion, film and advertising are close cousins), and if he wasn't exactly in the vanguard, he didn't waste any time turning in his jazz uniform for a pop one. The change in the musical and cultural climate also affected the music business in general, which periodically and fairly thoroughly closes ranks. Then, as in 1977, the smell of fresh lucre had the talent scouts scouring London, and the

11

ever attuned Bowie (still Jones) realized this, and wasted little time in getting a group (his vehicle) together.

Speaking later about the choices facing him at the time, Bowie told Timothy White:

> I wasn't one hundred percent into *performing* music at the time of the Mods, but I'd been playing saxophone since about thirteen years old, on and off. The things I'd considered doing once I left school were either to continue being a painter, start working in an advertising agency or be a musician if I could possibly get that good. [1]

As it turned out, he did continue painting, but not professionally and without much commitment until several years later. He did go to work for an advertising agency, with his parents' strong encouragement, but he was more concerned with self-advertisement, and working for someone else left him unsatisfied. Of course, Bowie did become a musician, though he has repeatedly denied the title (perhaps because he's not a "technocrat" on any instrument) preferring to call himself an actor, a generalist *et al*. Is it just that his standards are so high? Possibly, but for a long time the disclaimers worked as a foil, drawing attention away from the quality of his musicianship, while allowing for back-handed compliments. It also emphasizes what Bowie really is: a performer, be it on stage, in the studio or during an interview.

Upon leaving school David immediately went to work in an advertising agency. For six months Bowie was a "junior visualizer" at the agency. He may have learned a thing or two, but the talents and tendencies that drew him to such work in the first place were only to flourish outside of that field. Bowie was repeatedly encouraged to go into design (as opposed to painting) by teachers who saw his talents lying there, and they have been proven right by the way Bowie has handled the concepts and artwork for all of his albums. He's also a natural with advertising-related enterprises in general, with a flair for promotion and P.R., and a sound grasp of the sensational, ephemeral and subliminal aspects of advertising. Publicity could have been his career if destiny hadn't called, compelling David to use his talents more directly.

About his stint in the advertising agency, Bowie is reluctant to say much except that for six months "he tripped on capitalism". He then tripped on becoming a pop musician, and as the legend (distilled from a combination of Bowie and record company publicity) has it, he met up with a group called The King Bees in a barber shop in Bromley, though they all hailed from Brixton. The fact that there was one "Richard George Underwood" in the band makes this story rather suspect, though a barber shop meeting would have been most appropriate. In any case, The Bees (taking their name from a Muddy Waters title) concentrated on rhythm 'n' blues, playing the local club circuit for about six months. That was enough time on the rock pile for the ever impatient David Jones, who was fed up with the poor equipment (and general lack of funds) to write a letter to washing machine magnate John Bloom, asking help for his poverty-stricken but "up and coming" group. Bowie apparently chose Bloom because of his reputation for throwing lavish parties for pop scene-makers (like The Beatles) and because he had a lot of money. While Bloom didn't actually part with the requisite couple of hundred pounds, he was apparently impressed enough with the audacity of David Jones to respond with a letter suggesting that David contact a friend and entrepreneur named Leslie Conn --which David wasted no time in doing. According to Conn, David's letter to Bloom had run: "If you can sell my pop group like you sell your washing machines, you're on a winner." Bloom relayed word about Jones to Conn, telling him that, 'I've just had a letter from a cheeky sod... but I like his style... give him an audition and tell me what you think!' 2 (Any such cheeky sod who would like to get in touch with Bowie will have to use other tactics. He brags that he gets so much mail that it's handled by a computer.)

Conn did audition the group, which also on occasion went by the name The Hooker Bros., (probably David's idea as a fan of John Lee Hooker and sucker for the idea of Brother) and liked what he heard. Confident, he booked David Jones and The King Bees at John Bloom's chic wedding anniversary party. Unaware of what awaited them, they arrived in jeans and T-shirts and played a raucous brand of R&B that lasted all of two numbers while the guests had hands over ears and took to screaming "Get 'em off!". Conn tactfully pulled David aside and told him that this wasn't "their audience", but a combination of real ambition and sensitivity with some insecurity thrown in had Bowie in tears. In spite of all this, Conn insists that 'David had total belief in his own talent... he was amazingly arrogant.' But Conn didn't mind the arrogance, because he had the same belief in David's talent. On the day after the anniversary fiasco when David called to apologize, Conn gave him the news that he'd just secured a recording contract for the group with Vocalion Pop. All apology calls should end that way...

At the time, Decca (Vocalion's mother company) tried to recover from their rejection of The Beatles with the signing of The Rolling Stones. Ever adventurous, they were looking for anybody vaguely resembling The Stones for repeat success. Davie and The King Bees were a likely choice due to their similar R&B stylings, but their first (and only release) with Decca was decidedly sub-Stones and consequently flopped. Aside from the lack of experience and the attendant weakness of the cuts, the choice of songs couldn't have helped matters.

The A side featured a Les Conn composition entitled *Lisa Jane* and the B side was a weak Paul Revere song called *Louie Louie Go Home*. Conn's composition was mainstream and unimaginative, and the only real interest (retrospectively) is in the squawking sax of David Jones, along with the similarly spirited and out of control vocal. The Revere tune is merely dismal and Charles Shaar Murray has said he'd like to think that one of the other Bees (Roger Bluck, Francis Howard, Richard George

Underwood or Bob Allen) was responsible for the inept Beatlesque vocals. After the flop, Decca lost interest, and The King Bees decided to part company with each other and with Leslie Conn. Although Conn's direction in some areas was less than sensational, he later claimed that the parting was due to the fact that he couldn't muster the resources which David's ambition required. There were some benefits from the experience even so. One of Conn's other clients was Marc Bolan, then also an unknown. Bolan was to become one of David's closest musical friends, as well as an advisor and inspiration. Conn went on to work with Doris Day, and says that the last time he saw David he was off to study mime at Sadler's Wells.

Instead, mime waited; David stayed in the music business, working with a man named Ralph Horton whom he'd met through Decca. Horton was a former roadie with The Moody Blues, who seems to have been unusually selfless, to the extent that he introduced Bowie to the man who would follow him as David's manager, apparently after realizing his own limits. The actual circumstances are vague; though three of Bowie's early managers were left on the sidelines of a "major career", all make it sound as if they bow(i)ed out graciously. Bowie is fairly expert in the art of gently discarding those no longer useful to him; even while extricating himself, he has seemed able to handle matters in a way designed to insure that little animosity is left in the wake. Generally, Bowie has been lucky with his managers. The field has always been full of sharks, and in 1963-64 with thousands of bands coming to London looking to make a fortune, there were as many unscrupulous managers looking to make theirs. While it can be argued that Conn, Horton and later Ken Pitt made mistakes regarding David's career, he was inexperienced and probably wouldn't have done as well by himself. They were dealing with a very raw talent which had yet to develop songs, a style or personality that were unique/individual and thus marketable. For some time, failure followed failure, and it is a tribute to David's charm, persistence and self-confidence (and to his managers) that the record contracts kept coming.

Ralph Horton secured a contract for David with EMI's Parlophone label, which resulted in two singles. For the first release of *I Pity The Fool*, backed with *Take My Tip*, David's back-up band (which is what they were) were called The Mannish Boys, another Muddy Waters' inspired name (from the song *Mannish Boy*). At this time, David was dividing his loyalties equally between the two bands (The Bees and The Boys) before deciding on The Mannish Boys for touring and support on the record.

I Pity The Fool is a Bobby 'Blue' Bland number written by "Deadric Malone", a name used either as a collective pseudonym for Bland's band or as credit for starving unknowns whose songs were bought outright for a couple of dollars. Davy Jones (as he was writing his name at the time) renders the tune down and dirty and alternately searing in the best blues tradition, although he sounds a bit young to make it totally convincing. He also takes off on Bland's delivery (which is rather dramatic), without direct mimicry but aiming for the same effect. This was one of his better early releases, and was also the first record David made with producer Shel Talmy who was also producing The Who and The Kinks (and to both of whom David owed a few musical debts). Talmy's arrangements are excellent, varying considerably from A side to B. *I Pity The Fool* also featured guitar fills by a ne'er do well named Jimmy Page, as well as the use of a brass section to create a blues meets soul feel for the cut. (This is available in several re-released formats — many featuring a classic photo of David and his next band, The Lower Third.)

The B side is David's first recording of one of his own songs, and while it isn't strikingly original, it is energetic and light-hearted. With rapid fire lyric delivery reminiscent of Mose Allison, it has a catchy melody and arrangement that points to one of the sounds that moved London at the time. The style is from the "flamingo school", so named for the music then featured at the Flamingo Club. The style was a jazzy, swing version of R&B with a lightly swinging backbeat and an organ-dominated sound. To those unfamiliar with Georgie Fame and Zoot Money (one of whose guitarists was Andy Summers of Police fame), the sound wasn't all that different from the Mersey sound which was enjoying its heyday. At this point, David's songwriting was fairly straightforward, addressing his concerns and those of his peers, here giving two tips. The main one is to "get on out", after telling his (presumably male) listener how to get in, "You gotta act tall, think big", "Gotta get ahead, get a car, fancy clothes..." That was his "tip" and one key to his later success.

The Mannish Boys didn't last too long (one record and a tour) but they did generate a bit of press coverage, thanks to their lead singer. The band was scheduled to appear on the BBC program *Gadzooks, It's All Happening* (Horton was hustling) to introduce *I Pity The Fool*. The show promised "the latest" in musical offerings and Davy Jones and The Mannish Boys were distinguished for their "sax sound", featuring two saxophone players in the band. (For posterity's sake, The Mannish Boys comprised Paul Rodriguez, Wilf Byrne, John Edward, Bob Solly, John Watson and John Whitehead with Jimmy Page also playing on vinyl.) For this occasion, David Jones showed the same ability to create a scandal (and garner media attention) that would serve him so well as David Bowie, by refusing to have his long hair shorn for the show. Though David would soon take the plunge and cut his hair, (and grow it and cut it *ad infinitum*) he wasn't about to be ordered to do so by producer Barry Langsford, who claimed that 'kids today just don't want this long hair business anymore', and this in 1965! To which the melodramatic and always quotable David replied:

> I would rather die than get my hair cut. I wouldn't have my hair cut for the Prime Minister, let alone the BBC. It took me nearly three years to grow and it's part of my stock in trade.

In this context, with the press finally paying attention, Bowie/Jones not only declared his trade, but defied the powers that be while making a direct appeal to the youth with his stance. He then went on to make another statement which seems like a warm up for his later attention-grabbing statements on sexuality. (In fact, with the response he got on this occasion he may have learned a few good lessons about the press and public that hadn't been action-tested yet.) After putting the BBC in its place, Jones went on to say that his girlfriend didn't particularly like his hairstyle either, and mused that: 'Maybe it's because I get asked for more dates than she does when we're out together.' Bowie also won the battle with the BBC, stating that if they received any complaints, the band's fee would go to charity. If this happened there were no reports of it.

The Mannish Boys were destined to go the way of The King Bees; one reason being the contradictions in the ego of Mr. David Jones. While David said at the time that he 'would rather achieve the status as a Mannish Boy that Mick Jagger enjoys as a Rolling Stone than end up as a small solo singer' (small may be the key word here), The Mannish Boys tell a different story. According to Paul Rodriguez (tenor sax and trumpet player) there was a "furious row" when their EMI single was released without a separate credit for Davy Jones. The record came out at the end of a tour opening for Gerry and The Pacemakers, The Kinks and Gene Pitney, and with another single to be cut. David opted for another band. In case you missed their shows, the group was described as having tried to adapt John Lee Hooker's foot stomping blues to the "big beat, never terribly successfully". Describing them at another time, Bowie claims rather different roots and a raucousness that wasn't to resurface until *The Man Who Sold The World*:

> We were too loud on stage. We used feedback and didn't play any melodies. We just pulverized the sound, which was loosely based on Tamla Motown. We had an ardent following of about a hundred mods but when we played out of London we were booed right off the stage. We weren't very good. [3]

So much for The Mannish Boys.

So Bowie went back into the studio again, once more with Shel Talmy producing, but with an older and more experienced band with which Bowie had joined forces, called The Lower Third. Since one of the fascinations of David Bowie lies in the discrepancies (and apparent contradictions) between what he says and what he does, the EMI issued a biography accompanying *You've Got A Habit Of Leaving* which is both interesting and humorous. When asked what his ambition was, Bowie/Jones replied: 'The group's ambition'. This is to be taken in light of similar comments made about his earlier bands, which were abandoned because of Bowie's personal ambition. Likewise, though Bowie claimed he was "really" determined to stick with The Lower Third, they cut only two singles together. It's also amusing in light of the other band members' responses to the same question. Dennis

Taylor wanted 'to be a good musician', a comment which Bowie has also made on occasion. Phil Lancaster wanted to 'make loads of money and keep playing', which Bowie might have said if it weren't so crassly obvious. Graham Rivens wanted 'to end up with a line of garages and pubs', for which Bowie might have substituted TV studios and film companies. It was also for the purpose of this bio that Bowie decided to add a year to his age, giving his birthday as January 1, 1946. The extra year was probably because everyone in The Lower Third was older, though it's interesting that he changed the date so slightly. This kept him within the same astrological sign; he might have chosen New Year's Day because of its association with change, without knowing yet that he shared his real birthday with Elvis.

Bowie also demonstrated a keen and subtle sense of humor, combining flattery and a sarcasm that puts the onus of belief on the reader. Example: David claims Graham Rivens (The Lower Third's bass player) and Sammy Davis Jr. as his "favorite artistes", and stated that his favorite food was "rump steak". Delectable as the rump cut may be, this statement indicates that Bowie's mastery of the P.R. medium was almost complete, and that sexual innuendo was fast becoming a standard item in his arsenal.

And the record? The songs were both D.J. originals: *You've Got A Habit Of Leaving Me* backed with *Baby Loves That Way*. Both were lyrically vague love songs with a less raw sound than David's earlier recordings. Musically, they owed a fair bit to The Yardbirds and early Who, apart from Bowie's fey vocals which are most pinched when trying to be emotive. Overall, both cuts are rather stiff but with the same backing band things went better (especially in the vocal department) next time out.

With a single released, David and The Lower Third embarked on the time-honored tradition of combing the country in a series of one-night gigs. In addition to being a collector, Bowie is also a natural "junker", with a good eye for quality and bargains in everything from clothes to glassware to apartments and vehicles. In this last category he found and purchased an out-of-service ambulance from the local town council, and furnished with mattresses it became the band's transportation and occasional abode. Kenneth Pitt, the man destined to become Bowie's next manager, met him at this point and described the ambulance:

> They kept it white because they found this helped them getting through traffic. It was a wonderful old vehicle, and for a while they were debating whether they could instal a blue light on top as well and have the word AMBULANCE painted along the side....' [4]

The ambulance was later dumped because their road manager left and David couldn't drive (he didn't own a license), but this wasn't until the band had driven and parked all over England. They could regularly be seen parked somewhere in the vicinity of the Marquee Club, where

Horton had managed to book them in a series of Sunday afternoon gigs. The shows were also being broadcast by Radio London, which at that time was the major alternative to the featherweight fare being offered on the government controlled BBC.

On a couple of these Sundays the band was backing The High Numbers, soon to be known as The Who, but then still fairly obscure. David has commented:

> We were second billing to The High Numbers, and even then Pete Townshend was writing great stuff. In fact, he and I were the only ones with anything to say.

Except perhaps for Ray Davies (and Lennon and McCartney); it is the influence of Davies and Townshend that are felt most heavily at that point in his development.

It was at one of these Marquee gigs that Kenneth Pitt first met and saw David perform. Pitt had been invited by Horton, who at the time might have just been seeking some advice, or perhaps the publicity services of Pitt who was manager and/or publicist for such then-breaking acts as The Kinks and Manfred Mann, as well as the more established Anthony Newley. Whether Horton knew it or not, Pitt had certain ideas of his own about what sort of entertainer was "needed" in pop music at that moment. He took as his model for the "all round entertainer" a man named Tommy Steele, an early Elvis imitator made good in films and light entertainment. The fact that Steele wasn't at all known in the U.S. points to one problem with the model and, although Pitt's scope was generally on target, the prototype was too parodic and corny for David ever to take too seriously. In any case, Pitt was looking for what he called an "all round entertainer", and he was quick to recognize that David was more than a nascent rock and roller. As he put it:

> When I saw David for the first time down at the Marquee I thought he was someone who could be groomed in just the way I had in mind — from the way he moved on stage, by the way he held himself, and even just his eyes. Even then the songs he was writing were quite remarkable. [5]

The year was 1965, and although Ken Pitt wouldn't officially become David's manager for another year, interest in and discussion about David's career began almost immediately. And there were some immediate effects. While David and The Lower Third were working on a single for Pye (with the deal arranged by Horton), Pitt had flown to the U.S. for discussions on assuming the British representation for Andy Warhol and The Velvet Underground. The discussions came to nought, but Pitt returned with acetates of The Velvets and The Fugs for David's perusal, a decidedly unstuffy move on Pitt's part. While the effects of these musical introductions weren't to be fully felt for a few years, the mere awareness of these sounds would have placed David light years ahead of his contemporaries who were still trying to work out Chuck and Muddy's riffs.

Of even more immediate importance was the fact that Pitt got wind of the newly formulated (which correctly describes the process of this made-for-TV band modelled on The Beatles) band called The Monkees, with a British actor named Davy Jones in its ranks. With great foresight (how did Pitt know they'd make it?) Ken wired London with the information, suggesting that David consider changing his name. David had already been playing around with variations on his first name (David to Davie and recently Davy), but Pitt's intelligence sparked the leap from Jones to Bowie. The Myth, supported by Bowie's own claims, places the origin of the name on the famed hunting knife, and Bowie's most famous comment on the choice was made to William Burroughs when he explained that he 'wanted a truism to cut through lies'. Ken Pitt says that he never asked about the name (when he got back to London David stopped by and casually mentioned that: 'By the way, I'm David Bowie now'), but Pitt thought it came from somewhere in his mother's family.

Whatever the origin of the new moniker, Bowie made his choice in a matter of weeks, and just in time for his first release on Pye and the usual promotion, with a press release entitled: "Davy Jones Is Back In His Locker." It announced the arrival of nineteen year-old David *Bowie* along with the info that Tony Hatch, his producer, had discovered him, which is hardly the case. The release explained that he had outgrown the pirate image that his name suggested (though in actuality he had some way and several years to go in his search for outlandishness.) It then went on to discuss Bowie in terms that would be as valid today as they were in '65, but the irony is that they were written pre-*Man Who Sold The World*, pre-*Ziggy*. The copy reads:

> Gone are the outlandish clothes, the long hair, and the wild appearance and instead we find a quiet talented vocalist and songwriter -— David Bowie.

The record which this press release accompanied hardly made Bowie's reputation, but it did feature two more originals. The A side was *Can't Help Thinking About Me*, which Bowie later called: "an illuminating little piece", no doubt because of the self-consciously egotistical title. (The B side wasn't much better, *And I Say To Myself...*) Someone once said that every first novel (or was it first play?) is about leaving home, and this track places Bowie firmly in the Grand Tradition. *Can't Help Thinking About You* is generally considered the best of the three Pye singles; the voice that Bowie was developing became obscured in the next couple of recordings (and years) thanks to a consuming quest which extended beyond David's music but which certainly affected it. Though Bowie made two more records with Pye, this marked the end of his association with The Lower Third (mainly because the people in

David's camp saw him as more than a mere front man) and the beginning of a managerial relationship with Kenneth Pitt.

In all, David's career was off to a solid, if unmeteoric beginning. Like Elvis, he had a record out within a year of leaving school (though Elvis was eighteen when he graduated) but his career didn't take off in the same manner, nor did Bowie earn the public's enthusiasm like the groups he so obviously admired. He didn't even make it as a one-hit wonder. In retrospect, a slow start probably worked in Bowie's favorl but there has been much speculation of the "He could have made it then if only..." variety. While these first two years as a professional (one bio called him "fully professional") formed foundations that Bowie would build on, he must have often doubted the unshakeable certainty of what he calls his "destiny". The broad outline was there, but the day-to-day decisions were difficult. Moments of self-doubt, disappointment and frustration there must have been but David's sense of his own direction was strong enough that all the tangents, influences and distractions which captured his attention were ultimately synthesized, contributing to the complexity that makes Bowie perpetually fascinating.

The fact that fame would be deferred (for what must have seemed forever at that time) allowed Bowie to develop and explore himself more fully than would have been possible had he immediately attracted the spotlight. His desire to succeed, coupled with the realization that it would have to be on artistic terms, saw Bowie exploring his creativity to the point that it became a lifelong obsession. Compulsion.

THREE

████████████████████████████████████

'Because You're Young...'

'Because You're Young' — *Scary Monsters (And Super Creeps)*

From here on out the subject is David BOWIE, who in early 1966 took on Kenneth Pitt as his manager for a five year contract which would last for only three years. By the end of their association a song called *Space Oddity* would have been written and recorded, but the space from A to B is strewn with failed experiments as well as searches that would take years to bear fruit. What follows is an account of the relationship between Pitt and Bowie in both its positive and negative aspects, as well as Bowie's growth in directions Pitt would never have imagined, and of which he generally didn't approve.

Kenneth Pitt is an urbane man, well bred, well read, with furniture, art and rare book collections, as well as the professional experience which David needed. That is presumably why Horton brought Pitt to see David in the first place. Soon they were discussing a management deal, but as Pitt describes it, it was their mutual interest in art and collecting, rather than musical ideas, that formed the basis of their relationship. Pitt tells of the first time that David saw his apartment:

> He ran his fingers along the bookshelves, lingering over the better editions saying: "Oh, you've got that one!" and then, "Oh, that one, too!" He was obviously interested in books and art; that strengthened our relationship because he was reading one of my books on graphic drawing when he suddenly turned to Ralph Horton and said, "Let's do a deal with Ken!". I think the thing that made such an impact upon me was that here was a young singer and writer who was interesting as an artist and who had a mind as well. [1]

It was David's mind, his artistic predilections and his sense of style that were nurtured under Pitt, and although Pitt got David acting for the first time, his concept of "the all-round entertainer" seemed both to stimulate and frustrate David. While the idea was appropriate to David's talents, it was based on a pre-rock image of the entertainment industry, and this conflict caused most of the problems between them in the long run.

While David never completely swallowed Pitt's concept (partly because it was based on Tommy Steele), David's father was sympathetic and saw David in similar terms. David's parents were included in the negotiations over the management contract, and once it was signed, their communications continued. The following are Ken Pitt's observations on Mr. and Mrs. Jones:

> They both obviously wanted David's career to go right, and I think Mr. Jones realized that he had bred a rather unusual son, but he coped very bravely with it. He tried to be open-minded, though I suppose there were times when he thought David was going off the rails — and then he'd sit down and have a chat with him about it. [2]

According to Pitt, Mr. Jones did everything he could for David, by way of offering advice, taking care of his banking and national insurance, as well as keeping a room for him at home. This fits in with the image Pitt creates by describing him as one of those 'rare men with beautiful handwriting'. He also went on to say that Mr. Jones didn't have a creative bone in his body, but this seems an extreme judgement; after all, he'd started his own theatre troupe, and could well have been a Sunday painter.

With the approval of David's parents, David and Ken Pitt signed a five year management contract in April of 1966, with David already under contract to Pye records. The Lower Third had disbanded, and without a group to ground him in R&B, the forthcoming Pye releases were lackluster and fairly tentative. The other problems seem to stem from the fact that David had a manager with ambitious though cautious ideas, and he was working with a producer who was generally unsympathetic. Tony Hatch was Pye's star producer, which says something for the way David's career was being handled, but by all accounts he and David didn't see eye to eye. Pitt claims that he didn't really know what went wrong, and having just come into the contract with David, he stayed out of their "contretemps". Undoubtedly David was impatient, and with three "professional" recordings under his belt he was beginning to have definite ideas about what sounds he wanted and how to get them while Hatch, the seasoned professional, must have thought David was an upstart. Hatch put it a little differently:

> David was the first real singer/songwriter and was very stimulating in the studio, but I knew he would not have a hit with me because he was not ready. For every great artist there is a time when they happen, and that time hadn't come yet. [3]

Hatch's remarks were made years later, which may have had something to do with his perspective, but with a negative working situation, David's time wasn't going "to come" with Hatch.

Despite their difficulties, the promotion as usual painted a glowing picture of their collaborations, and also provided the first public statement on David's interest in film and theater. The following is

Melody Maker's almost word for word reprint of the press release, although the first line belongs to the M.M. writer:

> Without doubt, David Bowie has talent, and also without doubt it will be exploited. For Mr. Bowie, a nineteen year-old Bromley boy, not only writes his own numbers, but he is also helping Tony Hatch to write a musical score, and the numbers for a TV show. As if it wasn't enough, David also designs shirts and suits for John Stephen of the famed Carnaby Street clan. And his ambition? "I want to act," says Bowie modestly. "I'd like to do character parts. I think it takes a lot to become somebody else; it takes some doing." [4]

Aside from the purported collaborations with Hatch, the rest speaks for itself and though John Stephen isn't mentioned elsewhere, Bowie's clothes fetish and his own designs do figure strongly, with the mention of acting being especially interesting. (Special note should be taken of the word "modestly" when used in how Bowie presents himself). While the impetus to act was being encouraged by Pitt, Bowie went on to talk about other long-standing interests, particularly astrology and Buddhism. After saying that he'd also like to go to Tibet, he mentioned a dilemma for any intelligent songwriter:

> As far as I'm concerned, the whole idea of Western life --that's the life we live now — is wrong. These are hard concepts to put into songs though.

So instead, he concentrated on writing for and about the kids of London.

Unfortunately, the single David came out with at that moment wasn't as good as some of his earlier work, nor even on a par with songs that he was performing at the time. The titles were *Do Anything You Say*, and *Good Morning Girl*, two more originals again on the "love" theme. The sound was another product of the "flamingo school", with more Who and Kinks thrown in, but there isn't much to recommend in these cuts. In fact, the next (and last) Pye release was even more dismal, which if it wasn't so quickly forgotten, could have been an embarrassment. The titles are indicative. Says Bowie: 'I Dig Everything' and he also claims, 'I'm Not Losing Sleep', an early assertion of self-assurance which didn't quite come off as the disbandonment it was intended to be.

After three releases on Pye, there was silence from the label, presumably because things weren't working out between Hatch and Bowie (and the records weren't selling). Hatch had written *Downtown* for Petula Clark, but only succeeded in making Bowie petulant. So much for that. The next time around Bowie effectively produced himself, though this may have been partially by default. Pitt had secured a contract for Bowie with a new label called Deram, founded in 1966 by Denny Cordell. The first two acts he signed were Cat Stevens and Bowie; the fact that the Cat's "time had come" had repercussions on Bowie's place in the Deram scheme of things. Ken Pitt talked about the time between contracts and even after the deal had been worked out, saying that: 'We did rather suffer at that period'. The records weren't really going anywhere and David was beginning to flounder, partially due to Pitt's urging to try other things, although David's choices had a range and intensity which also disturbed Pitt.

Bowie was performing solo on acoustic guitar at the time, with his major bookings being summer gigs for tourists and students at the Marquee. They were entitled the *Bowie Showboat*, and his audience included a contingent from Bromley, along with David's mother who reportedly often sat in the front row, sporting a straw hat and greeting David's friends as they arrived. Though David may not have been too close to his mother, her loyalty is touching, even if it must have embarrassed David somewhat. By all accounts the Marquee gigs went well, but the show stopper was *When You Walk Through A Storm*, not one of his originals. Bowie told a white lie on this subject speaking with Melody Maker:

> And remember, with all original numbers the audiences are
> hearing numbers they've never heard before — so this makes
> for a varied stage act. It's risky, because the kids aren't familiar
> with the tunes, but I'm sure it makes their musical life more
> interesting. [5]

In fact, one of Bowie's hallmarks is to pack his original tunes full of musical and lyrical references to other work, which must have also helped retain interest in his own songs (familiarity breeds acceptance), along with the cover tunes that he was doing.

Bowie's own musical life was one thing, but not his only pursuit at that time. With Pitt pushing the Tommy Steele model, the one area where they could agree on in terms of direction and possible other avenues was film. To this end, Pitt secured David a role in a film entitled *The Image*, which Pitt later described as 'dreadful'. Without going into a shot-by-shot description of what sounds like a less than mediocre student film, Bowie's own summary will suffice:

> My first true film appearance was in a movie called *The Image*, an
> underground black and white avant garde-type thing done by
> some guy (Michael Armstrong). He wanted to make a film
> about a painter doing a portrait of a guy in his teens, and the
> portrait comes to life and, in fact, turns out to be the corpse of
> some bloke. I can't remember all the plot, if indeed it had a plot,
> but it was a fourteen-minute short and it was awful.' [6]

For this godawful film, which was to resurface circa Ziggy in a Soho (London) porn theatre, David was paid the grand sum of thirty pounds. During a scene in which he appeared through a window in the rain,

David had to hang from a ledge while buckets of water were poured on him. Somehow he persisted, though all was not glamor, apparently realizing that the experience was worth it in the interests of his film education.

Pitt encouraged David to pursue modelling and dance work as well, and though the time period from 1966-68 is full of tales of David's various projects and jobs, the chronology has never been clear.

Before getting into the details of his other acting work, there was one thing that preoccupied David throughout this period. Following up on his early interest in Buddhism, especially the Tibetan brand (and later Zen), he became more involved when several Tibetan religious leaders fled to London following the Chinese "invasion" of their country. He took up studies of Vajrayana meditation with Chogyam Irungpa Rinpoche, and became involved in the Tibet Society through their efforts to help the refugees, which finally led David to work on the establishment of a monastery in Dumfriesshire, Scotland. When this work was completed, he spent time there and nearly took the vows of a monk. He recoiled at the last moment (mumbling something about nearly shaving his head), returning to London and more earthly considerations. At the time, Bowie was reluctant to over-emphasize his association with Buddhism, due to The Beatles and their fiasco in India, which had tainted such romances with Eastern religions.

Bowie's next film role, lined up for him by Ken Pitt, was in *The Virgin Soldiers*; although David's part was minor, it was a bigger, better film and a more educational experience than his previous effort. Essentially an extra, David claims that he's never seen the finished film and doesn't know if his scene ever made the final cut. If you happen to see the film, shorthaired and wearing a soldier's uniform, David gets thrown over a bar. Bowie submitted to the haircut without fuss, partly because it was executed out of the glare of media attention, but particularly because he was more prepared to be pliant as an actor than as a rocker. Even when his film career began to blossom, a film director's will was one of the few that David would bend to.

While on the set of *The Virgin Soldiers* in Ascot, David had little to do while waiting for his scene to be shot. He called Pitt in frustration telling him, 'If that's what Hollywood is all about, you can stuff it!' Because of this attitude, frustration in the lack of progress with his acting career, and the reascendancy of music as his top priority, it was years before David took on any more acting. His interest really seemed to wane after auditioning for the part of a homosexual boy in *Sunday Bloody Sunday*, which went to Murray Head instead of David. While his fascination with films didn't end, his overt attempts and auditions did.

Before abandoning acting, David engaged himself in all manner of short term film, TV and dance appearances, but his music career kept on rolling, albeit rather slowly. David's first Deram release was issued on December 2, 1966, shortly after the label was formed. The two songs were *Rubber Band*, backed with *London Boys*. Putting *London Boys* on the B side was a strategic error. There is general agreement that it was one of the best songs David wrote prior to *Space Oddity*. In fact, he had been performing it for at least a year prior to recording it, and had even plugged it in Melody Maker calling it, *Now You've Met The London Boys*, and saying that it went over very well in performance. The Deram release described the song as:

> David Bowie's partly autobiographical cameo of the brave and defiant little Mod racing up-hill along Wardour Street to an empty paradise." Bowie recently described it as 'another one about being a Mod. It was an anti-pill song. I wasn't particularly pro the thing — after a bit.'

Charles Shaar Murray refers to *London Boys* as 'The inevitable comedown from the high of *My Generation*.' While Bowie may have been unconsciously answering Townshend, the other song on the single was in the style of The Kinks and the Edwardian Beatles tunes, a sentimental throwback in the show tune tradition, complete with tubas. *Rubber Band* had a "plot" based on losing a lover to the leader of a brass band. It was followed up by more silliness in the form of *The Laughing Gnome*, backed with *The Gospel According To Tony Day*. The "Gnome", with its sped-up vocals, has been compared to everything from The Smurfs (and Chipmunks) to similar songs by Syd Barrett and The Beatles, both of whom Bowie was listening to. This attempt at a hit didn't succeed in '66 but was pulled from the vaults in 1973, causing Bowie a small measure of embarrassment and probably some amazement when it sold over 250,000 copies. The B-side was a real mismatch with its tone of darkness, despair and defeat.

One of the other influences beginning to show in these last two releases is that of Anthony Newley, whom Bowie hadn't met, but had become fascinated with, fueled by Pitt's inside information. While most people have expressed amazement at the choice of Newley for "idol", Bowie and Newley did share some common interests in the form of acting, singing and composing as well as another possibility that has somehow been overlooked. Bowie may well have been intrigued by Joan Collins, figuring that if he imitated Newley he could win his woman. In any case, he studied letters from Newley that Ken Pitt possessed, even bringing xerox copies home to show his parents, while he looked at film clips and watched Newley in *Gurney Slade*. Newley's influence reached full flowering on Bowie's first album, released in June '67 on Deram. The album was simply titled: *David Bowie*, and while it was a somewhat ballsy move on the part of Deram to devote a whole album to Bowie's work, the risk was minimized by the fact that almost nothing was spent on the recording, the whole thing being completed in four or five studio sessions. David later commented: 'That first album I did in about fifteen minutes. You could say it was rushed!'. But the rush wasn't the only problem with *David Bowie*. Due to decisions undoubtedly influenced by Pitt, Bowie moved from the raunchier R&B stylings of his early records, to something almost straight out of West End musical theatre. The best of what can be said about the record was printed on the songbook jacket, though these words mostly fit the category of general description rather than specific testimony. The copy read:

> He has the eye of a newspaperman who knows his way around, the insight of a gifted psychiatrist, the heart of a loving child, the mind of a philosopher, the pen of a poet... and the ear of a nineteen year-old Englishman who knows what makes today's hits happen!

Actually, Bowie hadn't quite mastered the hit-making machinery, although he would soon do so, and there were enough indications of his potential.

In terms of his songwriting, Bowie was already examining several of his recurring themes, beginning with himself, though sometimes getting quite outside of his personal sphere with fanciful scenarios. Age and change figure strongly in his songs, though with more resistance than he would later manifest, and apocalyptic visions recur. Of the material that made it onto the album, there were some odd choices. Neither *Gnome* nor *The Gospel* made it, while *Rubber Band* was included and *London Boys* was not. This was probably because *Rubber Band* fit the quaint vapidity and sentimental sound of the rest of the album, while the more memorable and significant *London Boys* would have been out of place.

Love You Till Tuesday was one of the songs on the album which Ken Pitt liked so much that he made a film of the same title, featuring Bowie and his music. It seems that around that time there was some interest on the part of a German television station to do a Bowie special. Pitt may have personally helped generate their interest, but in any case, with the resources of the Germans combined with his own money, Ken Pitt began to plan a promotional film featuring David's music. This shows some foresight, but unfortunately the film itself was a disaster. There were some positive side-effects, but the film took quite a while to organize and shoot. In the meantime, quite a lot was happening to David.

Among David's longstanding interests were dance and mime. These talents fit in with Pitt's concept of the all-round-you-know-what. David had also reached a crisis point concerning Buddhism, seriously considering taking monastic vows before withdrawing right at the brink, apparently realizing that what ever he'd learned through Buddhism would be more significant (in terms of his own life) if applied in a larger context than a Scottish Buddhist community. Thus he returned to London, wandering around one day (as legend has it...) when he stumbled onto a lunchtime mime performance by Lindsay Kemp. (It may not have been an accident at all. Marc Bolan also studied with Kemp, though it's not clear who started who on this course of study; Bolan was generally leading the way for Bowie at that time.) During the show's intermission, David walked outside for a cigarette break when he heard his own Deram album being played inside. Flattered and encouraged, he walked backstage and introduced himself, with the result that he began taking classes from Kemp in return for the promise of writing some material for the shows. The extent of their relationship has been inflated, as the time period of actual study was fairly short and David appeared in only four Kemp-associated performance runs, usually in the guise of "Pierrot In Turquoise". This was not unlike Kemp's purported studies with Marcel Marceau. Said Kemp: 'I talk about studying with him and don't tell anybody I only had three lessons.' But even if Bowie's work with Kemp has been exaggerated, the move from the extremes of Buddhism to that of Kemp's milieu seemed to suit David's needs at the time. As Bowie put it: '... he (Kemp) was so earthly that I learned from him that people are more important to me than ideas.' Lindsay Kemp was an internationally known mime performer who took the traditional mime figures of Pierrot, Scaramouche and wedded them to Joyce, Genet, Artoud and the like. Kemp's idea that the extraordinary and the strange were the proper subject matter for art, held some sway over Bowie's opinions for quite a while. Later on, Bowie talked about the experience in general, saying that:

> Lindsay was the man who I ended up studying with, working for, and living the most degenerate kind of life with. It was all wonderful, incredible. It was a great experience living with this sort of rancid Cocteau-ish theatre group in these bizarre rooms that were decorated and handpainted with elaborate things. The whole thing was so excessively French, with Left Bank existentialism, reading Genet and listening to R&B. The perfect bohemian life. [7]

This experience had many repercussions. It was through the Kemp troupe and classes that David met a woman named Hermione Farthingale, a solicitor's (lawyer's) daughter from Kent, with whom he was to "fall in love". Evidently, the acquaintance blossomed while they danced a minuet in powdered wigs and full regalia for a BBC production of *A Pistol Shot* and they soon moved into a small bedsit in Gunter Grove. (Until then David had been living at home or in a spare room in Ken Pitt's apartment.) Ken Pitt liked Hermione (the opposite of his reaction to Angie), although he was quite aware of the differences between her and David. He described her as a quiet girl, very attractive with beautiful red hair, 'the sort of girl who wanted a quiet life, who would have been quite happy to marry, settle down, raise a family, without anything very hectic ever happening to her.' They lived together for nearly a year, but this was a very hectic period for David when he was "a Buddhist mime songwriter and part-time sax player, or it became like that", and it seems that the confusion was too much for her. Testimony to this affair is one of David's purest love songs, *Letter To Hermione*, and though the lyrics suggest that she left for another man, if this was the case, it might have been by default. The mood of the song is tender, with Bowie sounding his most vulnerable, looking for solace and solidity, the likes of which would become increasingly difficult to find, even as he needed them more.

While David and Hermione were together, they and fellow mime and bass player John Hutchinson formed a mime troupe/group called Feathers. Their impact was also featherweight, generally performing to hippie audiences in art labs, without generating much response or money. It finally came to a halt after Hermione left David. Bowie and Hutchinson put on one show after her departure, then John also called it a day. Feathers were captured in performance by Pitt in *Love You Till Tuesday*, but the complete film was never released. The experience with Feathers also put David in the Arts Lab frame of mind, which was to occupy his time and public comments for a couple of years.

By the time *Love You Till Tuesday* was completed, David's Deram album was already cold and dead. Pitt thought that the film might benefit from some original material and sent David off to write another song. Ever compliant, he went home and wrote a hit (that must have been what Pitt had in mind) called *Space Oddity*, a parody inspired by Kubrick's *2001 – A Space Odyssey*. He also called it 'a mixture of Salvador Dali and The Bee Gees'. Whatever it was, people responded immediately. Pitt loved the song and devised a scene for it in which David crawled around in a space capsule, that looks more like an ad for the latest in air-filled plastic furniture, complete with mirrors for the space brothel look. But the story Pitt loves to tell is the filming of the scene when the hardnosed we've-seen-it-all-before film crew put down their girlie magazines and even started humming the song. But Pitt says David wasn't really convinced until he played the tape for Marc Bolan whose response, 'It's a hit, Davie!', quelled all of Bowie's doubts.

On the strength of this song, David was signed to Philips/Mercury, who assigned the production team of Gus Dudgeon and Paul Buckmaster to work on the singles, while Tony Visconti produced the bulk of the album. The release of *Space Oddity* was held up for almost six months, until July 11, 1969, in order to coincide with the coverage of the American moon landing, on July 20th. The song was chosen by the BBC as theme music for their reports, an irony that wasn't lost on anyone who actually listened to the lyrics. The song was eventually published by Essex House Publishing, for whom David had worked during the lean years.

According to Pitt, David was under a contract with Essex House as a songwriter, but the ostensible purpose was that David was having such trouble breaking through with his own material, they thought he might find his HIT through the publisher. David Platz of Essex House shared an office with a man named Geoffrey Heath, who had acquired the rights to a French song by Claude Francois entitled *Comme d'habitude*, and he suggested that David should try to write an English lyric. Bowie did write one, and although Pitt claims it was 'splendid', events conspired against David's version. With everyone agreeing that the song was a perfect vehicle for David, Heath called the French publisher to give him the good news that David Bowie would sing the song. The publisher knew his song but didn't know Bowie, and he replied: 'Look, we want Tom Jones and if you can't get him to record it, then send the song back'. Instead, Heath sent it to Frank Sinatra without Bowie's lyrics, so when Sinatra decided to record it, he had Paul Anka pen the non-existent English lyrics. Anka came up with something called *My Way*, a song better known for Sid Vicious' interpretation than for Bowie's lyrics — no doubt to Bowie's perpetual chagrin. (Eventually he made up for the loss with a song called *Life On Mars*, but that's a little later.)

David had been involved in quite a few enterprises during the course of a couple of years. Though he appeared in a TV commercial for Lyon's Maid introducing LUV "the pop ice cream", looking rather clean cut, his image had changed from Mod to hippie.

Sporting long hair, and a scruffiness that was undermining Ken Pitt's plans for him, Bowie also moved on to a new, more appropriate idol. Bob Dylan became Anthony Newley's successor in Bowie's pantheon, and besides the musical influence which is especially apparent on the *Space Oddity* album (alias *Man Of The Words, Man Of Music*), Bowie also took to adopting Dylan's image, wearing all black on stage and again arousing Pitt's ire. At that point, Pitt felt compelled to lecture Bowie on the need for a performer to dress up and project a positive image, which as he noted, Bowie certainly did learn to do.

As the decade of the 1960s drew to a close, Bowie began to get away from the "Flower Power" consciousness which he later considered "cloying" and "deadly". He met a new group of people that helped inspire a personal change in him, and on the musical front he began to realize that something new was needed, was in fact inevitable. He was still a couple of years away from "establishing himself", but events and developments accelerated. Soon Bowie was moving in an entirely different sphere, though as usual, elements of the old carried over until they became impossibly cumbersome. With Sixties culture losing its momentum, voids were being created, and Bowie (with Bolan and others) was preparing himself to fill them. As the new decade approached, Bowie began to position himself for conquest.

FOUR

'Time — He's waiting in the wings' ..

'Time' -- *Aladdin Sane* 1969,

Ken Pitt was still in the picture, but not for long. He didn't fit in with David's new associates, who were usually not much older than he was, and who were equally alienated by the so-called Establishment, as they were by the naive cynicism of the hippies. They were to become partners in Bowie's own version of Bohemia. As one who has always claimed to be deeply affected by his environment, the new lifestyle brought out a new Bowie. Friends played a major role, and one by one a new cast of characters entered his life. There was Marc Bolan, Tony Visconti, Angela Barnett, and later there was Freddie, Suzie, Mick, The Rats, Tony De Fries and so on until the old David (Jones) and even David Bowie were eclipsed, and a starman named Ziggy was born on the other side.

As sudden as some changes seem, the process was evolutionary, with the new displacing the old gradually, although there were a few sudden leaps. Marc Bolan had been a part of David's life for some time, much to Ken Pitt's displeasure, since Bolan was advocating such outrageous ideas as agent-free artists -- anathema to a professional agent. Bowie and Bolan spent a lot of time together, realizing alone that they were both destined to be stars while no one else seemed to recognize the fact. Bolan's favorite producer was Tony Visconti, a Brooklyn born draft resister who also happened to be Denny Cordell's assistant at Deram. Visconti eventually produced several of Bowie's albums (starting with *Space Oddity*), shared a house wih him, and constituted the third member of what Charles Shaar Murray called "an exclusive mutual admiration society", composed of Bolan, Visconti and Bowie.

In the meantime, David had some old business to work through. Still harboring some altruistic/idealistic aims, he became involved in the running of his own "arts lab". His interest extended back prior to the release of *Space Oddity* and he continued to work with the lab even after he started getting attention for his music, and for what also seems like an uncommonly long time for one with such a low boredom threshold. He seems to have been quite serious about the whole enterprise, talking more about the lab than himself or his music, when the pop press started knocking on his door. To this day he speaks about it with a certain fondness. A press release issued in November of 1969, which David had a hand in writing, is fairly indicative of his priorities. The arts lab gets more space than his upcoming LP.

Prepresent: Born London 1947

15   — Didn't attend school much — Played tenor sax with Modern Jazz Group — Buddhism
16   — Left school, went into ad agency and tripped on Capitalism for six months as a commercial artist — Re-read *On The Road* — Formed progressive blues group
17   — More groups
18   — Frustrated with amps, went solo with an acoustic
19   — First L.P.
20   — Dropped out of music completely and devoted most of my time to the Tibet Society — Helped get the Scottish monastery under way
21   — Acted, wrote and produced with mime company — Formed own mime, music, mixed media trio — Fell in love
22   — Solo again and making an L.P. for Philips — Started arts lab in Beckenham, Kent to try and promote the ideals and creative processes of the underground.

While David was inspired and enthused over the idea and its results, he finally bowed out when he realized that others weren't contributing and that the audiences were only interested in his solo performances.
    David ran the lab with a woman named Mary Finnigan, a journalist with two children, whose house David stayed in while he was working on the lab. Located in Beckenham near his folks in Bromley, the lab was actually a spare room next to the Three Tuns Pub. Mary ran the lab, leaving David free as the artistic director, with the mission of promoting a new awareness and appreciation of a cross-arts, cross-class creative process. Speaking with Chris Welch in '69, Bowie went on at length about the lab:

> We started our lab a few months ago with poets and artists who just came along. It's got bigger and bigger and now we have our own light show and sculptures etc. And I never knew there were so many sitar players in Beckenham. [1]

He went on to make statements like: 'There isn't one pseud involved. All the people are real — like labourers or bank clerks'. He added: 'There is a lot of talent in the Green Belt and there is a load of tripe in Drury Lane.' In this same conversation he began talking about the skinheads and his perception of them, which hinted at a coming change in David's orientation. (He was still looking sweet with his jeans and perm...)

> I think a lot of skinheads are better than hippies and the hippie cult is so obviously middle-class and snobbish, which is why the skinheads don't like them. The hippies don't know about people,

they really don't. They don't know what it's like to see three
heavies go after their sister, and all the other things that
happen in a skinhead's environment. [2]

By the summer of 1969, things were at a high pitch for David. He had
been introduced to a woman named Mary Angela Barnett a few months
earlier, and since she became his wife, the story is worth recounting.
David and Angie relate most of the same "facts", though with quite
different emphasis. (For Angela's full account, you'll have to read her
book, *Free Spirit*, as most of what she says can't be corroborated.) At the
time they met, David was about to be signed to Philips/Mercury for the
album featuring *Space Oddity*, and both a Mercury talent scout and the
man who signed David knew Angie. Angie claims that it was through
scout Calvin Mark Lee that she first met David. She had also dated Lee's
boss, Lou Reisner, while she was in college. These two contacts were
the extent of her relationship to the music business.

An American born in Cyprus, Angela had studied at St. Georges in
Switzerland, and then went to the Connecticut College for Women to
study drama. Acting had long been her ambition, but she was soon
expelled from the school for a certain sexual offense which compelled
her parents to send her to London and an Oxford Street Secretarial
School as "punishment". After she had served her sentence, she
enrolled in Kingston Polytechnic, and it was there that she began to
make the contacts, while she was studying economics/marketing, that
eventually led to her meeting with David.

Angie met Lou Reisner in an elevator while she was a student and
although it's not clear just how she met "Doctor" Calvin Lee, he was the
one who invited Angie to the Roundhouse to see "the new act" that
Mercury was about to sign. Angie claims to have been exhilarated,
saying that it was her first rock and roll show, and even with The Who
on the bill, she only had eyes for David. It's at this point that David's
version becomes amusing. In an infamous interview with Cameron
Crowe for Playboy magazine, Crowe asked: 'Didn't your wife Angela
have something to do with getting you your first recording contract?'
Bowie replied:

> Angela and I knew each other because we were both going out
> with the same man. Another one of her boyfriends, a talent
> scout for Mercury Records, took her to a show at The
> Roundhouse where I happened to be playing. He hated me. She
> thought I was great. Ultimately, she threatened to leave him if
> he didn't sign me. So he signed me. [3]

If the reasons for David's success were too boring (talent, hard work),
this story is rather flattering to Angie, and says a lot about her own
"charm". (David wasn't so delighted when former publicist Cherry
Vanilla claimed that her own sexual exploits on David's behalf had also
been essential to his success.) As it happens though, the deal was almost

a *fait accompli* when Angie entered the picture. Her influence was probably greater on David than on the folks at Mercury.

As for the rest of the mythical meeting, it was continued the next night with dinner for three (arranged by Calvin Lee) and a show at the Speakeasy, which is amusing because Angie subsequently described the evening and events in breathless terms, seeing King Crimson and láter dancing to Donovan after being asked the "famous question", "Do You Jive?" David's recollection was a bit more jaded, describing the Speakeasy scene as just another in an endless round of record company promotions, proving magic is a state of mind.

In any case, the dancing did the trick, and it wasn't long before David and Angela were sharing quarters at Mary Finnegan's Foxgrove Road house. This was until *Space Oddity* came out in July of '69, when David and Angie departed with Ken Pitt to attend the Italian and Maltese Song Festivals. Things were starting to pick up careerwise for David. Later in the year he won the Ivor Novello award for "Most Original Song" (for *Space Oddity*) and in the meantime he won awards in Italy and Malta for *When I Live My Dream*. The tales of the song festivals are a comedy of ineptitude, with no accompaniment provided in Italy aside from three local accordian players, but even then David's music was going over quite well in Italy and such appearances helped. *Space Oddity* was later given the title *Ragazzo Solo, Ragazza Sola* (Lonely Boy, Lonely Girl) and became a favorite of young and old in Italy.

Any enjoyment of the trip was eclipsed by the death of David's father on the day he returned from Italy, August 5, 1969. According to Angie, David's father was suffering from double pneumonia, unbeknown to them while they were in Italy. She claims that a call came, forcing David to rush home, but that he arrived too late and his father had died four hours earlier. The fact that her story contradicts David's account wouldn't be significant, were it not for the changes others began to notice in him after his father's death. The major differences in the two accounts are that whenever David speaks about his father's death, Mr. Jones was still alive when David arrived, as if he made it just in the nick of time. But if what Angie says is true, it hints at something that may have deeply wounded David. Stories abound of parents dying just before their children achieve "success", which was just then finally happening for David: He had a song entering the charts and on TV, and he had received songwriting awards, even if they were just kitsch statuettes. The fact that David became very angry with his mother for not getting his father to the hospital seems to have been a reason for the breakdown of relations between those two, and the fact that David took all funeral arrangements upon himself, hints that he might have been trying in some way to make up for not being there at the end.

According to Pitt, when David arrived home his father was semi-conscious. Pitt quotes Bowie as saying: 'I showed him the statuette, and I know my father understood, because he smiled.' Pitt correctly noted that his father's death marked major changes in David. In all fairness, there were certain hints of the changes in David on the *David Bowie* album. (Later reissued by Mercury as *Man Of Words, Man Of Music*, and by RCA as *Space Oddity*.) Lines like "I'm a phallus in pigtails" were the kind of thing that Pitt would have seen coming from the new Bowie rather than the old. Mellow folkie David was on the way out, and without the "moderating influence" of his father, David burst with musical and image changes that could hardly have been guessed at, unless you were looking at what his friends were up to.

Marc Bolan in particular led the way for Bowie. Most importantly, he forged the "glam rock" image and he also did what he could for Bowie when his own career took off. David had done a one-man mime show in the spring of '69, opening for Tyrannosaurus Rex (Bolan's band). The mime was based on a young religious boy's experiences during the Chinese invasion of Tibet. Though it confused and disgruntled the fans, David earned another booking with another old friend's band, this time on the same bill as Humble Pie, Peter Frampton's group. These shows took place in the fall of 1969, David's first public appearances after being in virtual seclusion following his father's death. The motivation was partially to promote his Mercury album which was to be released in early November.

THE song on the *David Bowie* album was *Space Oddity*. Shortly after it came out, David said he never should have written it, because he didn't have any other material that was nearly as good at the time. From a later perspective, the song seems like even more of a weight, since the fans won't let him forget it. It is an unforgettable song, and though there are many who find the Gus Dudgeon arrangement featuring Rick Wakeman on piano a bit saccarine, it reinforces the melancholy mood of the song. Much of its power comes from the imagery, that of the lone astronaut, Major Tom, stranded in space either by choice, or due to circumstances beyond his control. And while the song stands out for being "impersonal" (Bowie is not literally Major Tom) in contrast to his first person songwriting, this song has been linked as much to Bowie the man as were his later personas. For various reasons, people related to the alienation of the song, and it served its part in ushering in Space Age consciousness. The idea of the astronaut as the latest type of hero (previously it was movie stars, rock stars and sports figures) with the line "And the papers want to know whose shirts you wear", was right on target. There are also hints of what started happening to some of the real astronauts whose perspectives were so altered that life on earth never quite seemed the same. The song also helped sales of an early prototype of the synthesizer, something called the Stylophone, which Bowie used on this and other songs. As he described it, it was a thing that went "eh, eh, eh, eh, eh,....". He appeared in some of the company's ads, and also put a few pennies in the pocket of his old employer, Essex House when they became publisher for Bowie's first "hit".

The other song released as a single with *Space Oddity* was called *Wild Eyed Boy From Freecloud*. It featured more spacey, psychedelic imagery in combination with Teutonic mythology, another theme that would creep up in Bowie's later songs. The other cuts on the album give a fair indication of Bowie's frame of mind, both personally and musically. *Unwashed and Somewhat Slightly Dazed* might have been Ken Pitt's description of David at certain points, and this song also represents an amalgamation of several of Bowie's musical influences. The lyrics owe a lot to Dylan, and the music is a combination of everyone from Dylan to The Doors, The Who and The Yardbirds. *Letter To Hermione* segues nicely into *Cygnet Committee*, the favorite song from this L.P. of True Bowie Fans. *Cygnet Committee* is a swan song for the lofty observer who sings the song.

With Beatlesque musical touches and a Jim Morrison opening line (Bowie's "I bless you madly" versus Morrison's "Love her madly" of the same year), the song established several other trends in Bowie's songwriting, from the quasi-religious themes, to the excellent handling of simultaneous changes in music and point of view. This song, like so many others, shows Bowie's predilection for musing on the future, be it his own, someone else's or the world's. By thinking things out beforehand via creative imagination, he was able to prepare for both and create what was to come. For instance, even before creating Ziggy, he wrote: "I gave Them Life/I gave Them all./They drained my very soul... dry." As an obvious example of Dylan's influence, Bowie sings of "desolation rows". What's remarkable in looking at the lyric sheet is the number of words and ideas Bowie felt compelled to pack into one song, as if it was the last one he'd ever write, whereas his most recent songs are Zen like pop jewels.

Like the rest of the album, *Janine* isn't exceptional, but it contains one of Bowie's most often quoted lines. Speaking to a woman who'd like to get inside the author, he explains: "But if you take an axe to me/You'll kill another man/Not me at all." This is most often cited when an attempt at making sense of Bowie reaches an impasse. One other song on the album is interesting mainly for its theme. In *God Knows I'm Good*, Bowie recounts the story of a petty criminal, this time an old woman shoplifter, who can't quite rationalize her action (though Bowie can: "Through her deafened ears the cash machines were shrieking on the counter") and is reduced to crying "God know's I'm good" *ad infinitum*. Life is cruel to the conscience-ridden desperate ones.

This was the album that Bowie hoped to promote on tour, though in fact he only had "that one song" that had much hope of appealing to virgin ears. Bowie's promotional plans were news to Andrew Loog Oldham, the former Stones manager who had booked David on the Humble Pie tour, expecting David to perform his mime act. Pitt had arranged these gigs for David, but due to the timing of the album, and the placement of mime on the back burner, David decided to perform on his acoustic guitar anyway —David also had problems with the tour's organization. As he put it: 'It was my first tour and I never stopped being surprised that the concerts even went on. It appeared to be badly organized to me, but I supposed everybody knew what they were doing.' He went on to say that the shows were nothing near an artistic success, because although he'd been playing one-off gigs all along, they were for folkier audiences, and he discovered that Northern England and Scotland were a million miles away from blase' London. Here is some of Bowie's description of the scene he encountered:

> It was very hard. I was on in front of these gum-chewing skinheads. As soon as I appeared, looking a bit like Bob Dylan with this curly hair and denims, I was whistled and booed. At one point I even had cigarettes thrown at me. Isn't that awful? It turned me off the business, I was totally paranoid. [4]

Recalling the ill-fated '69 tour in 1983, Bowie put his experience in perspective:

> I'd written this little thing about Major Tom and gotten it recorded and I was told I had a concert tour if I wanted it! I thought haughtily, "I'll go out and sing my song!", not knowing what audiences were like in those days. Sure enough, it was the revival of the mod thing which had since turned into skinheads. They couldn't abide me. (Laughter.) No! No way! The whole spitting, cigarette-flicking abuse thing by audiences started long before the punks of 1977 in my own frame of reference. [5]

Something else that began around this time was that David started getting fan mail from girls "promising to do strange things to him" and sending "gonky little things" and stuffed animals to their idol. Said Bowie at the time: 'I stand amazed by it all!'

Though David had gone along with the tour, it was becoming clear that Ken Pitt's decisions were out of tune with both David's personal and career needs. A rift grew, helped by the fact that most of David's major influences were coming from elsewhere, particularly from the Marc and June Bolan, Angie, and Tony Visconti group. And then there were people like Calvin Mark Lee, who were more akin to David's new lifestyle than Ken Pitt could ever be. Bypassing Pitt entirely, David and Calvin Lee organized "An Evening With David Bowie" at the Purcell Room on November 20, 1969. By all accounts, it was one of David's great performances, but not a single member of the press was there to write about it. Pitt was angered and upset by the increasing distance between himself and Bowie, especially when David prevented him from doing things which he was well qualified to do. As a member of the Society of Theatre Press Representatives, Pitt was quite disturbed when Lee, that "American-pharmacist-turned-show-business-wheeler -dealer" had bungled notices to the press, and David was equally upset when he learned that no one was there to review his brilliant performance. At this point in his career, the attention of the press was crucial, and a great opportunity had been blown, fueling speculation that Bowie might have made it much sooner "if only..." These early frustrations contributed to the process of educating David in the use of the media to his own advantage.

As the gulf between Pitt and Bowie grew, so did more of the career-oriented changes that David would make became inspired by changes in his private life. The end of '69 found David and Angie moving into a residence which they would occupy for several years. They had been living temporarily with David's mother, but evidently she didn't appreciate the help, their relationship or having another woman in her kitchen. Angie left England (and David) for Cyprus over Christmas to escape from Mrs. Jones' new tactic of "telephonic abuse", which was too much for Angie to bear. Mrs. Jones didn't like them "living in sin", and let her feelings be known. So the decade ended with David and Angie a thousand miles apart, planning their next moves.

FIVE

'Watch that Man-Oh Honey Watch that
Man/He talks like a jerk/But he could eat
you with a fork and spoon' ..

'Watch That Man' — *Aladdin Sane*

It was 1970, the year that The Beatles disbanded after working a rather thorough transformation on rock and pop music, and David Bowie was to all intents and purposes just getting started. No one emerged who was to capture the international imagination on the scale that The Beatles had done, and for the most part people retreated into narrower and more particular musical tastes. There are people who would claim Neil Young as the major artist of the Seventies and others would give the crown to Springsteen or to Bowie, whose persona was certainly the most bizarre. At the same time, there were several other musical trends progressing simultaneously; the mainstream efforts of the Carole Kings and Stevie Wonders; the Grateful Dead dragged hippie music into a new decade, and heavy metal came to the fore with the help of Led Zeppelin, while electronic/textural music became popular through the likes of Pink Floyd. This is not to mention the rise of disco or birth of reggae and punk, and such forms as country music, which developed alongside rock. The one thing that can be said of Bowie is that he was one of the few artists exhibiting a power to both synthesize and generate new styles that were comparable to what the Beatles had achieved. And without belaboring the point, for all the other influences that were working on Bowie during the 1960s, there can be no doubt that The Beatles were his greatest teachers. When Bowie teamed up with John Lennon in the mid-Seventies, he said that Lennon "set him straight" on subjects ranging from the essence of rock music to how to survive in the music business, not to mention how to cope with Fame.

In the meantime, without Lennon's direct guidance, Bowie set to work with a few friends, trying to figure out just how to crack the oyster of the music business. While Marc Bolan gets credit for beginning the so-called glam-rock or glitter rock movement, Bowie introduced certain heavy metal elements, though both were smart enough to realize that they had to go "pop" in order to make their music and acts truly popular. And since all of these ideas arose from a combination of personal predilections and social observations, the personal deserves some attention.

As 1970 began, Angie was with her parents in Cyprus, trying to decide what to do about her relationship with David. She hadn't heard from David for almost two weeks, due to an English postal strike that she hadn't been aware of. When the mail finally did arrive, there was a pile of it, including a postcard from David which read: "Please come back. We will marry, I promise, this year." That was all she needed to hear, so when David called her that evening wondering why there was no response from her, she promised to return immediately. David also played the acetate of a song he'd just written for her called *The Prettiest Star*, which was released as a single early in 1970, although it didn't appear on an album until *Aladdin Sane* a few years later. This is indicative of something happening then and throughout Bowie's career; his songwriting was so prolific that at any moment he had a backlog of material just waiting to be polished and recorded.

So Angie returned to Haddon Hall, their favorite name for a place which was actually Flat 42, Southend Road, Beckenham, which they turned into a home befitting their tastes and lifestyle. Going back to what David had in common with Ken Pitt, we have Pitt's description of what he found on his first visit to "The Hall":

> Whenever he received a sizeable check in his years with me, the first thing David would do would be that he would go down to the antique supermarkets in Marylebone and Kensington, and choose himself another piece of glass by Lalique or Galle, or another volume with prints by Rackham, Caldecott or Kate Greenway, or another piece of pewter or a vase — and then David would bring his latest trophy back here to my flat, and show me proudly what he had been able to buy himself with the proceeds of his latest record, or his latest series of concerts.
>
> The first time I went down to Haddon Hall, I saw all these "trophies" that he had collected over the years decorating the flat, giving it a character all its own. [1]

With a baroque, Victorian feel to the flat and the space for a music room, a wine cellar ('that is not as well stocked as we would like it to be because we're both very fond of wine') and a bedroom big enough for a seven foot wide Regency bed (which David discovered unassembled for forty pounds and which was 'fabulous, like a huge coffin with a canopy'), they had created a distinctive and artistic environment.

The flat at Haddon Hall was eventually filled with or occupied by most of the people who figured in David's life during the next two years, from Mick Ronson and the other Spiders, to Freddie Burretti their costume designer, to nannies, hairdressers and just plain friends and acquaintances. The association with the Arts Lab continued into the time they lived in the Hall, and David's friends and admirers from the lab were also frequent visitors at Haddon Hall.

The setting was also the inspiration for several things, including the infamous original cover to *The Man Who Sold The World*. An earlier casual photo of David reclining on the settee in their dramatic living room was fashioned into the image of David in his Mr. Fish dress. It was also the scene of David and Angie's wedding reception, and keeping to the promise of marrying, the date of March 20, 1970 was decided upon. The reasons commonly given for their marriage point to Angie's expiring visa, and while this may have had something to do with the timing and the decision to make things "official", mere convenience wouldn't necessarily have had them living together or deciding to have a child. No longer one to be taken in by the stereotypic image of love (he gave up that idea after Hermione), David later gave an understated explanation of their relationship to Cameron Crowe of Playboy magazine. 'I realized that she'd be one of the very few women I'd be capable of living with for more than a week. She is remarkably pleasant to keep coming back to. And for me she always will be.' He went on to explain the reasons why: 'There's nobody more demanding than me. Not physically, necessarily, but mentally. I'm very strenuous. Very intense about anything I do. I scare away most people I've lived with.' On a note of consistency he gave similar reasons for the demise of the marriage. 'I'm a very solitary person, actually, kind of selfish that way... I find it hard to be perpetually enthusiastic about somebody else's life all the time.'

Not realizing at the time that he "went into it wrong", the wedding was arranged and took place in a largely secret ceremony at the Beckenham registry office, with David's mother somehow finding out about it. Mrs. Jones wasn't invited, but she did some detective work and arrived before the bride and groom. Angie and David came late wearing some fairly outrageous nuptial costumes and further flustered the Registrar by pulling out four Peruvian bracelets to be exchanged in place of the traditional wedding rings. They each wore two of them, though David's original pair are now the proud possession of some fan who managed to slip them off David's arm in a moment of adoration (since then he's worn copies). In a classic low budget wedding, the bride, groom and a few friends retired to Haddon Hall, and depending on who tells the story, they either watched television while it rained, or had a rather uninhibited celebration including wine, dancing on tables and some crockery smashing in the Cypriot tradition. According to Angie, she and David managed to sneak away to the bedroom unnoticed, as they were to do on other occasions when some privacy was called for.

The first couple of months in 1970 saw David playing some solo gigs in Scotland and at the Marquee Club, as well as picking up his Disc magazine award for "Brightest Hope" on the British music scene. Foregoing these inroads to success, David let his perm fall, and on February 28th announced the formation of a new band called "Hype", which turned out to be the prototype for a later group known as the "Spiders From Mars". The line-up of "Hype" included producer and friend Tony Visconti on bass, John Cambridge (who played on Mercury's *David Bowie* album) on drums and a certain Mick Ronson on guitar. The story of how David and Mick met varies, typically, depending on who's telling the story. One version pivots on Visconti who had met Ronson during a session for Michael Chapman's *Fully Qualified Survivor* LP. Knowing that David was looking for a guitarist he introduced them, correctly guessing that they'd "get along". Charles Shaar Murray says that the introduction came through Gus Dudgeon and Paul Buckmaster who had worked on sessions with Ronson.

Melody Maker ran an article on the band in their March 28th issue, in which David discussed the concept behind "Hype"; it is illuminating, considering that Bowie would soon meet up with Tony De Fries and begin one of the biggest hypes in music history. The interview points out the dilemma facing someone with certain beliefs or ideas about how things should be, who also happens to be intelligent enough to recognize the way things actually work (in this case in the music business). Here the idealism and realism were still battling, though later the pragmatism emerged victorious. So David talked about his reasons for choosing the name "Hype": 'I deliberately chose the name in favour of something that sounded perhaps heavy because now no one can say that they're being conned.' He went on to talk about the public image of the business, of "free music" being presented for "free people" which he called "a crock", since the people involved were so hypocritical in everything else. So he said: 'I suppose you could say that I chose "Hype" deliberately with tongue in cheek.' As evidence that there was really no overnight change, he described one of the recent "Hype" gigs, which sounds like a test balloon for Ziggy Stardust:

> We've had these costumes made by various girlfriends which make us look like Dr. Strange or the Incredible Hulk. I was a bit apprehensive about wearing them at the Roundhouse gig because I didn't know how the audience would react. If they think it's a huge put-on the whole thing will backfire, but they seemed to accept it which was nice. [2]

His comment about the "put-on" is interesting because it indicates Bowie's correct sense of proportion. Rock has quite a bit of put-on, send-up and rave-up inherent in it, but if people think that's all they're getting, they're likely to be put off. No one likes to feel the fool, but they usually won't mind a little teasing. Bowie's been treading this same thin line ever since.

Meanwhile, *The Prettiest Star* was released on Mercury, with essentially the same line-up as Hype except that Bolan played guitar. He had time for the sessions but was too busy with his own career to play in David's band. On *Aladdin Sane*, Ronson played guitar, but he barely strayed from Bolan's original line. As an indication that Bowie was becoming a "name artiste" (thanks largely to *Space Oddity*), Decca reissued the first *David Bowie* album in their budget "World Of" series. This time they included *London Boys* and three other songs that had never been on an LP, partly because as Bowie began sounding more like a rock musician, they decided to change the orientation of the album. This tendency to update previous work would become a hallmark of record company dealings with Bowie, and this same package came out again in 1973, with the sole change being a new cover photo of David as Ziggy Stardust.

While the material for what would be called *The Man Who Sold The*

World was being worked out, another older song called *Memory Of A Free Festival* was released as a two-version single. The song had been included on the *Space Oddity* album (alias *David Bowie* alias *Man Of Words, Man Of Music*) with Visconti producing, as well as remixing these versions. The songs were about a festival organized through the Art Lab, and the sound is a mesh of psychedelia and back-to-basics rock. Things were finally beginning to sort themselves out, and rock was definitely on the rise.

Since *Space Oddity*, (the L.P) was what's known as a "sleeper", taking several months to climb into the charts, Mercury (probably with Bowie's approval) floated several singles prior to the release of *The Man Who Sold The World*, only one of which appeared on the album. That song was *Black Country Rock*, originally the B-side to *Holy Holy*. *Holy Holy* was an almost perfect imitation of Marc Bolan; in fact, many people couldn't be convinced that it wasn't Bolan. If nothing else, it proves that Bowie is an excellent mimic. Using a mock Oriental sound, Bowie ritualistically buried Buddhism and claimed his allegiance to the forces of the night. On this score there are all kinds of stories of Bowie's membership in a coven of witches which may have been true but could also have been assumed on the basis of his music alone. *Black Country Rock*, on the other hand, makes light of these Bolanesque influences, telling the listener that if the view from the Rock is much too hazy, "You can leave my friend and me with fond adieu". At this parting, Bowie opted for hard rock, a lead Bolan eventually followed, though he'd beaten Bowie to stardom. The time was approaching for their self-prophesies to come true. Bolan had long been telling anyone who would listen to him that he was gonna be a star, and as Mick Ronson simply put it: 'David just knew he'd be famous one day.'

At this time, the work towards manufacturing the "total package" was beginning, starting with the all-important matter of "image". The angle of theater and costuming was being explored, for which Angie deserves some of the credit. (She also worked on lighting and staging but was replaced with pros when De Fries arrived.) A believer that show business was glamor business, she did her best to convince the boys in the band of the need to maintain their glamorous images off-stage as well. The "boys in the band" still included Visconti on bass, although his time would soon be taken up by his role as Bolan's producer, leaving him little time for playing with or producing anyone else. The problem was solved by Ronson who, as the need arose, drafted members of his former Hull-based band the Rats, into David's services. Woody Wood-mansey was recruited on drums and the band was complete when Trevor Bolder turned up on bass, forming a cozy family all living in Haddon Hall. At this point, the only ingredient missing in the success formula was a suitable manager. Pitt was then having little contact with David (apparently David's choice) and there were some financial problems as well. With this as a basis, David sought some advice early in 1970 that would have drastic results on his career. The man David went to for guidance was a certain Tony De Fries, and as Bowie has been mythologized, so has De Fries, with nicknames like "Deep Freeze" or "De Freak" and with more than a few comparisons to Col. Tom Parker, Elvis Presley's notorious manager. It's important neither to under-estimate nor to over-emphasize De Fries' role in Bowie's career, which was of considerable importance.

It's worth considering what De Fries had done prior to becoming Bowie's manager; a role which became the logical next step for a man who seemed to possess the same internal gyroscope that Bowie possesses, which in De Fries' case led him into artists' management. Born in Shepherd's Bush (home of Roger Daltrey and the BBC), the son of a market trader, De Fries says he was "fated" for either the rag trade, show business or law, and he chose law. It's not certain that he ever became "articled", but people accepted his advice anyway, especially when the subject was entertainment, a field to which he soon gravitated while working for Martin Boston and Co.. His major case, beginning in 1964, involved representing Mickey Most in a dispute with The Animals. While representing Most, he took on the role of financial/business advisor when he tried to straighten out Most's affairs with Allan Klein. This project led in turn to De Fries meeting Laurence Myers, then part of the accounting firm of Goodman Myers and Co., who were handling Most's accounts at the time. Shortly afterwards, Myers gave up accounting to begin his own management company, while De Fries busied himself representing various top British models, a project which Michael Watts muses may have led to the decision to launch Bowie as the "Face of the Seventies". (It helped that Bowie had the face and that he happened to be agreeable — from fashion consciousness to promotion was a small step.)

In early 1969, De Fries began gravitating more towards management, through a loose association with the company Myers had created called GEM (which eventually gained Bowie as a client, as evidenced by their logo on the early RCA records). De Fries brought in clients and had use of the office, while also working for a firm called Godfrey David and Batt when his dealings were legal. It was in the offices of Godfrey David that Bowie and De Fries first met.

As usual, different people are credited with this fateful introduction. Some point to Visconti, and though the connections become increas-ingly hazy as friends met friends of friends etc., the more common version of the introduction points to a man named Olaf Wyper. Wyper was then heading the Philips operation in the U.K., when he heard that David was frustrated in his relationship with Pitt. He suggested that David contact his lawyer, De Fries, for some advice and assistance. The following is De Fries' description of his first meeting with David:

> He came wandering in very unshaven, hollow-cheeked, bleary-eyed and nervous, chewing his fingernails and sat in my office looking like a refugee. [3]

De Fries then added that 'he always looks like a refugee unless he's been properly dressed and put together for the day', which should bring heart to those who aspire to the immaculate fashion of Bowie's recent incarnation. Here are some more illuminating remarks from De Fries, offering a key to Bowie's charm and ingratiating manner:

> I felt sorry for Bowie. That was David really, because when he wants people to do things, he usually gets them to feel sorry for him or gets them on his side in some way. I thought "poor little chap. He's got himself in a terrible mess".

De Fries' reputation for being able to get people in and out of contracts was well justified in Bowie's case, as they managed to convince Ken Pitt to waive the remaining two years of the original five-year management contract. Though there was probably some sort of financial settlement, Pitt was magnanimous, saying, 'I had to consider the atmosphere. Each of us had to consider the situation. He (Bowie) blamed himself too saying, "Ken, I'm sorry I can't be a cause".' Presumably meaning Pitt's cause, because Bowie would certainly become his own greatest cause with De Fries' help. Ken Pitt rather disparagingly considered De Fries to be "an Angie protege'", but David's remarks make it clear that the ensuing relationship was his decision (although Angie and De Fries got along quite well), and was based on his needs in conjunction with what he thought De Fries could do for him. As David put it, when Tony told him that he could get David out of his contract with Pitt: 'I just sat there and openly wept. I was so relieved that somebody was so strong about things.'

The reason for David's relief was that it was a tough time for him, especially as his music had yet to crystallize and since he was working simultaneously on two different albums worth of material, the usual creative blues were intensified by the insecurity of wondering just how his efforts would be received. He had also been living in virtual seclusion within Haddon Hall, and while necessary, the situation had become oppressive and laced with self doubt. With an entire household depending on him as well, what De Fries represented at that time was just what Bowie needed. As David described it:

> I was always stronger than everybody else around me, more determined and wanting to do more things and everybody else was mousy and didn't want to take any risks. It was like going uphill trying to drag kids with you. "Oh come on will you!" — and nobody would go with you. And then there was this pillar of strength. It was like everything was going to be different. [4]

Needless to say, everything changed for Bowie once De Fries became his manager. It turned out to be one of Bowie's most fruitful and profitable collaborations. They accomplished a great deal during their partnership, but there was also much that went on that Bowie couldn't abide, and displaying a tendency for assuming ever more control and responsibility over his own career, Bowie eventually became self-managed. De Fries, for his part, never expected this would happen because, as he put it: 'I've never been able to think of either of them (David and Angie) as anything but a couple of children.' No wonder Bowie outgrew De Fries' constricted view of him. On this point there are many who consider De Fries a "svengali" for his manipulations on Bowie's behalf, but in reality a manager is only as good as his client, though it took a few years before this became obvious.

Initially, what De Fries offered Bowie was the chance to work on his music, without concern for the business side of things. He also offered much-needed moral support. After spending several months familiarizing himself with Bowie's music before taking on management responsibilities, De Fries came to the conclusion that Bowie was potentially "bigger than Dylan", which must have heartened David. This measure of artistic freedom was just what David needed at the time, since by the time De Fries entered the picture, work had already begun on *The Man Who Sold The World* and the long-haired feminine image that began to develop was David's own creation and choice. It could also make him look like a good hippie if need be, which came in handy for one of David's last appearances in obvious sympathy with that particular culture. He was invited to play at the Glastonbury Fayre in June of 1970, sharing the bill with the likes of the Grateful Dead and Gong, with De Fries, Angie and Dana Gillespie in attendance for David's dawn performance in druidic Somerset. Although David donated a tape to the album which was released to support the event, his live set wasn't recorded, furnishing another example of "the one that got away". Angie claims that it was one of his best performances ever, and that people still write to her about it, as late as 1980 anyway.

So 1970 closed with Hype performing about and David's next album due out in January of 1971. It was at this point that he began to get the kind of attention that he's famous for, as well as providing the frequently ambiguous responses that his equally ambiguous images provoked. In the preceding year, David had let his hair grow and his perm fall, and had taken publicly to wearing what he called his "man's dress". The garb first came to notoriety when it was worn by David on the original cover to *The Man Who Sold The World*. (Bowie told one writer that it was a take-off of a Gabriel Rosetti painting 'slightly askew', prefaced by 'You probably won't believe it...', which should suffice as fair warning.) In the U.S., collectors, and those who buy Bowie books, are the only ones familiar with this cover, as the American record industry can recognize a threat when it sees one, and the Chicago offices of Mercury balked at the cover, substituting a cowboy cartoon instead and leaving Bowie quite angry and resolved to leave the label at the first opportunity. There was a second, and still in print version, issued when RCA bought the Bowie back catalogue, which features David with leg in air on a black background (Ziggy in performance), which is a visual clue for the "hard rock" enclosed. American audiences like to know what they're getting, or so goes the prevailing wisdom. In

England, things seem to work a bit differently, and though Bowie may not have known just how it would work out, 'The reaction of the English critics (to the cover) was predictable. They lapped it up but at the same time felt threatened.' It was this paradoxical/contradictory state of mind that Bowie and De Fries had the genius eventually to exploit. There were some people actually paying attention to the vinyl inside, prompting Charles Shaar Murray to claim that this is where things *really* begin. He's right in the career sense (Bowie had become an identifiable entity), though musically Bowie would later go back even further than this point. But this is where "Rock Bowie" really begins, and it's also where the calculated packaging job becomes an element, and neither should be underestimated. So if you own the original English pressing of this album what you see might influence what you hear, though what you hear will be largely hard rock with some almost "pretty" embellishment.

The hard edge will likely be undercut by your image of the singer and his voice, which is still a bit reedy, and not as sinister as the music or lyrics might suggest. You'll hear some Marc Bolan and some Nietzsche and traces of a folk singer who won't die.

And if you've got the U.S. version, you're likely to pay more attention to the music and amaze at the lyrics (which can be heard) and you might notice the contrast between the tone of voice and the crunch of the music. The drums are solidly present, but it's Mick Ronson's power chording and Tony Visconti's full volume bass that really define the sound of the album. The other side of it is that Bowie's vocals (plus the background voices), and Ralph Mace's synthesizer give the whole effort a musicality usually lacking in the genre known as "heavy metal", which in so many words was what they were toying with. Overall, it's rather finely balanced with some brilliant, far from heavy (handed, anyway) touches. The reactions to the album varied, and while Bowie later referred to it as one of the few albums that he considered an "artistic success", the overwhelming reaction was to ignore it. For some reason some American critics picked up on it and also gave it generally favorable reviews. Bowie later taunted the American critics in particular for their need to intellectualize and analyze the music, but in this case it worked to his benefit. Chris Van Ness writing in the L.A. Free Press began his critique by posing and answering a significant question:

> What happens to a flower-child, when all of the world around him is going slightly crazy and power struggles are taking over everything, including his music, is that he harnesses his genius, conforms to the insanity, outpowers the loudest group around, and does it all just a little bit better than anybody else. [5]

Van Ness went on to note that, 'The concepts of the title song, *The Superman* or the *Saviour Machine* are not your normal themes, but then David Bowie is not your normal writer.' Rolling Stone reviewer John Mendelsohn was similarly impressed, making the following comments:

In an album that, save the impotently sarcastic *Running Gun Blues*, is uniformly excellent, at least four tracks demand special attention; *Saviour Machine* demonstrates that Bowie far from exhausted his talent for quietly moralistic rock sci-fi in his earlier *Space Oddity*. The almost insufferably depressive *After All* contains the strangest refrain perhaps ever conceived — a haunting mantric "Oh, by jingo". *The Width Of A Circle* is both a hallucination with religious overtones that recall both Dante and Adam and Eve and a sound of enormity. And *She Shook Me Cold* contains some of the most bizarre sexual imagery ever committed to vinyl: "She sucked my dormant will" or "She took my young head, smashed it up/And left my young blood rising".
6

As much as Mendelsohn liked the album, he and many others were glad to see *Hunky Dory* arrive, making *The Man* appear transitional, but the fact is that either everything Bowie does is transitional or nothing is. The albums stand out like landmarks (Bowie favors the more ephemeral analogy to polaroids), reference points to which Bowie is prone to return in true traveler fashion. This hard rock approach would be applied on at least two other occasions (*Aladdin Sane* and *Scary Monsters*), with variations of course. Not only was he almost immediately recognized as a songwriter, but his arrangements (here in conjunction with Visconti and Ronson) would make his music as distinctive as his themes and his voice. Another trait which Bowie has displayed throughout his musical career is the inclusion of "borrowed phrases", be they musical or lyrical. It is so obvious that Bowie has referred to himself as a "tasteful thief" (with the emphasis on "tasteful"), saying that the only art worth studying is that which you can steal from. In the case of *The Man*, a couple of the most obvious appropriations are from The Beatles and their psychedelic period in general, and the use of borrowed introductions on a few songs which work to immediately catch the listener's ear. On *She Shook Me Cold*, Ronson does a pretty good impersonation of Jimi Hendrix, and the title song starts off sounding remarkably like The Yardbird's *Over Under Sideways Down*, while *Running Gun Blues* sounds generally like The Who. Of all the themes that Bowie has explored, his psychotic tales have been consistently criticized, but they must hold some deep appeal for the author who nearly repeated *Running Gun* as late as 1980.

On the subject of Bowie's "thievery" though, it should be noted that all culture is self-referencing and is a matter of accretion, so his references are nothing to get irate over (unless you have a copyright on the original) and the manner in which Bowie incorporates these other elements into his songs is one of the reasons for his popular success. He regularly gives his audience these musical straws to grab hold of, and they make the doses of originality easier to absorb, more accessible. The biggest problem comes with his imitators, who have usually lost the spark of the original inspirations and only tyrannize with their emptiness.

As fine an album as *The Man* proved itself to be, sales weren't very impressive even with the positive reviews. To bolster sales, Mercury arranged for Bowie to visit the U.S. on a promotional tour. They were unable to arrange a work visa, so Bowie was limited to radio and press interviews (and a spur of the moment live appearance in Chicago, where Mercury was based and had some clout) through which he managed to stir up some interest and outrage. Bowie's first stop was New York, his first visit to a city that he would return to often. Wearing his Mr. Fish dress and carrying a handbag, he was hardly out of place, and he found New York very sympathetic. The timing also points to this possibly being the visit on which Bowie met a few people who would have more than a passing influence on him, namely Lou Reed, Iggy Pop (alias Stooge) and Andy Warhol. Bowie tells a funny story about visiting Warhol's Factory and repeatedly riding up the elevator only to encounter a brick wall facing him, at what should have been the studio entrance. The paranoia was partially due to Warhol's recent run-in with Ms. Solonas. Despite this perturbing first impression, Bowie went on to meet and paint a musical portrait of Andy Warhol "the artist" on his next album.

David was already familiar with Warhol, and he'd also been listening to Lou Reed and the Velvet Underground, thanks to Ken Pitt's introduction. Lou and David finally met while Bowie was in N.Y.C. Bowie likes to tell this story, beginning with, 'Did you know how I met Iggy and Lou Reed?'

> I was at an RCA party at Max's Kansas City in New York and was introduced to Lou. He immediately started telling me about a guy who injected smack through his forehead — that's typical Lou. Anyway, up comes this funny, ragged, ragged little guy with broken teeth and Lou says, "Don't talk to him, he's a junkie" — that was Iggy. You can't help loving him, he's so vulnerable. [7]

As it turns out, Bowie's friendship with Iggy has been among his most enduring, and the fascination with this retinue continued during Bowie's travels across the States. There are tales of David in his dress being asked to leave a Texas town at gunpoint, so it's not surprising that he found more sympathy on the West Coast. Visiting a San Francisco radio station, he explained that *The Man* was the story of a 'shaven-headed transvestite', and L.A. was even more fun to play with. An interview with John Mendelsohn begins with a description of Bowie leaving his own party to watch Ultra Violet hold court from her milk bathtub. This environment had Bowie sufficiently at ease to speak frankly (after his fashion) on a few crucial subjects. While he was intentionally playing up the sexual ambiguity (or maybe it wasn't ambiguous at all) with lines like 'Tell your readers to make up their minds about me when I start getting adverse publicity; When I'm found in bed with Raquel Welch's husband.', he also made a couple of frequently quoted remarks that clearly state just where Bowie was coming from and where he was heading. They also echo statements he'd made before and after on the relationship between himself and his music. Leading in from a discussion of his mime background, this is what Bowie had to say on the subject:

> What the music says may be serious, but as a medium it should not be questioned, analyzed or taken so seriously. I think it should be tarted up, made into a prostitute, a parody of itself. It should be the clown, the Pierrot medium. The music is the mask the message wears — music is the Pierrot and I, the performer, am the message. 8

This tarting up, dressing up and generally theatricalizing rock was a major part of Bowie's formula for success. He still understands this to be an essential ingredient of rock music, and even if he's performing in a pin-stripe suit with a watch, his moves still have a bit of striptease in them. But in the meantime, he took it all to an extreme before reeling it back in. The period between the release of the *Man Who Sold* and the introduction of Ziggy is tumultuous and finds Bowie at his most prolific. It also marks the beginning of the sale of Bowie to the world, and while there is no evidence of contracts written in blood (the man who sold the world to somebody for something...), it becomes clearer just what some of the prices were that Bowie eventually had to pay for the rapid rise to recognition that was just a few brilliant strokes away.

SIX

'Do you remember the bills you have to pay/For even yesterday' ..

'Young Americans' -— *Young Americans*

In the period between January of 1971 and June of 1972, David Bowie released three MAJOR albums, which if nothing else indicates that he's prolific, and essentially hard working. He's forever mentioning work as an overriding concern, even a need, and because he has worked so consistently on material for albums, it makes it very difficult to determine just when and how they were written. For instance, if *The Prettiest Star* hadn't been released as a single, who would know that it wasn't written in the control room during the *Aladdin Sane* sessions? Bowie's been known to do that on occasion. The one thing that helps date some of the material on David's next release, *Hunky Dory* is the references to his son Zowie, which means that at least two songs were written around the time of Zowie's birth in June of 1971. The other material is harder to pin down; the songs could have been started much earlier or written just before the tape started to roll. There seem to be both types of song on the album. In any case, the pace of Bowie's progress was beginning to accelerate. While *The Man* was being promoted, the acetates of *Hunky Dory* were being taken around by Tony De Fries. It also came about through the auspices of De Fries' former associate Mickey Most, that Peter Noone recorded a version of *Oh You Pretty Things*, which preceded the release of Bowie's version and even made it into the English charts. This helped *Hunky Dory* win some acceptance, but Bowie reached a new level after he gave his famous interview to Michael Watts -— at a time when the Ziggy tapes and tour plans were already a reality.

By the time *The Man Who Sold The World* was released in early 1971, Bowie was a father-to-be, had a new manager, and something of a reputation, at least amongst the London gay community, which had formed a faithful fan club for the latest Bowie incarnation. All of these factors came into play, with an emphasis on De Fries' help in the areas of defining his image and his performances. Angie tells about De Fries at rehearsals armed with a stop watch, at least in the early days. One of his main contributions was a new professionalism which brought discipline to David's act. De Fries also had some definite ideas on the proper strategy to take with Bowie's career, decisions largely in keeping with certain ideas shared by Angie and David, but he also became possessed with the idea that David was the beginning of an "empire syndrome" which worked as Tony's motivation, and classically, led to his demise. Though he was to prove himself right in seeing Bowie as the center of an empire, the syndrome was his own problem. De Fries often mentioned that he thought of David as a building, something like the Pan Am building, possibly because he was as solid and enduring, but more likely because with De Fries behind him, Bowie could generate the money to buy such a property, and then no doubt charge exorbitant rents. In the short term, De Fries' greed and ambition worked in Bowie's favor, and they remained partners for just that long. Bowie had already tried out a "nice man" for a manager and that didn't work (says Bowie: 'You've gotta be a bastard in this business.'), so for the time being, De Fries was perfect.

One of the things that De Fries helped Bowie develop was the matter of "image", of which David was already conscious and innovative to a high degree. What De Fries contributed was taking it all the way out, with all the trappings of glamor, which produced an effect (and envy, the stuff of which dreams of fame are made) and guaranteed notice. When De Fries first entered the scene, David was in his Lauren Bacall lookalike phase (he preferred to be thought of in terms of Garbo); and though it was a step in the right direction, it was premature to be planning the limos and entourage. First they had to sell David as songwriter (and will-be-star) in order to get the financial backing for the real deal. Only then could the face and persona of David Bowie become as estabished through music as Garbo had become through film, exerting a not dissimilar effect on culture and imaginations.

What De Fries initially had to work with was Bowie's swishy, occasionally dress-wearing image, and though it attracted a staunch following of gay men (which pointed out just how many people were waiting for something like this), there were others who found the image sufficient grounds for suspicion if not rejection. This was what Tony De Fries encountered as he began to take the tapes of *Hunky Dory* around to various record companies. (David had decided he wanted out with Mercury after their treatment of his last L.P.) Clive Davis, then president of CBS in New York had been interested in Bowie, liked the music, but was put off by "the sexually ambivalent Lauren Bacall lookalike" of 1971. This was after English A&R man Dan Loggins was ready and willing to go ahead with Bowie, proving if nothing else that the conservative U.S. record company execs were digging their own graves (since when have businessmen been the keepers of morality?) and to this day continue to depend on the British for most significant developments in their artists and repertoire.

CBS had been a "real contender" for Bowie's hand, but it's only appropriate that Bowie ended up at RCA, since it had been Elvis' label ever since Tom Parker brought (bought) him from Sun. Besides, Lou Reed was with RCA too, and De Fries had a few words to say on just what he expected from the relationship:

I want RCA to be Bowie, and I want Bowie to be RCA — in the

same way that Presley was RCA. Elvis Presley is their bread and butter and I want Bowie to take that position. [1]

For several years that was more or less the case; Bowie reaped benefits from being RCA's star performer (he was flown to New York to see Elvis perform for example) and in return he put money back in their pockets. He continues to do so, even while signed to another label since they've got his back catalogue (although he maintains some control) and if Elvis is any indication the reissues might continue forever.

One thing that isn't necessarily obvious now is that RCA took quite a risk with Bowie, because De Fries was "asking quite a lot", especially considering that David had "just come off a couple of loser albums for Mercury". As it was, De Fries must have been able to turn on a persuasive sales pitch with his talk of The Next Big Thing, but the clincher seems to have been the tapes of *Hunky Dory*, including a couple of songs that had "hit" written all over them (Peter Noone's version of *Oh, You Pretty Things* was in the charts by then). An unprecedented deal was worked out by that master of contracts, De Fries, whereby RCA picked up David's two "loser" Mercury albums, and on the strength of his arrival as Ziggy Stardust, turned them into winners. This also poses the question of whether or not De Fries also hinted that Ziggy was about to come out of the closet, but with RCA's conservative reputation it's doubtful that they would have bought into glitter, even given the chance. Instead it seems that De Fries sold Bowie on his singing, songwriting, intelligence, charm, and the promise of someone who would be a great performer, in whatever guise or situation, someone who would practically sell his own records, with just a little push and backing from the label.

Those *Hunky Dory* tapes must have sounded sweet to the first ears that heard them. RCA probably would have been quite happy if everything he did sounded just the same and many others felt the same way. This is the point at which people begin to have their favorite Bowie albums, and while *Hunky Dory* would be near the top of many people's lists, David himself is not among them. He called the song *Changes* neurotic, and probably had doubts about the extremely sweet pop sound he'd created, when his own taste runs towards music with more of an edge to it. The one song on the album which he claimed to like at the time, and continues to do in performance, is *Life On Mars?* Bowie talked about the song to Mick Rock, in part explaining the cryptic "(INSPIRED BY FRANKIE)" note next to the song on the album cover. Bowie told Rock that he'd written the song around the same chord pattern as Frank Sinatra's *My Way*. He didn't mention his intimate relationship with the song and the reason that it might have become an obsession, but rather spoke about the lyrics; 'I couldn't believe those lyrics. You know, "I'll get pissed my way". Really evil.' He went on to say that he loved the arrangement on *Mars* and that he would have preferred to put that out as a single instead of *Changes*, 'but I decided to leave it up to RCA.'

RCA knew what it was doing, because *Changes* is still getting airplay. If Bowie wasn't crazy about the song when he wrote it, the fact that the very word has become a permanent tag and ubiquitous adjective could make him wish that he'd never written it. *Changes* may have resulted from some of Bowie's "neurotic" musings on his future, (and that of his friends) qualifying as personal in themes, though the differences between *Changes* and *Mars* are major, and almost define the two poles of Bowie's songwriting. *Changes* is one of the simplest and most direct songs Bowie's ever written, and happens to be thoroughly pop, with its dramatic tension and the infectious "Changes" explosion. It also happens to be written for a young audience, whereas *Life On Mars?* is less accessible, with more personal quirky references and shifting points of view which make it more intriguing and mysterious.

Its beautiful melody and the almost other worldly vocal performance by Bowie render *Mars*, all in all, a far-away song. Speaking with Mick Rock about the album Bowie talked about the different points of view (where in a song like *Mars* a pause in the middle of a phrase may be the only cue for a phase shift) and it is Rock's voice that you hear first.

> He's been working for a long time not really knowing where he was going. Now *Hunky Dory's* made him very aware of his own style of songwriting, in a way that he wasn't before. "Part of it is not singing like an American, and then using lyrics that really meant something to a lot of people, not just me. So, often it's not my point of view I'm putting across. I'm more like a focal point for a lot of ideas that are goin' around. Sometimes I don't feel like I'm a person at all, I'm just a collection of other people's ideas." [2]

This last idea is one that Bowie's frequently expressed, and others have made the same point or accusation, but it's not that simple an issue. While he may absorb a lot, discrimination enters into the process. On the absorbtive side, Mick Rock gives a good picture of the man behind the songs, which has also been corroborated by many that know Bowie (including his father, who mentioned to Ken Pitt that David sometimes needed a chance to relax, 'something he always finds hard to do as you no doubt know.') Here is Rock's image of Bowie:

> He sits with his knees drawn up to his chest. His hands flicker about, touching indiscriminately anything which finds its way into their range, stroking briefly, lightly, soon dancing off again in search of new textures. His nerves run very close to the surface. [3]

Rock went on to describe Bowie as 'vulnerable at times, although at others no one seems more confident, more worked out.' This is the essential paradox, complicated by the fact that both extremes are subject to the further manipulations of Bowie the actor/performer. As Bowie's grown older, the ratio of control has also increased. The vulnerability is still there, though quite well buried most of the time, and he's no longer as vulnerable in terms of his career. Not much in the music business could surprise Bowie at this point, and since he has taken so many "risks" and still maintained his fans, further risks become more possible and essentially less risky. He has almost been given a mandate to change, although there are many who would like to freeze him at whatever is their favorite point in his career.

For all the problems that Bowie had to face and work out at this time, *Hunky Dory* marked the beginning of wide recognition and both popular and critical acclaim. What follows is a fairly typical review by John Mendelsohn in Rolling Stone, which points out some of the reasons why others loved the album, and which are the same reasons that Bowie gave for its being less than artistically fulfilling.

> For the most part, Dave is back after an affair with heavy, high energy killer techniques, back into his 1966-ish Tony Newley pop rock thang, and happily so; *Hunky Dory* is his most easily accessible, and thus most readily enjoyable work since his *Man Of Words, Man Of Music* album of 1969.
> ...Hunky Dory not only represents Bowie's most engaging album musically, but also finds him once more writing literally enough to let the listener examine his ideas *comfortably* (my emphasis)... Here the backing, including strings, doesn't oppress him as it sometimes did in the *Man* but rather creates a casual pop atmosphere in which Dave's voice, which loves to entertain company, is free to perform all manner of little tricks for us. [4]

Maybe Bowie didn't like the album because he did consider it something of a throwback, but it is true that in the matters of production and singing he was becoming a master. Aside from singing in his own natural accent he also hit his singerly stride with a fair amount of purity. The singer's "tricks" were there but didn't sound as artificial as they later became, and while some of Bowie's vocal characteristics have become trademarks as much as Elvis's, at this point the style had yet to supplant the substance.

In returning to the actual music, there are a couple of things to consider: one is the intent and the other is the effect, which seem to oppose each other throughout the album. Bowie claimed that it was a 'very worried album' and yet, he gave it the title *Hunky Dory*, suggesting either schizophrenia or more tongue in cheek humor. The album is almost equally divided between the worried and the hunky dory, with a few rather inconsequential songs thrown in for good measure. Actually, even the lighter tunes have an underlying tension to them, which helped make them good pop. In this category, there is *Changes*, ("Every time I thought I'd got it made/It seemed the taste was not so sweet") and *Oh, You Pretty Things*, both of which have an air of optimism in mere forward momentum, but hint at disturbing possibilities. With a son on the way, Bowie was psychologically preparing to be passe', "they're the start of a coming race/The earth is a bitch/We've finished our news" but with Rick Wakeman's piano dominating the sound, this song (like most of the album) is deceptively "pretty". Here the piano bounces along and in general, the luscious chords disarm even the most disturbing songs.

These songs are followed by *Eight Line Poem* with a haiku sound and feel, a reminder that the Sixties had just ended. It also happens to be nice poetry, as is the case with other songs on *Hunky Dory*, though this one makes less concessions to pop/rock music. *The Poem* is followed by *Life On Mars?*, the only song Bowie's ever written with a question mark at the end. In addition to offering proof that he's always drawing from his own musical past (which increasingly became a cache for him to raid) by rewriting *My Way*, it also hints at the future and the Spiders From Mars with lines like "I wonder if he'll ever know/He's in the best selling show/Is there life on Mars?." Another line that becomes more resonant with the later friendship between Lennon and Bowie is "Now the worker's have struck for fame/'Cause Lennon's on sale again." The mere occurrence of the words "fame" and "Lennon" in such close proximity is enough to make one wonder just what was the inspiration for what. Did this song make "Fame" inevitable or is Bowie prescient? *Mars?* is especially interesting lyrically, with leaps that somehow are followed, and images that are highly suggestive. And while this one doesn't focus directly on the "homo-superior" theme, it hints at another trend on this album and in Bowie's work, an unsentimental reading of America and its mass culture. David says that the song's written from the perspective of a sensitive young girl overwhelmed by the media and its machinations. "It's on America's tortured brow/Mickey Mouse had grown up a cow". (Get the original copy with the lyrics, listen and look at those cave men go...)

On the subject of sentimentality, *Kooks* is one song that Bowie has said just proves how sentimental a writer can get sometimes. Written for "small Z.", it's a light song about what their son can expect from life with a "Couple of Kooks/Hung up on romancing". Describing the affectionate touches applied to the preparations for Z's life, it also echoes Bowie's realization that one can't possess a child, posing the main question of "Will you stay (in our Lover's Story)", and promising that "If you stay you won't be sorry". At a later date, David the single father says that occasionally Zowie/Joey will remind him of the song when he's being forced to do homework, especially the line, "And if the homework brings you down/Then we'll throw it on the fire/And take the car down town.".

It's back to himself and continuing concerns in *Quicksand*, another favorite among those fans who share Bowie's open mind and philosophical bent, not to mention the resulting confusion. *Quicksand* is another of the "worried songs", because Bowie was intelligent enough to realise where certain systems of thought that interested him might lead, contrasting a reference to Alistair Crowley with one to Himmler. More references to Churchill ("I'm living proof of Churchill's lies" gets back to his obsession with the state of things in England), Garbo and Bardot indicate the range of his obsessions, along with his realization of the danger in constructing a new system out of such disparate awareness. He states the case clearly enough, "I'm sinking in the quicksand of my thought/And I ain't got the power anymore." There is also the reaffirmation that is typical Bowie: "I'm not a prophet or a stone age man/Just a mortal with potential of a superman", raising the Nietzschean influence, which along with all the others stands side by side with a Lovecraftian belief in such supermen, whatever their actual point of origin.

The second side of *Hunky Dory* is fairly inconsequential with the exception of the final cut. Beginning with an odd choice for a cover tune, Bowie takes on Biff Rose's *Fill Your Heart*. Since at least a couple of lines stand out as particularly Bowiesque, the lyrics may account for the choice. For something Bowie might have said, how about "Things that happened in the past/Only happened in your Mind"? Rose also postulates love as the only salvation, which is something the Bowie of the mid-Eighties just might agree with if he didn't quite in '71.

The next three songs were tributes of a different sort. Beginning with *Andy Warhol* as a second thought for *Andy Monument*, it starts with a recording of pre-take chatter that sounds distinctly late night and sub-oceanic, pronouncing Warhol's name for his unenlightened crew. With his accent, it's "War-hole". Notwithstanding that some of Warhol's concepts would be applied to Bowie's career, the picture of the man is amusing, and rather to the point with lines like "Dress my friends up just for show/See them as they really are." And like everyone else, Bowie couldn't resist mentioning his appearance, "Andy Warhol looks a scream".

Song For Bob Dylan is probably the worst on the album, but here again there are a couple of redeeming lines, ones that hint at Bowie's insights to personality and character. Bowie tells Dylan that "You gave your soul to every bedsit room/At least a picture on my wall" and though the rest sounds rather trite ("With a voice like sand and glue") it's a fair enough tribute when Bowie proclaims that Dylan could overcome Babylon herself (or Bowie) with "a couple of songs from your old scrapbook." With Dylan's influence all over Bowie's music, it's fitting that Bowie should wish Dylan back on the scene, although the absence of people like Dylan made Bowie's entrance possible in the first place. That the two were so different also shows in Bowie's cliche'-ridden writing of the song.

The third tribute in a row is *Queen Bitch*. This time the inspiration is Lou Reed, though Bowie sometimes denies it. The note next to the song title reads "(some V.U., white light returned with thanks)" and when Bowie said later that he was just trying to see if people would take the reference literally if he wrote Lou's name next to the song, he gave away the game. He didn't write Reed's name, but "White Heat/White Light" is practically his signature, although it was veiled just enough to please those who figured out the riddle. And here the venue is Reed's all the way with lyrics that point to both Reed and Dylan, though somehow lacking the authenticity of either. It's been called the greatest Lou Reed song that Lou never wrote, but it seems there's a good reason why he didn't write it. (Self-parody?)

Bewlay Brothers, on the other hand, is one hundred percent Bowie. For that reason, it has fascinated and mystified fans for years. The song is long and poetic, and extremely veiled as if written in the private language of intimacy. The imagery and references are dense and personal, and most attempts to decipher them have failed to reach any firm conclusions. The mood of the song is suggestive, and when Bowie was later to remark that keys to his sexuality were found in his lyrics, this is one of the first songs that came to mind. Bowie referred to it as 'another in the series of David Bowie confessions — Star Trek in a leather jacket.' While some have seen Bowie's brother Terry in the song, justified by several lines, the boyhood secrets hinted at could have been shared with his brother or with any number of others. There's no hard and fast evidence to justify any claim, the only thing that betrays is the pillow where "The Factor Max (Max Factor) that proved the fact/Is melted down". There are all sorts of things in this song to interest the Bowie Egyptologist, such as why is "Mark" capitalized when it's not clearly a name. Whatever the real meaning, to Bowie it's somehow quite significant and he went so far as to name his production company after the song, or the original Bewley Brothers, which for all we know is the name of some small dusty store in an obscure corner of London. It's Bowie's "Rosebud".

This song has the word "fakers" in it as does *Changes* which brings up the cover, and the work of friend George Underwood (and his partner Terry) who did the artwork for David. The front has a retouched airbrushed photo of Bowie at his loveliest, in a quasi-Garbo pose, while on the back he's looking like Bloomsbury on a bad day. The notes are of as much interest as anying else (looking like Bowie's hand) and this is where he refers to himself as "the actor" for the first time in print. For the album he was acting the part of assistant producer, to Ken Scott who took on production responsibilities when Visconti was no longer available. Scott had been Visconti's engineer on *The Man* and with the now experienced Bowie by his side, they formed an excellent team for three of Bowie's most successful albums. The rest of the team also survived for approximately the same length of time, and though they were originally known as The Rats, the combination of Mick Ronson on guitar, Woody Woodmansey on drums and Trevor Bolder on bass are better known to the work as The Spiders From Mars. The other member of the team who also went on to a degree of fame was Richard Wakeman, alias Rick, who had also played on the Dudgeon — and Buckmast-produced *Space Oddity* for Bowie. Recognizing a good pianist when he hears one, Bowie invited Wakeman back and he made a major contribution to the overall sound of the album.

SEVEN

'And so the story goes they wore the clothes/They said the things to make it seem improbable' ..

'Bewlay Brothers' — *Hunky Dory*

Before delving into the Ziggy phenomenon, the creation Bowie at one point called 'the most talked about man in the world', it is worth mentioning that in 1972, and even in 1984, it is possible to find people who don't know David Bowie's (or Ziggy Stardust's) name, much less who he is. For all the hype and claims of revolutions begun by the concept as well as the music, Ziggy and His Spiders played to many near empty houses (though this is seldom mentioned). In general, the entire enterprise was fraught with contradictions, most pertaining to image versus substance, though playing with just these elements was what the whole affair was about.

The album *The Rise And Fall Of Ziggy Stardust And The Spiders From Mars* was finally released on June 6, 1972, but the Big Event was prepared for well in advance. That the music apparently led the way for the persona is significant and is evidenced by the fact that David got his costume designer, Freddie Burretti and a band called Runk to masquerade as Arnold Corns, the group which would supposedly blow The Rolling Stones off the map. The whole thing was a joke, but through it Bowie floated a single with *Moonage Daydream* backed by *Hang On To Yourself*, which if nothing else allowed him to work the songs out, since he was producing, singing (with Freddie, alias Rudi Valentino alias A. Corns) and still working on the lyrics. At that point *Hang On To Yourself* was a more thinly disguised version of Reed's *Sweet Jane*. Meanwhile Freddie and his girlfriend Daniella were working on the costumes (with input from Angie and David), and RCA had also been prepped and convinced to make a low interest loan for touring and promotion on behalf of the rise of Ziggy Stardust. There was only one thing really missing, and that was a little hoopla, since the world at large was still unaware of the Starman in its midst.

At several points in the not-too-distant past, a lack of press attention had been a thorn in Bowie's side, and in the interim he had come to understand the machinations and the needs of headline hunters as well as anyone. Presumably the interview between Bowie and Michael Watts of Melody Maker was fairly routine and probably would have been relegated to a few paragraphs on page nineteen was it not for the turn around that Bowie effected. While the eventual title was taken from *Oh, You Pretty Things*, (Melody Maker's title was *Oh, You Pretty*

Thing) the discussion didn't stay in *Hunky Dory* for long, though it was probably the reason for the interview in the first place. After an introductory description of Bowie and his vocabulary which is three parts parody, Watts ends with "I wish you could have been there to varda him, he was so super." But then comes the clincher; the line that made both this exchange and Bowie himself instantly (in)famous. Wrote Watts: "He's gay, he says, Mmmmmmmmmm."

The whole article is of interest, (as Bowie later reassured Watts, it was "archetypal") but everyone's attention focused on the sexual comments, and Watts must have sensed that this would be the case. He laid out the rules of a game that is still being played today (especially in the prurient U.S.A.). What follows is the pivotal paragraph from Watt's article.

> David's present image is to come on like a swishy queen, a gorgeously effeminate boy. He's as camp as a row of tents, with his limp hand and his trolling vocabulary. 'I'm gay,' he says 'and I always have been, even when I was David Jones.' But there's a sly jollity about how he says it, a secret smile at the corners of his mouth. He knows that in these times it's permissable to act like a male tart, and that to shock and outrage, which pop has always striven to do throughout its history, is a balls-breaking process. [1]

The slight smile, or what sometimes emerges as a chuckle, seems to be a reflex reaction on Bowie's part when he's hooked a journalist and is about to start bringing in the line. He still does it, and with all the self-control he possesses this seems to be one way that he gives others a fair chance and lets them keep him honest. Watts understood:

> The expression of his sexual ambivalence establishes a fascinating game: is he or isn't he? In a period of conflicting sexual identity he shrewdly exploits the confusion surrounding the male and female roles. [2]

It's doubtful that Bowie realized just how long others would want to play this same game, and he seems rather bored by it all at this point. When asked about his sexual "orientation" he'll either flatly deny that he was ever homosexual or bisexual, admit both if he's in the mood, or chalk it all up either to youthful experimentation or a gigantic publicity ploy. All of these explanations seem to be true, since by Bowie's reasoning "what happened in the past only happened in your mind", but the publicity aspect was the most important. Bowie had no interest in leading legions of gays out of the closet. A staunch individualist, he mentioned that to Watts immediately after he made his "admission", though the tedious process of being asked the same questions perpetually was all a necessary evil in the quest for attention, opening Bowie (would-be star) to public scrutiny and "possession". The decision to play the mystery of his sexuality to the hilt had been made before the interview. It was a calculated risk.

This gets into an area of conjecture, posing the question whether the whole thing was a scam masterminded by De Fries; whether it was part of a mutual strategy, or whether the responsibility was Bowie's. It seems that the inspiration came from David (which he in turn has credited to Ziggy, alias Mr. Hyde), with De Fries being said to have "quickly adjusted" to the new agenda. If things got sticky they could always put Angie and Zowie on display, and besides, they were both men of the times, cognisant that there was an audience for androgyny. The appeal was developed not only along sexual lines; Bowie's audience was composed of the generally disenfranchised, be it sexually, politically, philosophically or otherwise. Angie made the point that David Bowie became someone for those "with no banner to wave". Beginning with the sexual, Bowie offered an entire cosmology and new society complete with fashions and anthems, at least temporarily. Eventually, he got bored with his new religion just as quickly as with the older ones which he's studied, the role of savior and sex symbol becoming too taxing for a living mortal.

Since the Ziggy Stardust concept and image served Bowie so well, it can be studied for its success, though what's less clear now is that the entire venture was fraught with risk. Beginning with the notion of centering a work around Ziggy, Bowie, whether consciously or not, went straight to archetypes, thereby giving the project a solid foundation. Even in explaining the origins of the name "Ziggy Stardust" Bowie has used the words "archetype" and "derivative". Besides being highly suggestive of the space-age setting, the name conjures both Iggy Pop and Twiggy, with the Z added for a more bizarre effect. The "Stardust" Bowie says was derived from a character called The Lonesome Stardust Cowboy. The story goes that having spent a lifetime perfecting his country & western singing act he appeared on *Laugh-In* where the audience thought he was hugely funny, though his act wasn't intended to be comedy. Devastated, the old man walked off stage and wept. Bowie could probably empathize with the situation, and the name was perfect for the character he was developing.

Resonance became a key to the idea and if we believe Bowie's explanation that the music came first and suggested the character, once the idea of Bowie playing Ziggy arose with the. full backing and encouragement of De Fries, the driving force became the creation of the ultimate "plastic rock 'n' roller". Without pushing the point too far, one reason that Ziggy was so quickly embraced was that Ziggy was "formulated" with the full weight of culture behind him. This is apparent in the music and in the qualities of the character. The essential songs to the "Ziggy Myth", especially *Lady Stardust* and *Ziggy Stardust* are sung by a second person in the manner of a gospel, while *Five Years* functions in the same manner as Revelations and *Starman* is essentially the equivalent of Genesis. This is not to say that Bowie took the Bible as his model, but he taps into the same mythic archetypal structure. He even calls Ziggy "the nazz", jazz slang for 'the Nazarin' and from there introduces Lovecraft in a rock 'n' roll setting with the combination of reality and fantasy that made Ziggy so appealing. From this base, Bowie made the leap to the Twentieth Century and as he put it, 'packaged a totally credible plastic rock star.' And his was 'much better than any sort of Monkees fabrication. My plastic rocker was much more plastic than anybody's.' This "fabrication" was marketed with the help of De Fries who would have been the guy selling the 3-D Jesus photos and T-shirts at the foot of the cross.

Before getting into the actual sale, there was at least one other "archetypal" element in this conglomeration that was to be Ziggy. This was the matter of sexuality, which first began to get David media attention, and which made up an essential aspect of the "outrage" and "enigma" that was Ziggy. Bowie's reaction to the Michael Watts article hints at his own awareness of the situation because while friends were calling and telling him not to buy the magazine, and that he 'was ruined', his reaction was that 'nobody is going to be offended by that. Everybody knows that most people are bisexual.' With this enlightened opinion, Bowie found an audience that agreed with him while he disturbed the straight world. The timing was right for shaking up sex role stereotypes and Bowie just took it all a couple of steps further than most would have dared. This was partly based on the view of various arcane systems of thought, that the hermaphrodite is the consummate form of humanity. Since Bowie didn't have all the right equipment for that image, he took the androgynous route instead which, in addition to being highly fashionable, was all inclusive in its own way. It left Bowie's maleness intact and allowed him to play around with other things. This was reinforced by comments from De Fries to the press. As he put it: 'Alice Cooper is always reminding everybody he's really a man. David doesn't need to; He *is* a man.' In fact, a lot of critics (especially males) were happy to point out the same thing.

The handling of "Ziggy's" sexuality developed into both an obstacle and a somewhat unexpected bonus, partly owing to the confusion. Depending on who was hyping whom, David/Ziggy was either gay, bi, straight (bring out the wife and kid!) or the whole thing was irrelevant and the concern of petty minds. But what's usually as important to the public as "who's shirts you wear", is the sex life of their star. Curiosity and confusion about this were created both on and off stage. Bowie took his play with sex roles to where it counted most; he dredged the mass subconscious to create his effects. Of all the elements (theatrical and otherwise) that eventually became part of the Ziggy stageshow, the mock-fellatio performed on Ronson's guitar was the most popular and sensational, effectively subverting the image of guitar as phallus, and the whole macho world of rock 'n' roll. For the shock value, no one else had gone so far. If Bowie had merely intended to make a point about the guitar as a phallus, a little Townshendesque penetration of amps would have done the trick, and if the point was to feminise things he could have followed the lead of Elvis with his make-up or just engaged in more of Jagger's prancing. But the image of the blow job (some prefer to describe the scene as "Bowie playing Ronson's guitar with his teeth" a' la Hendrix with a twist) was infinitely more powerful and disturbing because there was no gender limitation implied. Needless to say, critics and fans lapped up this piece of theater, and the only other feature of the Ziggy performances that got nearly as much comment was the fact that Bowie sometimes made three (!) costume changes.

Long before the album came out followed by the full-fledged promotion and performances, work had begun on the set and the costumes, in turn preceded by at least some of the songs that would comprise the album and the heart of the performance set. Knowing that at least the outlines of *Moonage Daydream* and *Hang On To Yourself* were extant in early 1971, it seems likely that these songs, and possibly others led the way to *Star*, *Starman*, *Lady Stardust* and *Ziggy Stardust*, which are all of a piece and give extra resonance to the other songs which could easily have stood alone. If Ziggy began to take shape in David's mind's eye thanks to his sense of theater, he (Ziggy) quickly began to influence the songs. Once the rudiments of the idea were presented to Tony De Fries, he recognized that Bowie-as-Ziggy-as-Star was just wild enough to be used in making Bowie the star he was supposed to be. With this sort of encouragement, the responsibility was back on Bowie's shoulders to create an alter ego he could live with and that would achieve his aim. In the end Bowie fashioned fame out of infamy, noteworthiness out of notoriety.

The process of becoming (both on and off stage) another character was something that Bowie has frequently attributed to his shyness and his discovery that he could overcome his personal insecurity by having "someone else" (be it himself in disguise) sing his songs for him. Predicated on an assumption that the best rock performers are acting out a part, Bowie just took the role-playing and the character development to an extreme. In Ziggy's case, by creating a character that was a rock star, (as opposed to an Average Joe) it was that much easier to play the part on stage. For those who find it hard to imagine Bowie as less than the ultimate performer, the fact that he may have needed to hide behind characterizations in the attempt to overcome himself is borne out by descriptions of some of Bowie's early solo performances (circa *Space Oddity*), which suggest that in those days he looked rather lost and desperate on stage. That was before he learned about parody as distance.

Before making the leap to creating and performing as other characters, (Ziggy, Aladdin, The Duke) Bowie had long been in the process of exploring and modifying his image. On one level this process was just a manifestation of David's acute fashion consciousness, but as his image changed so did he subtly change himself. By the time *The Man Who Sold The World* was released, David was beginning to cut quite a distinctive figure; the emphasis on the feminine became even more pronounced with the cover of *Hunky Dory*, though all this was still just an exaggeration of what others like Marc Bolan were already toying with.

The leap that then took David from Bowie to Ziggy was a leap in imagination and aplomb, something that Bowie had been staking out if a little diffidently for some time. Some people, more than others, need physical form as a conduit for self expression. One might imagine Bowie going through a similar metamorphosis to the one that created Elvis Presley as we know him. A passage in Albert Goldman's book *Elvis* suggests another Bowie parallel between the King and Bowie:

> The cause of Elvis' troubles at school was, significantly, the first unmistakable expression of his genius. On a summer's day in the year 1951, Elvis Presley decided to crown himself with the world's most celebrated hairstyle. This momentous decision was arrived at only after years of earnest experimentation. Elvis recognized early, apparently, that his strength lay in his hair; his dirty blond, baby fine locks. Billy Wardlow remembers going downstairs once after school to visit with Gladys and discovering that Elvis' mother had given him a kinky curly permanent. Another time, Billie screamed with shock when Elvis appeared in a Mohawk. Now, all these experiments were about to conclude in the making of a masterpiece. [3]

The vision of "earnest experimentation" comes as readily to mind with Bowie as with Presley, and though Bowie's success (as Elvis') was dependent on more than a haircut, it is hardly an exaggeration to describe it as the true stroke of genius wwhich crowned all that preceded it. Bowie would never allow himself to become stuck for long, however, Elvis proved less adroit at moving with (let alone ahead of) the times. Of all the haircuts that Bowie has ever launched the "Ziggy" cut-and-dye job was the most imaginative, outrageous and forward-looking. Johnny Rotten as well as countless fans are testimony to its enduring compulsiveness. Now in its third generation, the idea behind the Ziggy coif still adorns green, orange spike heads in London today. It was perhaps more effective (if not taken quite so far) in 1972, by which time the long unwashed locks of the hippies had become more boring than radical.

In this regard, Bowie took a leap of imagination and transformed himself in the process; a process similar to Elvis' experience.

> At first, this bad-assed Elvis is little more than a shell: a haircomb and a costume inhabited by a shy, self-doubting, self-effacing kid. Eventually though, this shell begins to fill with the man it proclaims, *artor resartus*. Clothes make the man. Five years later, Elvis had become the tough punk that he set out unconsciously to emulate as a boy. [4]

Bowie's image was more extreme than Presley's, and within a year it led to him becoming A Lad Insane; within Five Years (as the album informs us) the end had come — at least for Ziggy —and Bowie was on to the next major phase of his career. But in the meantime, Bowie made a go of playing the space-age rock star, prophet and spokesman with personal as well as social repercussions. Since the vision and the music were so interrelated (though thanks to photography the image may outlast the music) the music remained crucial as the base from which the invasion was launched.

The album, *The Rise And Fall Of Ziggy Stardust And The Spiders From Mars* was almost universally recognized as a work of comprehensive genius. Charles Shaar Murray called it:

> the definitive *rock 'n' roll* concept album, and by far the most cogent comment any artist has ever made on his own art form.'

If that wasn't enough, he goes on:

> It was also a virtual advance diary of the next action-packed year of Bowie's career, a year that was its own artistic justification...It was also nothing less than an investigative journalism project on the grandest possible scale. How else can you discover precisely what rock 'n' roll superstardom is like without actually going out and becoming a superstar? [5]

The songs testify to the fact that Bowie had pre-visualized it all quite clearly, and perhaps this helps account for his coping so well. Murray also makes the point that if it had backfired 'it would have been the most embarrassing personal disaster in the history of the music industry.' In summation, Murray lays it on the line. The album was:

> Rock 'n' Roll's greatest analysis of itself, an object lesson in how to record and layer vocals and the blueprint for rock stardom all in one package. [6]

Thanks to Bowie's successful construction of stardom from these blueprints, he has almost singlehandedly rewritten the rule book on such stardom, for better or worse.

Working with the same crew that accompanied him on his rise, Bowie recorded *Ziggy* at Trident Studios, again as a co-production with Ken Scott, with arrangements by Ronson, who also played piano for the tape. The Spiders were the same personnel who had worked with Bowie on *Hunky Dory*, that is Ronson on guitar (and keyboards), Trevor Bolder on bass and Mick "Woody" Woodmansey on drums. All songs, save one, were written by Bowie. Although the order of composition isn't clear, the result was a complete and self-contained entity, more like a novel in its faithfulness to theme than even *Sergeant Pepper* with its vignette structure, although *Ziggy* owed a lot to The Beatles masterpiece on every possible level.

From the opening drum intro of *Five Years*, joined by Ronson's piano and Bowie's vocals, the production is virtually flawless, testimony to the mountains of experience Bowie had gained by the ripe old age of twenty-four. He gives himself and the world five years in typical apocalyptic musings from a brain that hurts "like a warehouse, it had no room to spare, I had to cram so many things to store everything in there". The mood created by Ronson's tasteful piano and Bowie's plaintive vocal is potent, preparing the listener to hear the rest of the tale that leads onto a rollercoaster between high and low, inside and out. As the drum fades out on *Five Years*, it becomes supplanted by the shuffle of *Soul Love* which informs that "Love is careless in its choosing" and that "Love descends on those defenseless". Bowie as theologian then contemplates *Soul Love*. The striving ever upward leads to "my God on high is All love though reaching up my loneliness evolves By the blindness that surrounds him." Here, consumately unconsummated love is rendered lightly and matter-of-factly.

The lofty preoccupations of *Soul Love* are evaporated with the opening chords of the next number. Blasting back into rock 'n' roll reality, *Moonage Daydream* is all electric guitar and a quick descent to earth on the tail end of the Sixties, complete with references to "ray guns", which may have been a bonafide tool of Ziggy's trade, but recall Country Joe McDonald's zero-ing in on Ronald Ray-Gun (zap) while he was still Governor of California. The first line sets up the promise and the threat as well as the dual role of Ziggy. Bowie announces "I'm an alligator, I'm a mama-papa comin' for you/I'm a space invader, I'll be a rock 'n' rollin' bitch for you", promises he was able to keep for the first year of his term. Here Bowie also introduces the "I-dare-you-to-destroy-me" sexual theme that runs through the most raucous songs on the album, climaxing (literally) with the now classic "Wham Bam Thank You Mam" at the end of *Suffragette City*. Here the spaceman wants to experience the genuine earthbound article: "Don't fake it baby, lay the real thing on me." Instead there's the first touch of the supra real.

In the Ziggy cosmology, Mr. Stardust himself is the radio listener in the song, soon to carry the message of the *Starman* who's speaking to Ziggy and a few other "chosen". The reaction of the singer is joy and anticipation of the promise of the Starman's arrival in the communication which he realizes "weren't no D.J. that was hazy cosmic jive". The Starman's transmission was preceded by some "Rock 'n' roll, lotta soul", and the intro to this one is almost identical to *Somewhere Over The Rainbow* which might be jive if it didn't have all the right resonance for the song. The "soul" comes in before the chorus in the form of an appropriated intro from *You Keep Me Hangin' On*. In dealing with forces larger than himself, the narrator might have been inclined to echo Diana Ross' "Ain't nothing I can do about it". So here Bowie clearly lays out the situation/plot, "There's a starman waiting in the sky/He'd like to come and meet us/But he thinks he'd blow our minds", and in the last line he gets to the impulse that moved his fans. They just wanted a little flash and he promises that "if we can sparkle he may land tonight". Then, turning to something that must have been an adolescent problem if his lyrical preoccupation is any indication, Bowie implores "Don't tell your poppa or he'll get us locked up in fright".

To put perspective on the "rise" and continuing struggle, Bowie ends the side with a cover of Ron Davies *It Ain't Easy* which Ziggy and the Spiders put their hearts into as if it's a magical incantation. The soulful delivery of the title line serves to remind the listener that the intent isn't entirely selfish.

The "Star" cycle continues onto the B side. *Lady Stardust*, another observer/fan narration, is an amalgamation of several "stars" though it's commonly agreed that Marc Bolan was one inspiration for the song. This was given some credence when Bowie performed the full scale Ziggy set for the first time in London with a slide of Bolan projected during the song. Bolan didn't appreciate the veiled references to him and harsh words were passed between them with the help of the press. Bowie goes for the pathos of the situation with lines like "people stared at the make-up of his face/Laughed at his long black hair, his animal grace". While *Lady Stardust* is called a "creature fair", the pivotal line (especially if you were Bolan) was "I smiled sadly for a love I could not obey". No one wants to be pitied, and Bowie probably wouldn't have liked it either.

Star rolls around as the ultimate statement, essentially an adolescent fantasy on stardom, with a naive belief in the efficacy of fate, though the actual process is left vague. Ziggy tells the sad tales of the unfulfilled lives of Tony, Rudi, Bevan and Sonny, the assertion being that he'll be able to accomplish what they couldn't "as a rock 'n' roll star". The song is interesting partly due to Bowie's frequent talk of getting back to the roots of why he wanted to make music in the first place. The lure for Bowie and Ziggy is in the power of rock 'n' roll and in the elevated status of the rock 'n' roll star. Bowie intentionally chooses working class names for his failed friends in keeping with the thought that as a kid in England the only way to buck the class system is through rock and roll. Besides, it would be fun, "So inviting — so enticing to play the part/I could play the wild mutation as a rock 'n' roll star". All the fantasies are laid out ("I could fall asleep at night... I could fall in love...") and another typical Bowie element is included, that of responsibility. He could make a "transformation" as a rock 'n' roll star and "make it all worthwhile". Just as it begins to sound too cosily altruistic, the line "I could do with the money" is slipped in and the social significance evaporates, precluding any accusations of selling out because there was no pretense of purity in the first place. But even after all the dreams came true, Bowie still had trouble falling asleep. Even for a rock 'n' roller, old habits like hyperactivity die hard.

From the man who once said the three things that interest him are "politics, myself, sex..." comes *Hang On To Yourself*, another number that continues the tradition of sex, as opposed to love songs. The earlier version of *Hang On To Yourself* sounded more like *Sweet Jane* than the album version. Ronson's guitar line takes it far away from copy and Bowie's vocals sound sweetly innocent while delving into such Lou Reed inspired themes as thighs and Vaseline.

The bottom drops out in the song *Ziggy Stardust*. The essential tale is told by one of the members of the Spiders From Mars, fully chronicling the whys and wherefores of Ziggy's ascent and fall from grace. This song has usually been taken quite literally, and while the tale is realistic enough, especially in terms of Bowie with lines like "he could lick 'em by smiling/He could leave 'em to hang", not to mention his "snow white tan", the perspective belongs to the jealous band members in the shadow of the star "with beer light to guide us". (That's dim). There have been many interpretations of the song based on the final line, which is usually taken at face value. The line is "When the kids had killed the man I had to break up the band". While some have seen this line as a reference to the dangers of self-parody, it seems to relate directly to the line preceeding it: "Making love with his ego Ziggy sucked up into his mind". This would point more to the reactions of the fans, and sometimes Bowie himself to Ziggy as a projection, because the love for the "leper messiah" was a false one and to believe in it would be psychic suicide. This is what *Rock and Roll Suicide* is about, but in between there lay one more good roll in the form of *Suffragette City*.

This song has been as influential as anything Bowie's ever done, and seems to be one of his favorites, if the frequency of its appearances on B-sides of singles is any indication. It's a rock song to end all with relentless drive and breathless lyric delivery, not to mention the audacity to make it another instant classic. Ziggy/Bowie finally found the one woman that could blow him away, and true to the rock 'n' roll stereotype, nothing else matters. The music takes its lead from the subject. It's total "blam-blam" and Bowie raises the phrase "Wam Bam Thank You Mam" to new heights.

The end of the album is appropriately final, with *Rock And Roll Suicide*. It might just as well be *Rock And Roll As Suicide*. The song returns to the theme of time versus rock 'n' roll, somewhat echoing *Five Years*. Bowie must have determined that five years is the usual cycle of rise and fall of any rock entity and by now in the context of the album, the star has "lived too long". The song progresses through more Clockwork Orange imagery to the last lines which sound like a built-in finale, allowing for a moment of union between the star and his fans before the show ends. Bowie's routine of reaching out to the front rows of the audience may have been a genuine attempt at communion, but the effect seems largely calculated by virtue of the fact that it worked so well in performance. Audiences were elated to hear "You're not alone.. You're wonderful, gimme your hands" but of all the moments in the show this was the most frightening to the performer. (All that adulation...) Bowie had created a monster, and luckily for him Ziggy became the martyr, allowing Bowie to survive.

Of all the things that Bowie had to endure as a "Rock 'n' Roll Star" among the most personally strenuous were the tours, of which the Ziggy performances were the most crucial. Facing an all or nothing situation they went for all. Some things were made easier due to the shared conviction (through a De Fries obsession) that the trappings of stardom would serve to convince everyone that a star was in fact what Bowie/Ziggy was already. Everywhere Bowie was supplied with a limo to whisk him to and fro, burly security guards and of course, *the entourage*. In order to heighten the theatricality and glamor of it all, De Fries drafted several actors from the English cast of Warhol's "Pork" to work as publicists and "figures about Bowie". With the exception of the bodyguards (whose burliness was beautiful), the rule was that only the beautiful, the famous and the outrageous were allowed. This worked for a time, serving to reinforce the image of Bowie as a celebrity. Although he may have only been on the scene for five minutes, when he appeared it was as the ultimate instant rock star.

All the gears were in motion, with the thoroughly titilated pop press having put Bowie on the map. Freddie kept busy turning out new outfits by the hour, while hairdresser Suzie Fussey continually wrought improvements to the Ziggy coif. The tour began with Bowie promising "theatre", "entertainment (that's what's missing in pop music now)" and "outrage". After all, Bowie was "old enough to remember Mick Jagger." The man had been studying and now it was time to test all his theories on the road.

There were a few British concert dates scheduled in the winter and spring of '72, before the album came out, with the purpose of working the kinks out on the road, and outside of London. Bowiemania had yet to really blossom, and while many of the halls were only half full, Bowie played for his life every night, with consistent standing ovations as his reward. For those who had been following Bowie all along (and there weren't very many such people), the show was a shock. The acoustic guitar and long hair were gone, mellowness had been thrown out the window, and in blew Ziggy playing hard electric rock. Bowie had hit on just the right mixture for suspending belief and creating it, and the response to the music, character and "theatrics" was as desired. Now it was time for the big publicity push to begin, the stuff that Bowie later considered "too much too soon". With the album due out in early June and an American tour planned for the fall, De Fries gave the American critics a couple of weeks to listen to the album and then arranged what has become one of the most infamous press junkets in big-media-music history. De Fries decided to fly two dozen American media heavies to London to see a carefully arranged performance of what was by then the well-oiled "Ziggy set", with provisions for excellent accommodation and the chance to meet and speak with the Star. Suddenly all the small journals that had been supporting and promoting David since the days of *The Man* felt jilted and angry that the favors were going to the likes of New York Times and Playboy. A compromise was worked out, extra tickets were added and a great time was had by all (except those who stayed home). Since David put on a great show, there were no guilty feelings amongst the press about being bought, and nearly all the journalists dutifully returned home to write raves for the moment and for years to come. The show was followed up with what turned out to be a temporarily fateful group inteview at the Dorchester Hotel. All of the American guests, key British journalists, Angie, Lou Reed and Iggy Pop, who happened to be in town, plus their bands and bodyguards were invited. At one point, Reed, who said that the Ziggy album was 'at least 99% perfect,' walked over and planted a kiss full on Bowie's mouth. The pandemonium escalated when Angie took a bite out of Lillian Roxan's breast while David held court in the center, occasionally slipping out to change his costume. Somehow Charles Shaar Murray managed a "real" interview in this environment. Bowie predicted that others attempting to follow his theatrical lead would produce a lot of tragedies, and he posited his own sure success on hard work, professionalism and on his concern for all aspects of performance. At this point, he also directly contradicted his previous and much touted statement 'I, the performer, am the message.' This time Bowie said:

> I wish myself to be a prop, if anything, for my own songs. I want to be the vehicle for my songs. I would like to colour the material with as much visual expression as is necessary for that song.

If anything, the contradiction points to the unity between the man and his music. This scene pointed out to De Fries that the situation had very nearly gotten out of control, that anything might be said or could happen, and he declared this interview the LAST ONE.

While this move has been discussed as being a well calculated ploy, its basis also lay largely in self-defense. It certainly did have the effect of heightening interest in Bowie, who if he hadn't already thoroughly captured the imagination of the press, did so now by virtue of his absence. As it turns out more interviews were given, but they were very strategically timed and placed. In the meantime, every detail that could be unearthed was faithfully published, which is why half of England knows the name of Bowie's hairdresser.

The conquest had begun, but even while plans were made to take the capital, Bowie was hard at work on other projects. In addition to revamping the stage show, David spent the summer producing two albums, whose success testified to Bowie's Midas touch. The first project involved working with Mott the Hoople, whom Bowie had long admired, mainly since they were the unselfconscious rockers that he could never be. Besides, "the kid's loved them", and through his friendship with various band members, Bowie knew that they were in trouble; without a hit, they were sinking fast. He sent them a tape of *Suffragette City*, but even that wasn't enough, and with financial pressures plaguing them they decided to break up the band. Newly unemployed bassist Overend "Pete" Watts gave Bowie a call thanking him for the tape and asked Bowie if he needed a bass player. The news prompted Bowie to call De Fries immediately, urging him to help them. Although De Fries was essentially a one-artist-manager, Bowie called on him every time any friend needed help, which brought De Fries some rather unwelcome business that he had to take on just to please David. While

De Fries worked on Mott's contractual problems, Bowie sang them a song called *All The Young Dudes* which he thought "might do the trick" (i.e. give them a hit). Just to make sure it did, David took on the responsibility of producing the song and album for them.

Since most people who've worked with Bowie have said almost exactly the same thing about his attitude and approach, it's worth quoting at length from Mick Ralphs' description of the collaboration with Mott:

> It was a revelation working with Bowie. He's a much more together bloke than most people believe he is. He has a very firm sense of direction, total control over his own career, and he knows exactly where he's going. And yet at the same time he is always looking for new ideas — not just big ideas but little improvements, little ways of doing things better.
>
> He works very closely with Mick Ronson and they are both very imaginative. Before recording with us, they both came to see us on tour and to see the way we performed on stage — because they were anxious not to project us differently to the way we were.
>
> Then, when we were recording in the studio, David was always looking for ways of making the sound that much better, for bringing out greater clarity or using a different sound effect —some of the very strange. When we were recording the album he brought a blacksmith's anvil down to the studio one day. He had decided that he wanted the sound you get when you strike an anvil with a hammer. But instead of using the studio equipment to get something close to it he got the real thing. [7]

This gives a pretty clear picture of Bowie as producer. The comments about his control and direction are pertinent, because although Bowie placed himself in the eye of a hurricane he made it not only safely, but triumphantly, to the other side by virtue of his talent, determination and sense of direction.

One thing that Ralphs didn't mention is the way Bowie uses people, taking from them just what he needs, though also giving something back. This was the case with Lou Reed, who was a tremendous influence on Bowie, and to whom Bowie was able to return the favor through his talents as a producer. At a point when RCA was about ready to let go of Reed, Bowie offered to produce an album for him, which went on to yield Reed the biggest hit of his solo career.

While Lou was in town for work on *Transformer*, he joined Bowie on stage for the concert that has been unanimously declared a turning point in Bowie's career. It was the night the act became real, even though a slightly earlier concert at Imperial College was equally auspicious. That show ended with an enraptured crowd carrying David out of the hall on their shoulders, 'while, dressed in shiny white satin trousers and white silk top, he continued to sing his encore'. Afterwards, David was heard to comment: 'You know I never do anything by half.' But the reason the night of June 8, 1972 is cited as a turning point was that the attention of the press was fully focused on David. The occasion was a Save the Whale concert (of all things...) which took place at the Royal Festival Hall. All the right journalists were there, as it turns out, competing with each other for mega-adjectives and analogies to describe Bowie. Music Week quipped that David Bowie 'will soon become the greatest entertainer Britain has ever known'. New Musical Express described the music as 'T. S. Eliot with a rock 'n' roll beat'. But of all the ravers it was Ray Coleman of Melody Maker who went the farthest and came closest to the truth. M.M. declared that "A Star Is Born". Said Coleman: 'When a shooting star is heading for a peak, there is usually one concert at which it's possible to declare, "That's it, he's made it."' Coleman went on: 'Bowie is going to be an old fashioned charismatic idol, for his show is full of glitter, panache and pace.' He also wrote about Bowie's 'detached love affair with the audience, wooing them, yet never surrendering that vital aloofness that makes him slightly untouchable... slaying us all with a deadly mixture of fragility and desperate intensity, the undisputed King of Camp Rock.' Coleman ended the piece by giving Bowie a suggestion for an album title, saying, 'Bowie has arrived -- a worthy pin-up with such style.' Lou Reed had also arrived, and he duetted with Bowie on three of his own best songs. But the crowd belonged to Bowie that night.

All Bowie could do at this point was consistently to top himself, which he somehow managed to do. He kept his London appearances to a minimum, and concentrated on reworking the show until his summer's end performance at the Rainbow, when the show that Bowie was exporting to America was unveiled. For this occasion, Bowie was released from his cocoon for an interview with Andrew Tyler. Bowie talked about his buddies and the latest "mutual admiration society", this one composed of Reed and Iggy Pop. Iggy had recently signed with Mainman, (De Fries' management company, in which Bowie was the Mainman and his friends were mostly headaches) at Bowie's insistence. Bowie proclaimed that he, Reed and Pop were the three best song-writers around, and went on to say:

> I really don't know what we're doing, if we're the spearhead of anything, we're not necessarily the spearhead of anything good. But people like Lou and I are probably predicting the end of an era and I mean that catastrophically. Any society that allows people like Lou and I to become rampant is pretty well lost.

There were a lot of people who agreed with this (and wondered why they hadn't been stopped) and others who claimed that the likes of Bowie and Reed were just what was needed at the time in order to wipe clean the slate of the Sixties. Confusion was convenient, and a lot of people approved of switching the emphasis from earnest to parodic, from activism to "entertainment". Bowie was smart enough to realize what was going on, but at that point he wasn't quite sure of how others might try to use him. He went on:

> I've always been scared about what I represent and very wary of being categorized because I'm not altogether sure of what I represent. I'm a ball of confusion, mentally, physically....

He managed to pull it together for the Rainbow show that night though, and he kept it fairly well together for the next ball-breaker of a year.

The performances were constantly being altered at this point and Bowie threw in a few touches for the British audience that were abandoned in the U.S. The constants were the *Clockwork Orange*-inspired Beethoven theme for Ziggy's entrance, the set with scaffolding galore and the now classic mock fellatio at the end of *Suffragette City*. Although many shared Lou Reed's sentiments when he described the show as 'amazing, stupendous, incredible — the greatest thing I've ever seen', there were a few dissenters, objecting to his excessive and even mawkish sentimentality. If the Busky Berley style extravaganza wasn't too much, the sight of choreographer and old friend Lindsay Kemp — overweight, wearing wings and smoking a joint during *Starman* — sent several people over the edge. While many touches were left behind in London, the shows remained upscale campy full-tilt theatre, with the music augmented by the addition of a pianist and saxophones in order to recreate the recorded sound in performance.

The show and entourage then moved across the Atlantic with Bowie traveling on the QE2 due to his much publicized fear of flying. He also had a few other phobias which he mentioned to Mick Rock just prior to the tour.

> I get worried about dying. At the moment it's this terrible travel thing. I keep thinking we're going to crash. Last month it was ' being killed on stage. Not here so much. In America, I know that one day a big artist is going to get killed on stage. And I know we're going to be very big. And I keep thinking —it's bound to be me. Go out on me first tour, get done in at me first gig, an' nobody will ever see me. And that would make me *wild*.

As it turned out, he didn't get killed, and he finally overcame his fear of flying, though not until several years later. Bowie's mode of travel by ship, train and bus also determined somewhat the experience he had in the U.S., and allowed him time to work on music between gigs. Since it was also the first time that Bowie had performed for American audiences he learned a few things about this temptingly large market that were put to use both in performance and on *Aladdin Sane*, his next album.

The process of touring, which occupied Bowie almost continuously for nearly one year from the release date of Ziggy, illustrates the reasons for the metamorphosis of the amorphous Starman into A Lad Insane. Ziggy never knew exactly who he was and his origins and mission were never as clear to him as they were to those whose ends he served.

Bowie had explained Ziggy as a conduit for the messages of some Invisible Infinites who made Ziggy a Star in an age of chaos, with music as the only surviving medium for mass communication. But when his ego became overly inflated he was destroyed, his mission accomplished. Ziggy was one of the *Young Dudes* who had to carry the news for the Others, in the period before they became incarnate and endowed with voices and bodies of their own. (They had to snatch them.) This helps to explain the mind frame behind some of Ziggy/Bowie's comments, such as his self-description as 'partly enigmatic, partly fossil'.

If all this sounds complicated, it becomes ever more unreal as the image of this space-age messiah, who only partially understands what he has to do and why, is packaged as a fashion item and sexual curiosity, who also happens to be intelligent and reasonably in control. A substantial burden to be carried on the thin frame of one man who has to give concerts and interviews, who happens to be quite determined but ultimately human, and who has to do and be all these things, while having his picture taken at the same time. This was the man and the situation that Tim Ferris encountered in a drab hotel lobby in Cleveland, where the King of Glamor sat in state over a subdued and joyless "party" which reminded Ferris of Roman legions camped out behind enemy lines in Germania. This was conquest, a grim business, with no allowances made for failure, yet supposed to make it look like fun because this was rock 'n' roll!

In a description of the first performance that Ferris attended which took place in Cleveland (again they began in the hinterlands) he got to the heart of the matter. With the emphasis on the performance, he wrote about freedom, the lack of which finally forced Bowie to abandon Ziggy and all his trappings.

> Bowie keeps moving, strikes poses reminiscent of a dozen
> earlier rockers and behaves much of the time like a puppet. He
> looks the way he says he feels — like an actor playing the role of
> a rock star. The thesis of the role is that freedom on stage is an
> illusion paid for by freedom. [9]

He was also happy to point out that there wasn't 'a limp wrist in the set', and he mentions another Bowie performance hallmark, that 'For all this preparation the show retains a lot of spontaneity in a period when most big-name concerts seem to come out of cans'. In a wide-ranging article he also mentioned the subject of influence, stating that Bowie has obviously borrowed from 'The Beatles, Elvis and a half dozen others, but what emerges is essentially his own.'

One of the other subjects that Ferris broached seems especially crucial to any discussion of Bowie's "career". Especially since he's as astute a businessman as he is an artist. Said Ferris:

> Perhaps the...Americans who have already signed over much of
> their lives to corporations won't mind if even their funkiest,
> most outrageous music springs from corporate mentalities, as
> we've been told for years that it inevitably must. Perhaps for
> the performers, it will be a relief.

In this respect, Bowie's delineation of the possibilities open to him has
to be considered in the context of retaining the status of "star" that this
whole enterprise was intent on making him. Assuming that he already
was a star he saw the alternatives as either becoming one of the 'large
entertainment-for-entertainment's-sake entertainers like Engelbert
Humperdinck...', or one of the people who would be large 'because they
have some kind of redeeming social value'. He said at the time that he
wasn't sure which road he'd take and 'I won't be able to say much about
it until maybe a year or so from now. I'll see where I've been pushed by
the public.' In fact he's been pushed in both directions, and many of the
swings in his career are attributable to Bowie offering just what he
thinks people want at the moment. He can give them something they
don't expect, but he never forgets that the fans have to be prepared to
buy what he's offering.

Working in a corporate context, with promises made to RCA, Bowie
had a few responsibilities. He had to release a lot of records and sell
them too. This later became rather oppressive, but Bowie kept up the
pace for about five years; including the re-releases of *Hunky Dory* and *The
Man Who Sold The World* in conjunction with the Ziggy promotion, David
released eight albums between 1972 and 1976. For his part Tony De
Fries always kept a very clear vision of Bowie in mind, which went some
way to accounting for their continued success. He knew what he was
dealing with and where to go with it.

> Bowie is setting a standard in rock 'n' roll which other people
> are going to have to get to if they want to stay around in the
> Seventies. I think he's very much a Seventies artist. I think most
> of the artists who are with us at the moment are Sixties artists,
> and Bowie certainly to me, is going to be the major artist of the
> Seventies. In 1975 he will be at his peak in music. What he does
> after that will depend on his talents in other fields. [10]

In the meantime there was a continent to capture, and after the
shows in Memphis and Cleveland, the tour came to New York City's
prestigious Carnegie Hall for David's full-scale American debut. He had
picked up a debilitating dose of the flu on the road and by the time he
reached New York could barely speak, but professionalism and discipline stepped in and the show went on. Ferris, who had seen the earlier
shows called it a "pallid imitation", but for those who didn't know
otherwise it was a triumph. New York has always been a good city to

Bowie, and this debut was no exception, with the bad and the beautiful coming out in force to welcome their hero. Warhol, The New York Dolls and their respective retinues showed up, along with almost everyone in New York who made-up, dressed up and always made the scene. With a Klieg light shining outside a' la Hollywood opening, the stage was set. Ruth Copeland opened the show singing mainly for herself while everyone else was in the lobby appraising eachother but, when the Beethoven theme from *Clockwork Orange* marking Ziggy's intro struck up, everyone dove to their seats, spellbound.

With Warhol in the audience, Bowie sang his song. He also managed to get one of his usual Jacques Brel songs into the set. That night it was *Amsterdam*, performed as part of the acoustic set which included *Space Oddity*. After an introduction of 'This is like bringing coals to Newcastle', Bowie and the band launched in Lou Reed's *Waiting For The Man*, *White Light/White Heat*, and finished off with a Chuck Berry classic, *Round And Round*. For those that didn't know any better the show was great, although Bowie was so run down that there was no party afterwards, just bed for the beleaguered star.

The tour was going so well that RCA and De Fries decided to extend it, adding another seventeen gigs over eight weeks. Contrary to the P.R. though, all was not gilded success for Bowie and the band. For instance, a show in St. Louis took place in a several thousand seat auditorium attended by scarcely a thousand behinds; and half of those were there courtesy of a radio station give-away. In spite of the small turnout, Bowie and the Spiders played like they had a standing room only crowd. San Francisco was another disappointment with a poor turnout, but many of those who saw the shows became lifelong Bowie fans, and did their best to convert their friends.

Traveling by train between the performances, Bowie continued to work on the *Aladdin Sane* material, previewing some of the songs in the U.S., and recording at the RCA studios along the way. He sent the masters of *Jean Genie* back to London for early release as a single — all part of the get-it-while-it's-hot theory. Bowie followed the tapes back to England for Christmas, where he took care of business, and again revamped the stage show. He appeared on the "Russell Harty Plus Show", previewing *Drive In Saturday* and Jacques Brel's *My Death*, and talked about the pace of his life. 'I never believe that time can be eaten away as quickly as it is when we're working as we are at the moment'. What he was working on was a major tour with dates being added daily, plus another album, again released within six months of his last one. He was also putting the finishing touches to Lou Reed's *Transformer* album.

With *Aladdin Sane* set to be finished on January 24th, Bowie faced more rehearsals, and a transatlantic crossing on January 25th for another high pressure New York concert. This one, at Radio City Music Hall on St. Valentine's Day, marked the beginning of the public transition to the Aladdin Sane character, though the differences between Aladdin and Ziggy were of degree. There was different staging, more costumes, more material. The *Clockwork Orange* theme was retained and Bowie added a film clip of the cosmos rushing towards the viewer at light year speed, with the climax provided by Bowie's entrance. In spite of the rehearsals, the band didn't quite have it together and as one reviewer put it: 'Bowie's persona and the music were competing for the audience's attention, and the music lost.' Some of the songs were reduced to pantomimed vignettes and with several extra musicians on stage, all that was left for Bowie to do was act and sing. Perhaps for this reason, his sax solo during *Soul Love* was called the highlight of the show (along with his harmonica on *Jean Genie*). Bowie also introduced his descent-to-stage motif, this time enclosed within a sphere, while more costume changes than ever (five!) somewhat hurt the pacing of the show (Mick Ronson did extended solos while Bowie headed for the wardrobe). While many of the fans had no complaints, the show's climax had more than a few wondering where to draw the line between art and life. Following *Rock And Roll Suicide*, a fan rushed at Bowie and gave him a kiss, leaving him lying apparently unconscious on stage. It turned out to be a genuine case of exhaustion, and it was faithfully reported by the still rabid press that he slept for twelve hours afterwards.

Recovered, Bowie continued with the second leg of his American tour, during which *Drive In Saturday* was released as a single, shooting to the top five in the British charts. As further proof that all the hoopla was working, *Aladdin Sane* was released with 100,000 copies sold in advance, a feat that The Beatles had been the last act to accomplish. With this marvelous news, Bowie headed off for his dates in Japan. He was able to play the tourist for a while, traveling to outlying areas to witness some Kabuki and other ritual theater and dance. Japanese theater had been a longstanding interest (he'd claimed the Ziggy show was heavily based on Kabuki) and Japan is a place that he's since returned to frequently. Likewise, his performances have always been excellently received in Japan, where the combination of high style and his "stripper's tricks" usually send the audiences into a state of ecstasy.

The actual concerts in Japan were different to those which took place elsewhere. As Bowie has put it:

> In Japan we were faced with an audience that we presumed didn't understand a word of what I was saying — there I was more physical than on any other tour I've ever done and I carried it back here (England) again. Literally, I activated the whole thing with my hands and my body. I needn't have sung half the time.

In response to his scantily clad body, his kicks and caresses, the Japanese fans went wild, and near riots ensued. The situation was exacerbated by the fact that the security, which had been so tight all along was undermined by the Japanese tradition of acquiescence. At one show the fans rushed the stage, leaving Bowie and the band trapped in the dressing rooms because the Japanese promoters had responded to all questions about the group's mode of exit with a polite "yes". (Will the bus be backstage? "Yes".) As it turned, people were literally crushed in the crowd.

Leaving Japan triumphantly, the circus made for Russia and crossed the country on the Trans-Siberian railroad. In one of his least enlightening comments ever, Bowie sought to describe his impressions of the trip. 'Russia is an impossible country to talk about. It's so vast. The people we found to be warm generally. When we got to Moscow they were colder.' He also said that he was the first person to take a movie camera to Siberia, and that in his Ziggy/Aladdin guise he was mistaken for a member of a real circus and that 'you can get away with murder with orange hair in Russia.' The troupe made it to Moscow in time for the May Day celebrations and though he found it hard to talk about the country, David later returned to Russia, gaining a deeper perspective which found oblique expression on the *Low* album.

From Moscow, he journeyed to Paris. A British press lapping at his heels faithfully reported that David and Angie missed the morning train, had to catch another and hop the Hovercraft in order to greet their patient fans at Victoria Stadium. The obligatory limousine was waiting, and while he was hustled into it Bowie made a few parting comments to Melody Maker reporter Roy Hollingworth, who'd been accompanying them on the tour.

> I'm sick of being Gulliver. You know, after America, Moscow, Siberia, Japan, I just want to bloody well go home to Beckenham and watch the telly. This decadence thing is just a bloody joke. I'm very normal. I am me and I have to carry on with what I've started. There is nothing else for me to do. I have been under a great strain though. For me, performing is indeed a great strain. I've also become disillusioned with certain things. I never believed a hype could be made of an artist before that artist had got anywhere. That's what happened you see. But when I saw that our albums were really selling I knew that one period was over. The hype was over. Well, it wasn't but at least we'd done something to be hyped about. [11]

Bowie took this occasion to talk at some length about Ziggy, and how being treated as if they were one and the same was 'a monster to endure'. I mean I never thought that Ziggy would become the most talked about man in the world.' Bowie also spoke about his audience, making some rather important statements, though he would later contradict many of them. He began by talking about Ziggy and his effect.

> The characters I have written about have indeed been the roles I wished to portray. Ziggy — that dead creature. I loved him. I feel somewhat like a Doctor Frankenstein. Although Ziggy follows David Bowie very closely, they are indeed two people.

What have I created?

Ziggy hit the nail on the head. He just came at the rightest, ripest time... I know I have created a somewhat strange audience — but that audience is full of little Noddy Holders and Iggy Pops. I know we used to attract a load of queens at one stage but then other factions of people crept in. Now you can't tell any more. They're all there for some reason. And we get young people. These lovely young people. And they have to be considered very seriously. They cannot be forgotten — as they might be. We cannot afford to lose them by continuing to make rock a cultural force. We must not leave the young behind. I repeat that. You see, I don't want to aim statements at them. Again, the whole idea of being a statesman is abhorrent to me.

As it turns out, rock has remained a cultural force, and Bowie has continued his input, but he might not have been saying all he could have for the benefit of "these lovely young people". As he mentioned in the same interview:

I've gone through a lot of changes on my way back from Japan. After what I've seen of the state of the world, I've never been so damn scared in my life. If I wrote about it, it would probably be my last album ever because I wouldn't be around very long after finishing it.

Bowie was finished with the idea of becoming a martyr, and instead opted for survival. He also hinted at Ziggy's demise which was only months away.

I became Ziggy on stage. That was my ego but I don't think Ziggy is my ego anymore. It's a more mature David Bowie now.

This mature Bowie came back to England, to his seven quid per week flat in Beckenham, and threw a small party with the Haddon Hall crew, many of whom had been with David throughout the tour. They had a lot of reasons to celebrate, with *Aladdin* at the top of the charts, and David an international sensation. After a brief respite it was on to more touring, beginning with a concert at the Earl's Court Exhibition Hall, an event that has been called a 'fiasco' and 'the worst example of a bad deal in the history of British rock'. Aside from the problems of the Hall itself, most of the blame fell on the promoters who actually owned up to the fact that they had scrimped on the sound (something over which Bowie and De Fries always wisely took pains) and the security, leaving fans free to surge up to the stage. The scene became even wilder with incidents of fans urinating in the aisles while others removed their clothes and tried to force a young woman to do the same. Anyone who had any interest left in the show on stage found it nearly impossible to see or hear. As a result, many in the audience left before the gig was over, convincing Bowie to cancel another date at Earl's Court which was scheduled shortly afterwards.

This show was followed by a forty date British tour of what was now essentially the "Aladdin Sane" show. While forty dates can be dismissed in one sentence, the grind as well as the split Ziggy/Aladdin personality were starting to wear thin on Bowie. In consequence he decided to put a temporary end to it on the last night of the English tour. The date was June 3rd, 1973, the place was the Hammersmith Odeon. After almost exactly one year of constant touring and promotion, David granted Ziggy, and himself, a well-earned retirement. It later became clear that there were also quite practical reasons for cutting things off at that precise moment, since Bowie had already scheduled studio time for work on his next album apparently without consulting De Fries, who had likewise added more dates to the tour schedule. Calling the break a "retirement" helped get them off of a few hooks.

The announcement of the "retirement" came at the end of the Hammersmith show. Following a duet with Jeff Beck on *Jean Genie*, David spoke the words which, as Charles Shaar Murray put it, 'sent every glitter kid in the world into mourning'. Said Bowie:

> Of all the shows on the tour this one will stay with us for the longest because not only is it the last show of the tour but it's the last show we'll ever do.

The crowd went into shock and instant depression; a few words had shattered the order of things. As testimony to Bowie's status, the story was carried by all the major UK dailies as well as by the music press, and the headlines were as sensational as Bowie's announcement. As it turned out, it was the last show the Spiders would ever do. Like an Egyptian burial, the vassals were placed in the tomb with their now dead King. The costumes were also put in mothballs as were most other items that could be associated with Ziggy (except the effect on the imagination). A film was shot of the Odeon concert by documentarist D. A. Pennebaker and for years fans have been waiting for its release. Most had given up hope of ever seeing it when Bowie announced that he would release it in late 1983. There were several reasons for the lengthy delay which owed as much to the state of Bowie's business in the ensuing years as to his state of mind.

Bowie's retirement called for a party, a shindig used as an opportunity to celebrate his new-found friendships as well as his fame. The post-show bash was held at the Cafe Royal on Regent Street, a sight of slightly decayed elegance which perfectly suited the campy Bowie entourage. Everyone was there, from old friends Lou Reed and Lulu to more recent companions like Mick and Bianca Jagger, Ringo and Maureen Starr, Keith Moon, Paul and Linda McCartney, Barbra Streisand, Sonny Bono, Tony Curtis, Elliot Gould, Ryan O'Neil, comedians Peter Cook and Dudley Moore along with the Spiders, Jeff Beck and Pennebaker. The party's guest list read like a Who's Who of then "in" showbiz, generously filled with the beautiful people of music and movies. Most of the photos released featured Bowie, Reed and Jagger (with a beaming Lulu in the background), a desperately good time being had by all; Angie and Bianca dancing together and sitting on each other's laps, David and Mick doing the same.

Out of this period of R&R following a tour which David described as 'grim business', have come thousands of unflattering anecdotes. Once he showed up for a Bette Midler concert in L.A., making a dramatic late entrance wearing a Kansai robe which affront he topped by sitting through a standing ovation. The divine Miss M was moved to snarl: 'That son of a bitch!' The actions of those working on Bowie's behalf were sometimes just as outrageous; Publicist Cherry Vanilla has claimed that they, 'peddled David's ass like Nathan's sells hotdogs', and to this end tells of gladly bedding key D.J.s for the sake of advancing Ziggy's cause. David would claim that 'most people still want their idols and gods to be shallow, like cheap toys', but he began to feel cheapened as a person due to the efforts on his behalf. The situation began to get out of control, and even though David was determined to bring things back in line, at that moment all he could do was ride with the tide, doing whatever he could to keep the over-enthusiasm of his entourage in check. His decision to "quit" was one such effort. At the time, Roy Hollingworth made a point of linking the two. He asked:

> Would it not be a very super move to "quit" in public even
> before he's reached his peak? To be very famous, one has to pull
> many tricks these days. And however lovely Bowie is in your
> eyes, don't think he won't pull tricks. To survive, he has to.

In Bowie's own mind survival was also an issue. The trade-off between business, personal and artistic priorities accounts for much of what he was to go through in the course of his career, though he'd made the first crucial leap. With his mythical creation, impeccable music, personality and performance, Bowie had done what he needed to do, which Mick Ronson put very simply: 'Bowie has to become a legend — that's the only way he can last'. And that's just what he had done. But Bowie also happened to be a living human being, and now the task was to further the legend while presenting a more human face because, after all, he wanted to be loved for himself. Such exposure is fraught with risk, so Bowie opted instead for the protection of masks/personas, each of which illuminated whatever facet of himself he was exploring at the moment. One might catch an occasional glimpse of "the man" between the costume and make-up changes, but the days of "candid" photos ended with Ziggy's birth. An image is a delicate creation and its handling and care were a prime concern.

(For all this concern with image it was clear to many people that as sudden as David's rise seemed to be, there was something of musical substance behind it all. No less of an "authority" than Dick Clark wrote in the closing chapter of *20 Years of Rock And Roll* — published in '73 —

that 'Performers like Alice Cooper and David Bowie seem to hold the key to the future of rock, and entertainers like Michael Jackson and Donny Osmond have only just begun to show us their talents.' Well, two out of four ain't bad...)

EIGHT

'Up the hill backwards, it'll be alright...'

'Up The Hill Backwards' -- *Scary Monsters (and Super Creeps)*

As much as he has claimed he'd like to, it seems unlikely that David Bowie will ever be able to bury Ziggy Stardust; the Ziggy mythos is so entangled in what is now the Bowie myth. Living the legend had become a real strain, and having reached the point where Bowie was unable to spread himself any thinner without breaking, he took his own version of rest and relaxation following Ziggy's retirement. Rest for Bowie involved a large dose of work, although he took on a less than usually demanding project, which ended up as the *Pin-Ups* album. But first *Aladdin Sane*, which was tied chronologically and spiritually with Ziggy. *Aladdin Sane* is a favorite with many of Bowie's American fans, and it was somewhat calculated to appeal to what Bowie had determined to be the American taste in rock music. He received inspiration from his new friends, The Rolling Stones, as well as from his own observations on the reasons for The Stones' success, though his views were tempered by the experience of his touring the country. Bowie described Aladdin as a 'situation as well as a character in his own right', and the situation was literally that created for Bowie by living the Ziggy character's rise. Aladdin found himself in the U.S.A., prompting many to consider the album as Bowie's musical version of *On The Road*.

Since the bulk of the album was inspired by and written in America, some of the comments Bowie made about the country and the audiences he found there are revealing. Speaking about his first tour Bowie said that 'In America, we'll just keep it down to simplicities. But Americans are very academic towards their rock and need it to have a cultural stability.' In contrast to Japan and England, he indicated that 'possibly in America we play a harder set. Even though the Americans are more inclined towards this cultural thing, they need it to be more primitive.' Bowie had more than the downbeat in mind when he made those remarks. Due to the circumstances of recording on the road and the general rush job to get the album out, there is less than the usual painstaking production detail and clarity to *Aladdin*, but Bowie apparently realized that this too would appeal to the more "primitive" taste of Americans (critics included), who were mostly nostalgic for the "feeling over form" days of early rock. And for those who needed their cultural thing, Bowie threw in a lyric sheet and some food for thought.

It seems that Bowie had the feel of the album firmly in focus before he even arrived in the States, but while Aladdin Sane has been considered another in Bowie's gallery of characters; in reality Aladdin wasn't as cleanly or as clearly conceived as that, but rather an extension and another facet of Ziggy Stardust. This is highlighted by the number of variations on the name that Bowie went through before arriving at the "correct combination". He mentioned to one interviewer that the original title had been *Love Aladdin Vein*.

> The album is about the States in some kind of small concept. Originally, I felt that *Love Aladdin Vein* was right, then I thought "Maybe I shouldn't write them off so easily". So I changed it. Also in "Vein" there was the drugs thing, but it's not that universal.

Pinpointing his audience as he did, he got the positive response from the Americans that he desired, helped by the fact that all the Ziggy hype accompanied its release. *Aladdin* still did better in Britain than in the U.S. both because it was Bowie's home base, and a smaller country. The great American rock music public wasn't ready for Ziggy, and the "everyman" concept that Bowie promoted was simultaneously too amorphous and refined. But Bowie pleased the spectrum of his new-found audience with a combination of sophisticated jazz sounds and some of the hot rock 'n' roll that he knew it wanted.

From *A Lad In Vein* to *A Lad In Sane*, Bowie came up with the winning mix of *Aladdin Sane* which turned the insanity on itself and made a virtue of encompassing it, while also conjuring the element of the exotic with *Aladdin*. These variations on the theme were borne out by a slightly different look from Ziggy's sleek line to a longer haircut, more flamboyant costumes reminiscent of David's Kansai robes, bare-all leotards and stage wear bikinis, with the final touch of the Pierre La Roche circle (sun) glued to his forehead. The transformation was gradual, as it would be with Bowie's later character of the Thin White Duke. Bowie may have felt safer working through sketchier characters in future, whose identities wouldn't so completely submerge his own. Nevertheless, the trademark thunderbolt (Ziggy's Z, perhaps uncon-sciously borrowing from Elvis' Memphis Mafia insignia) became quite popular and can still be seen adorning faces in the crowd at Bowie's concerts.

While the make-up job and the gatefold sleeve that continued the thunderbolt motif behind Bowie's body were turn-ons for some, most fans were equally delighted by the vinyl within. Without disappointing his *Hunky Dory* fans, Bowie went for the market The Stones had previously cornered, trying to make up to those who might have missed *The Man Who Sold The World*.

The glitter kids were more than willing to go along with Aladdin. The romance was still young and his fans' loyalty hadn't been severely tried. Bowie guaranteed the album's success by insuring it carried the statutory two hits, *The Jean Genie*, which was the first single released from *Aladdin Sane*, and *Drive-In Saturday* which followed it. *Watch That Man* and *Aladdin Sane* both had some potential, but overall the album had a rushed and incomplete quality, particularly to an audience spoiled by the unity of *Ziggy*. Among the truest Bowiephiles, opinion reigns that *Aladdin* is one of the master's lesser works, but for those generally inclined to consider Bowie pretentious, its very faults and under-produced feel are considered its greatest merits. What was important was that "it made you feel radical."

One of the curiosities of *Aladdin Sane* is that despite its sketchiness, it manages to reconstitute itself rather clearly in the mind, somehow leaving the impression that it sounds better than it does. The opening *Watch That Man* is a case in point. The manic energy that the song needs doesn't quite come together in the cut, while the lyrics have been criticized as coming across like a first draft, but within the roughness there are brilliant moments. In line with all of the songs on the album, this one has its locational inspiration printed next to it on the sleeve; in this case "New York". It sounds like it too, lyrically influenced by Dylan and Reed with a comic description of the mood and the characters at a party. After a round of name-dropping (Benny Goodman gets a plug) attention focuses on the man "who's only taking care of the room/Must be in tune", which arouses visions of Andy Warhol as "he talks like a jerk/But he could eat you with a fork and spoon".

The all-out rock of *Watch* is followed by *Aladdin Sane* with the same piano dominated, jazzy, theatrical sound that appears frequently on this album and in Bowie's work in general. The pianist is Mike Garson, a New Yorker whom David had picked up for the American leg of the Ziggy tour and who remained in the band for quite a while. A lot of attention has been lavished on Bowie's guitarists as indicators of where he's at musically, but the same could be said of his keyboard/synthesizer players who are rarely spotlighted. Since both Bowie and Ronson play keyboards (and have done so on albums) they have a respect for their role in the music.

Aladdin Sane is the only track annotated with dates as well as a place, and although the setting could be the U.S., the U.K. or Europe, the dates (1913-1938-1977) suggest a prelude-to-war theme. Dictatorial rule seems to be its subject, though the lyrics are particularly vague and the piano enjoys all the attention apart from Bowie's rendering of the line "Who'll love Aladdin Sane?", which finds him in an almost crooner-like voice.

Bringing the tempo and idiom slightly up to date, Bowie launches into *Drive-In Saturday*, commonly interpreted as another of David's futuristic musings on an age when sexual technique will be a lost art and the practitioners will have to pick up tips from film and videotapes. The setting of "Seattle-Phoenix" is a reference to a night-time train ride through the desert, during which Bowie tells of seeing strange lighted domes that no one could explain. Presumably, this inspired the song's futuristic vein. Perhaps the train's route passed a Drive-In showing *Performance* or *Gimme Shelter*. While *Drive-In Saturday* doesn't have an obvious Stones basis musically, the line "When people stared in Jagger's eyes and scored" is one of the best in the song. Leaving the two awkward couplets far behind, Bowie launches off on another name-dropping spree, mentioning friends, old and new. The Astonettes get a plug as do "Twig the Wonder Kid", Jung and Sylvain. The other aching lines tell us that "His name was always Buddy", which could have been Mac or Joe, but perhaps Buddy Holly's ghost was in the vicinity. Bowie gets to the heart of the matter with "She's uncertain if she likes him/But she knows she really loves him", a dilemma that he was to return to musically on several occasions.

In the next song, the characters don't stop at raving. *Panic In Detroit*, undoubtedly a sensation inspired as much by Iggy's accounts of the place as actual happenings, is somewhat based on the case of John Sinclair, the White Panther leader and manager of the MC-5 who was framed for possessing a couple of joints. It's one of the few songs on the album where the intent and the energy coalesce, with the guitar up front and the background filled in by Linda Lewis and Juanita Franklin. Angie and David always claimed to love Detroit — 'it was the real shit you know' — but the song finds its singer paranoid about guns, accidental sirens and police brutality.

Continuing the theme of desperate actions by deranged individuals, Bowie presents the *Cracked Actor*, who could only hail from "L.A." In the light of this song, it's amazing that Bowie ever chose to live there, unless compelled to live his own demise. The title became the name of a BBC documentary on Bowie and presages the Thin White Duke, who also hailed from L.A. via Berlin. Bowie was still performing the song in concert in 1983 with an "Alas poor Yorick" rendition to a skull, though it'll probably be rested for a while. Bowie may have been getting tired of that bit of theatrics by the tour's end — but the song remains powerful, with not a line of lyric that misses the mark. It bolsters the "most bizarre sexual imagery ever put to vinyl" tag given the album, mainly by virtue of its directness.

On the second side, Bowie enters another world which, with the exception of *Let's Spend The Night Together* and *The Jean Genie*, is simple, sparse, piano-backed and sweetly sung. Bowie puts *Time* (Kronos) through the motions, from the passive "waiting in the wings" to "Flexing like a whore" and falling "wanking to the floor", to finally carrying his victims away, specifically Billy Marcia of The New York Dolls, alias Billy Dolls.

The Prettiest Star is an oldie pulled out for the occasion. Its bouncy optimism carries a sting in the tail in its use of the past tense to describe this love. Maybe things didn't work out between David and Angie because "you've got everything but cold fire", possibly the one thing Bowie needed. This song was placed at "Gloucester Road", whereas *Time* was situated in "New Orleans", a sympathetic city which may have inspired the timeless and languid feel of the song.

David and crew raise hell with their rendering of The Stones' *Let's Spend The Night Together*. In typical Bowie fashion, it gives a clue as to where he's coming from (he doesn't let you know if he doesn't want you to) and simultaneously points out a few differences between himself and Jagger. Bowie's version turns the issue of sexuality polymorphous and perverse, and therefore much more intriguing than The Stones'. He invokes heaven in the middle break, then brings the song back down, vamping all the way to the end. He made the song exciting in a manner that probably had some Stones fans sweating for reasons they didn't quite understand.

The same holds true for *The Jean Genie*, a song that harks back to blues roots via The Yardbirds, bringing the idiom up to date in rock terms with more of Bowie's less than literal but thoroughly arousing lyrics. This song has usually been assumed to be a take off on Jean Genet (at least in title) but others figure Iggy in the picture and, as is often the case with Bowie's most effective songs, it develops a kind of composite image. Almost a mirror image to *Hang On To Yourself*, the essential message to the poor little Greenie is "Let yourself go". The score, especially the guitar line and intro, are almost straight out of The Yardbirds' *I'm A Man*. With *Suffragette City* and *Rebel Rebel*, *Genie* is one of the great favorites of fans of Bowie the Hard Rocker.

The final cut on the album is basically filler, written back in London, ostensibly for Claudia Linnear, a soul singer who was also the inspiration for *Brown Sugar*. This brings to memory Mick Jagger's comment that he finally learned not to wear a new pair of shoes in front of Bowie for fear that Bowie'd be seen in the same pair the next day. Bowie has gleefully taken the story a step further, admitting that Mick won't walk into the same room as him "even *thinking* a new thought".

Despite its many failings, *Aladdin Sane* succeeded somehow in making the listener hear what he or she hoped to find, and its harder rock moments were among the best of Bowie's recording career to date. The album did tremendously well — owing as much to the timing of its release as anything — even though the fact that Bowie had worked at greater speed and with more distractions than ever shows in almost every aspect of the finished product. Neither the writing, the song selection nor production were up to his usual standards. By way of a footnote, a song called *It's A Game* was recorded for the album, and seems to have been the seed for the two renditions of *It's No Game* that appeared on *Scary Monsters*. In the original form, it's available only on a rare bootleg (the original *John I'm Only Dancing* came from these sessions).

Between the release and impressive success of this album fell the tail end of the Ziggy/Aladdin tour and the retirement of both characters. In keeping with his six month release schedule, Bowie headed off to the Chateau d'Herouville (after a short vacation with Angie) on the outskirts of Paris for an overdue rest and period of intensive re-creation. The Chateau was quite popular for its isolation, but was also well suited to David's round-the-clock-work-when-you-want-to habits. In this setting he developed the entire *Pin-Ups* album as well as doing much of the writing for *Diamond Dogs*, mostly while the others slept. *Pin-Ups*, a retrospective, was also the end of a particular phase for Bowie and some of his associates. It was the last album with Ken Scott as producer, and the last with Ronson at Bowie's side. Bowie originally hadn't planned to bring either Woodmansey or Bolder with him, having requested the services of Aynsley Dunbar on drums and Jack Bruce on bass. Bruce couldn't make it so Trevor Bolder stayed on, for what was to be the last incarnation of the Spiders. The material written for what would become *Diamond Dogs* was recorded by a group of musicians handpicked for the sessions. At the time, Bowie was also said to be working on a musical version of George Orwell's "1984", which was the conceptual underpinning of *Diamond Dogs*, but Orwell's widow refused permission, so the musical never came to be.

Pin-Ups is another Bowie album that separates the wheat from the chaff; the fanatics loved it almost without exception. To a devotee, the track selection, arrangements and Bowie's singing style were all spot on, though to anyone who had never understood what the fuss was all about, *Pin-Ups* provided few answers. The album epitomizes Bowie's tendency to pay tribute to the artists from whom he's "borrowed", and/or those whom he thinks deserve credit or exposure. There are some notable omissions, especially The Beatles, Roxy Music and The Stones (who received their dues on *Aladdin*), as well as Dylan, Zappa, The Beach Boys, Lou, Iggy, and The Doors. The fact that the list could go on sparked speculation that there might be a *Pin-Ups 2*, though a second never materialized. The original *Pin-Ups* would have satisfied Bowie's interest of the moment, aside from which he would probably have been wary of getting too heavily into covering other people's material. Pointedly, all the songs "covered" on *Pin-Ups* were originated by British bands.

The album features music by two types of groups: the "one hit wonders" and, as Bowie put in on the liner notes, "some % that— are still with us". He claims that the sounds are those of bands which were his live favorites from early club-crawling days, though choices seem to have been made in some cases to rescue certain songs from obscurity, in others because the songs were fun to sing, and in yet others to allow Bowie take off on the original interpretations. The Who's music (Townshend's songs in particular) falls into this latter catagory, with Bowie compelled to drain it of its manic energy and see what's left. The notes on this album are minimal yet interesting. The time frame is noted as '64-'67, and the "Scene" as the Ricki Tak, Marquee, and the "eel pie island la-la" circuit. Bowie attributes *See Emily Play* to "Syd's Pink Floyd", Syd being Syd Barrett, one of Bowie's early favorite writers who "let the music take him over" (though in Barrett's case, such abandon led to his eclipse).

The front cover features Bowie and Twig The Wonderkid, whose faces are an excellent match, although their moods couldn't be more different. Lugubrious Twiggy seems to be looking inward and back, while Bowie's straight clear gaze takes him all the way through the Seventies into the Eighties. A baton is being passed from the Face of the Sixties to that of the Seventies, as Ray Coleman had predicted in

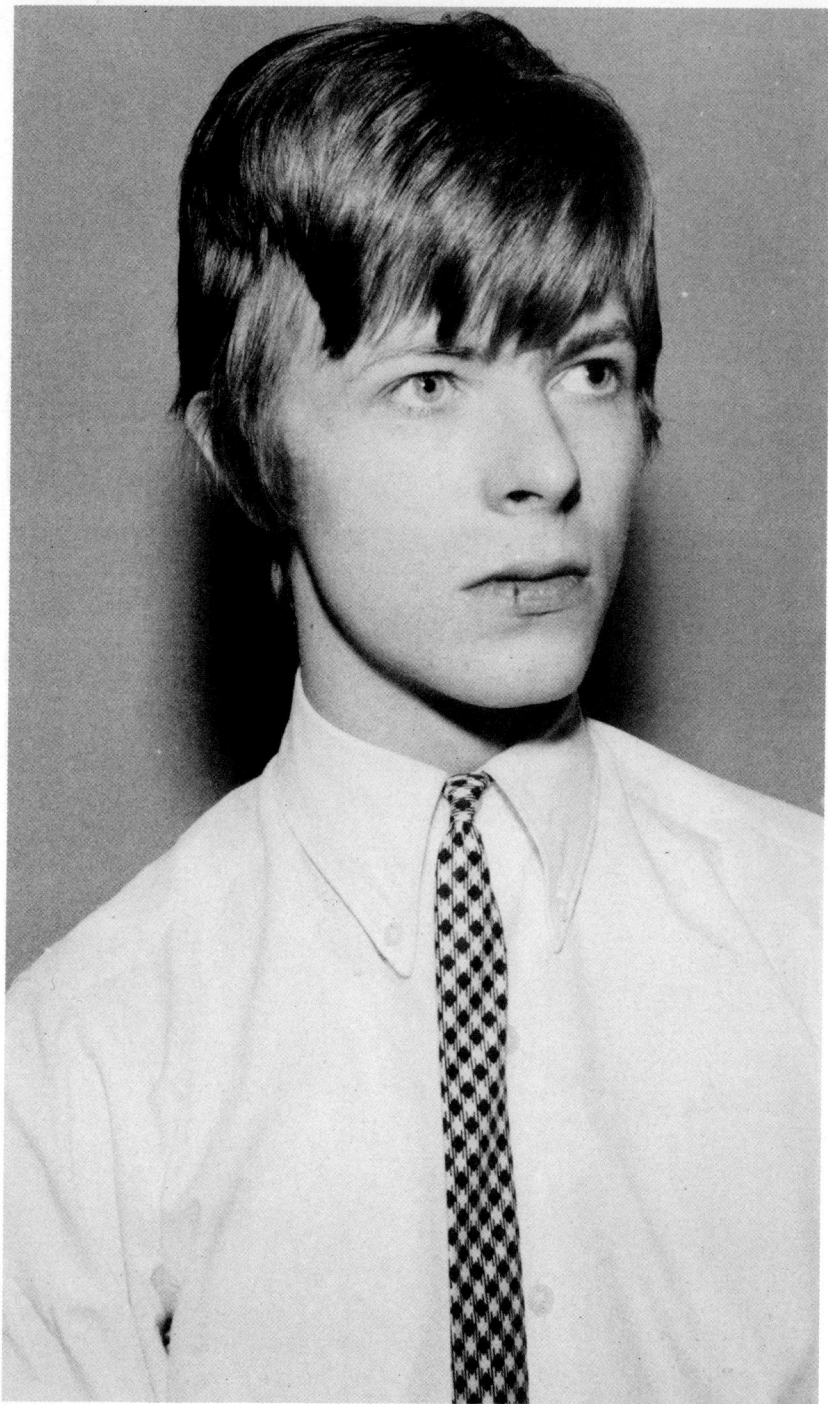

David Jones circa 1964

Left: The Space Oddity himself guests on Russell Harty's TV Show. February 1973.

Right: July '73

Publicity still from *JUST A GIGOLO*

Right: At the Cannes Film Festival for *MERRY CHRISTMAS MR. LAWRENCE,* with Ryuichi Sakamoto.

Below: On Broadway as John Merrick, the Elephant Man

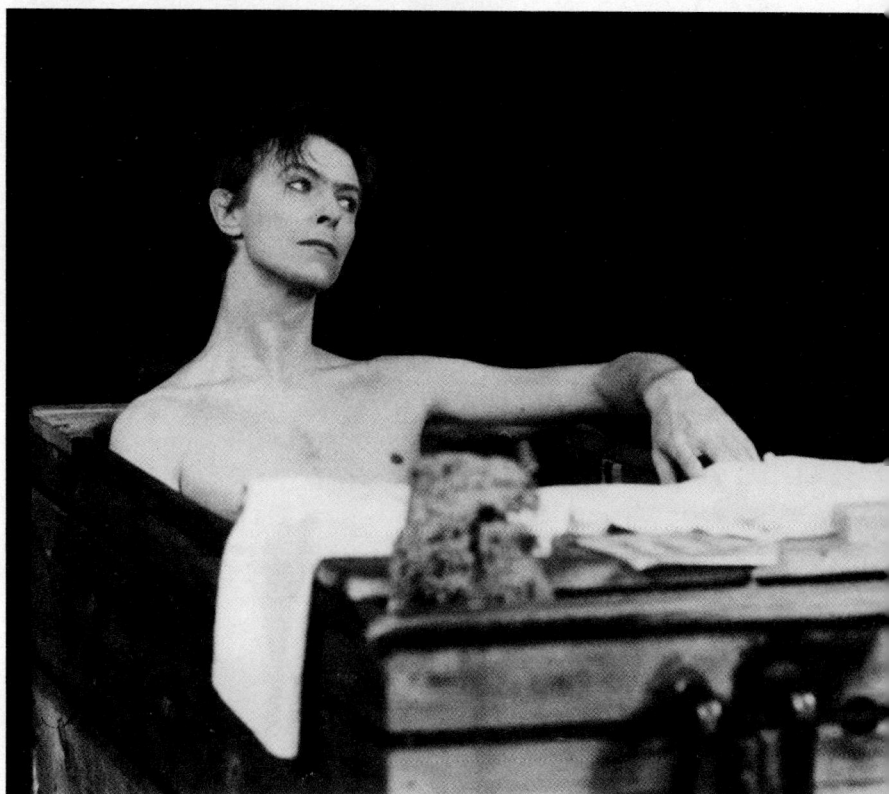

Above: A scene from *MERRY CHRISTMAS*.

Overleaf: On the European leg of the 'Serious Moonlight' tour. Brussells, May 18, 1983.

Melody Maker not much earlier. But if the faces are pin-ups, the songs are mostly rave-ups, the best ones anyway.

Things begin promisingly enough with *Rosalyn* by The Pretty Things, which may have been a more appropriate single than *Sorrow* turned out to be. Bowie truly found the spirit of rock 'n' roll for this one; it's driving and light at the same time. But the energy almost immediately dissipates when he takes on Them's *Here Comes The Night*. In contrast to Van Morrison's pure soul feel, this cut represents the first example of the crooning singer's bag of tricks from which Bowie was beginning to pull Elvis-like vocal knee drops which do nothing for the song, and pretentious enunciation that undermines its soul.

The next song up is The Yardbirds' *I Wish You Would*, a good choice with Ronson (the winner of the Jeff Beck play-alike contest in his earlier years) on guitar. The track receives an additional kick via the fiddle-playing of a member of the French band Zoo, who for some reason was uncredited. The spark is sustained through a haunting version of Pink Floyd's *See Emily Play*. As should be the case, the cut uses a synthesizer to excellent effect. It also suggests Syd Barrett's influence on some of Bowie's earlier and rather imaginative vignettes, whose subjects were not the normal stuff of rock 'n' roll. The album gets back into high gear with the next song, *Everything's Alright*, originally by The Mojos, which may owe some of its spunk to the fact that drummer Dunbar once played with The Mojos, though not on the original recording. The song contains rhythm changes which caused the original version to sag badly, but Dunbar makes an admirable job of holding the thing together for Bowie. Bowie seems to have had a lot of fun singing this one.

The upbeat quality and forward momentum of *Everything's Alright* are stopped in their tracks by the final cut *I Can't Explain*, a Who classic. Slowed down to a crawl compared to the original, it is one of the weaker cuts on the album (and would seem so even without the comparison). It is typical of Bowie's treatment of Townshend's material that he would strip it of its energy, leaving little more than a corpse.

Side two of *Pin-Ups* begins with *Friday On My Mind* by the Easybeats, whose sound is hit tune all the way. Bowie plays it up with some rather silly choruses while doing justice to the verse parts. The Mersey's tune *Sorrow* follows, and it seems that sentiment got the better of Bowie in choosing it as the single, because he croons his way through the piece shamelessly. (Maybe that's how he first learned to sing some of his early favorites, playing a post-Army Elvis in front of the mirror.) He obviously loves the song, including it in both the 1980 Floor Show and in his 1983 concert tour. The music and the sax break are nice, but the mock sentimental vocals make it hard to take.

From there on in its smooth and uphill sailing. *Don't Bring Me Down* by the Pretty Things matches *Everything's Alright* for high spirits, and Ronson shines again as a Yardbird-in-spirit on *Shapes Of Things*. By this stage the crooner has been truly let out of his cage, but Bowie is able to pull it back together and finally beats The Who at their own game on *Anyway, Anywhere, Anyhow*. This track features some patented mix tricks on the drums which went on to become part of Bowie's production stock-in-trade.

The final cut is the only Kink's tune on the album, *Where Have All The Good Times Gone*, which more than any other song on the album reflects Bowie's state of mind. It is also the only song whose lyrics are printed on the sleeve, testifying to Bowie's respect for Ray Davies as a songwriter/lyricist. The production on this one is sterling, Ronson is powerful and the staccato rhythm is reinforced by Bowie's singing. The mood changes are totally appropriate and only add to the song which, more than almost any other on the collection, Bowie seems to have made his own.

Indeed Bowie tried hard to do this with all the songs on the L.P., as witness the much reported fact that he didn't take any of the original recordings with him to France, only the lead sheets. The idea wasn't to do exact covers of the tunes —enough people were already objecting to the release of a cover album as it was, and simply copying the originals would have been a dangerous retrograde career move.

While Bowie took the opportunity of working on *Pin-Ups* to explore his musical heritage, he shared some of his views with the journalists who made their way to the Chateau for interviews. Speaking with Roderick Gillcrest, Bowie discussed his role as a superstar and talked about touring:

> Believe it or not, I didn't actually want to be a rock 'n' roll star. I had an awful lot of fun doing that but the reason I went on the road was to interpret the songs I was writing in an atmosphere that I felt was realistic for the songs. [1]

This statement was revealing in as much as it confirmed that the Ziggy and Aladdin material had been written for performance rather than record, though his observations later in the interview on touring — a subject about which he likes to expound regularly — need to be taken with a pinch of salt. He has said that he enjoys touring and dislikes it; that he only does it for the money and that he does not. Speaking with Charles Shaar Murray he got around to talking about his future hopes and wishes. Using the word "factory" straight from Warhol's lexicon, Bowie said that he had plans for 'a kind of factory. I'll put ye olde recording studio in, and then I want to follow up with other studios of sorts to see what I can do there.' "There" turned out to be wherever he was living, and since he was forced to move (by his fans) fairly regularly, for years Bowie had homes and studios all over the globe.

Around this time Angie began to move into the spotlight. Although there had been occasional photos and interviews with her (always doing her best to be as outrageous as David, and taking seriously her role as model for the new amorality) she had rarely been given the opportunity to be seen as anything other than David Bowie's wife. While they were in France, Bowie had promised to model some clothes for the Daily Mirror, but finding himself unable to abide the wardrobe brought over for him, he convinced the Mirror to work with Angie instead. The paper complied, including David in a few shots reminiscent of Elton John with his ubiquitous shades, and the session succeeded in getting Angie started on the modeling career she desired. Attention in the form of more photo-sessions, talk-show invitations and interviews began to turn on Angie, though she was never really able to shed her dependance on her relationship to a rock music superstar, and when she assumed the alias of Jipp (or Gypp) Jones it did nothing but confuse people. David was supposedly flattered that she used his family name, but "Jipp" only reflected the sense of dishonesty which plagued her efforts to carve a niche of her own.

Pin-Ups sold quite well on release. Shortly beforehand Decca decided to re-release *The Laughing Gnome*, which ironically become one of Bowie's largest-selling singles. Decca recognized and exploited the need to move Bowie "product" while the Ziggy Stardust buzz was still being felt.

Sorrow was released as a single on October 12, 1973 and Bowie's fans were heartened to hear that he would be performing, albeit for a limited audience, for the filming of a television special. The program was to be called "The 1980 Floor Show" in keeping with his interest in cabaret, as well as being a (somewhat lame) pun on Orwell's *19 84*; Orwell's book inspired the sentiment of much of the Diamond Dogs album. It was for this TV show that the song *19 84* was previewed, with human heiroglyphics spelling things out. The show was a major production for NBC's "Midnight Special", and the network chose the Marquee Club for its atmosphere, probably at Bowie's urging. Club owner Jack Barrie was rather taken aback when the network's art directors took the liberty of remodeling and repainting the place to get the visuals up to spec.

The show was a well planned spectacular, with three nights of performance edited down for the show; it featured all Bowie's most popular material, plus previews from *Pin-Ups* and *Diamond Dogs*. To the frustration of many, the show was staged for a small and select audience in England which might have made some sense if the show had aired there, but it didn't. The proud few were mainly members of the David Bowie Fan Club, members of the Marquee Club, a few friends and loyal members of the press. Melody Maker was invited (having done so much for Bowie's career), and reported that, "Show biz romantics" and good friends of the Bowies, Lionel Bart and Dana Gillespie were there, along with son Zowie -- "An incredibly beautiful child, he swore innocently at us arousing the spector of infant revolution."

The Troggs, another of Bowie's favorite groups, were also there. Their '60s hit, *Wild Thing*, is a rock classic, but they had fallen on hard times since then. Marianne Faithfull also appeared, duetting with Bowie on *I Got You Babe*, producing a musical experience reminiscent of Dylan and Johnny Cash on *Girl From The North Country*. Good-natured chaos was the scene. Dressed like a nun with nothing underneath, Faithfull provided one of the off-camera thrills with a dramatic exit in a slit-back habit. Bowie made countless costume changes, putting on the Ziggy persona for the appropriate numbers, then switching to Aladdin and so on like most of us change sweaters. This show also marked Ronson's last appearance as a Spider. Less than thrilled about the state of things, Ronson described his role somewhat cynically:

> I turned up, put me make-up on, got me guitar out, played, put me guitar away, took me make-up off and went home. [2]

Bowie seemed to enjoy his role more, the multiple costume and make-up changes, as well as major production numbers, wild enough to stand up to years of repeats. He was in mod-formal and make-up for *Sorrow*, wearing a feather encrusted breastplate costume for *19 84* (qualifying as the most ridiculous), while a gold net outfit with strategically placed artificial hands was the most outrageous. It was also the most problematic, as NBC (puritanical Americans that they are) couldn't abide the crotch grabbing pair of hands, and because their forced removal exposed Bowie's jockstrap, most of the shots were only from the waist up. Aside from bringing to mind the legendary stories of Elvis on the Ed Sullivan Show, this was a disservice to the costume and its full length effect, but all in all it was a wonderful show; while it still runs on television, segments of it crop up in the video presentations designed to satisfy Bowie fans year round.

The show was filmed on October 18, 19, and 20 and *Pin-Ups* was released on the 19th, approaching 1974 and the year of the *Diamond Dog*. But in the meantime, Bowie worked on an album with The Astronettes who had been mentioned on *Drive-In Saturday* and were on stage for the early London Ziggy shows. The Astronettes consisted of old friend and frequent back-up vocalist Geoff McCormack, Jason Guess and Ava Cherry, who figured in later work as well as some Bowie-related gossip. The material Bowie chose for them is maybe more indicative of his real musical preferences and influences than was much of *Pin-Ups*. The tunes included a number by Frank Zappa, one by Bruce Springsteen and the Beach Boys' *God Only Knows* (sounds like *God Knows I'm Good*...) from their *Pet Sounds* album. There were also four Bowie tunes and some jazz selections. This may have been a more honest view of where Bowie was coming from musically, or perhaps just yet a *different* view. In a way, The Astronettes' album was the equivalent to the rumored but unforthcoming *Pin-Ups 2*. What did in fact come next with the official Bowie imprimature was a new kind of surprise, the first real shock David administered to his ever-growing following.

NINE

'We're learning to live with somebody's depression'

'Fantastic Voyage' — *Lodger*

By the end of 1973 things had come to a head with the Bowies' housing situation, prompting a move from Haddon Hall. While they seemed to have been quite happy there, Bowiemania was spreading and word was out about their residence. While Angie claims that in the early days she would talk to the fans and "feed them cakes", their numbers and the vigils were growing, forcing the Bowies to run a virtual gauntlet to get out of their apartment. They moved temporarily into Diana Rigg's home at Maida Vale, and from there to a townhouse in Chelsea. It was also the last time David and Angie were to live in anything resembling wedded bliss, the move somehow symbolizing that the magic days of struggle together with their band, designer, and pals had come to an end. From now on it was just travel with a nanny or a friend, and it was rare for David and Angie even to live at the same address at the same time.

In November of 1973, writer Craig Copetas arranged for a meeting between Bowie and writer William Burroughs at Bowie's home. Entering through a room with a plastic couch and a surrealist painting ('A cross between Salvador Dali and Norman Rockwell', as Bowie described it) they were seated and served lunch by several "Bowie clones".

For the record, they lunched on Jamaican fish, avocado stuffed with shrimp and a French wine. The conversation was wide-ranging and fertile; Bowie learned about Burroughs' cut-up process and he talked about some of his work and plans. He didn't mention the upcoming *Diamond Dogs* (Bowie seldom talks about his work before it's been made public) but he went on at some length about Ziggy, Burroughs becoming gradually more fascinated. David described Ziggy as the receiver and carrier of the message of the Starman, making him a 'rock 'n' roll archetype', the star as false prophet. Bowie then drifted into a rambling explanation of the background for his sci-fi creation, and while much of his exposition was muddled, there was one idea that appealed to Burroughs. Bowie explained Ziggy's dependence on some Black Hole Jumpers called "The Infinites" who were Ziggy's advisors, the same Starmen referred to in the song. Going on to discuss the staging ideas Bowie had for a musical version of Ziggy's story (which never came about) they made the following comments:-

Bowie:

> The end comes when the Infinites arrive. They really are a black hole, but I've made them people ecause it would be very hard to explain a black hole on stage. Burroughs:Yes, a black hole on stage would be an incredible expense. And it would be a continuing performance, first eating up Shaftesbury Avenue.

The scenario Burroughs imagined nearly became reality on the Diamond Dogs tour as things conspired, first eating up David Bowie.

The album itself was wild enough to get quite a few people upset, not the least of whom was Mick Jagger. He should have known better, but he showed Bowie a painting by Dutch artist Guy Peellaert (of "Rock Dreams" fame) and mentioned to Bowie that the Stones were planning to ask Peellaert to do their next album cover. Bowie, the quick operator that he is, immediately got in touch with Paellaert and commissioned the album artwork for *Diamond Dogs*. This cover is as famous as any, though the final product was at least the third version. The first one submitted on the same design was rejected by RCA because of the anatomically more-or-less correct hindquarters of the "Bowie" dog.

While Bowie acted quickly in regards to the artwork, the actual production and recording schedule made the album one of Bowie's slowest projects. Many factors contributed to the extended timetable, but essentially it sprung from the fact that it was his third "post-stardom" album and the other two having been rather rushed prompted the desire for something that Bowie as an artist could be proud of. Partly because of this, he took most of the responsibility for the music upon himself, including duties on the guitar as well as vocals, sax, Moog and mellotron. He produced and arranged the album, rendering it as close to a one-man album as he has ever created. It also fostered his since regularly repeated tendency to invite either "heavies" or "technocrats" on their own instruments to fill in the missing pieces. Given time and patience Bowie could probably be completely self-contained in the recording studio in the manner of Stevie Wonder, but he seems to respond to the freshness and expertise of others, and doesn't like protracted sessions if it's possible to do things more rapidly.

The album was recorded in Holland (the *precise* address of the studio is given on the album cover) and at Olympic and Island Studios. He more or less sequestered himself in these respective studios, sometimes with the other musicians, of whom Mike Garson was the only holdover from the days of the Spiders (Ronson was working on his first solo effort, *Love Me Tender*, Woodmansey was doing whatever Scientologists do, and Trevor Bolder wasn't doing much of anything). The bass player Bowie brought in was Herbie Flowers, whom Bowie considered the finest in England and who'd played on *Holy Holy* way back when, or Tony Newman and Aynsley Dunbar shared drumming duties, Alan Parker played guitar on *19 84*, and Visconti helped out with the string arrangements.

One of the rumored early titles for the album was "Bowie-ing Out" which was what he did during the production process. As Bowie exclaimed at the time: 'I haven't walked in the light of day for ages except from my front door to the car and again from the car into the studios.' This intense state of mind may well have suited the sounds he was trying to get in the can, another instance of channeling environment and situation to creative good. The album is steeped in the Orwellian vision of decay and fascism to which Bowie lends an edge of decadence, drawing from his own observation as well as Orwell's. The ideas and moods were also influenced in part by Bowie's Russian "holiday", where the vision of crushed Vodka-drowned humanity was worse than he'd expected. These are combined with the imagery of any big city Hunger City) in the world and the corrupt and desperate folks therein. Claiming that the album was very much influenced by touring the U.S and the U.S.S.R, Bowie said:

> This one again has a theme. It's a backward look at the Sixties and Seventies and a very political album. My protest. These days you have to be more subtle about protesting than before. You can't preach at people anymore. You have to adopt a position of almost indifference. You have to be supercool nowadays. This album is more me than anything I've done previously. [1]

It also ended up being one of Bowie's personal favorites, one of his truest artistic successes, partially the result of the strong feelings that went into it. The album hints at an aspect of Bowie's aesthetic which isn't always obvious. Diamond Dogs shares with The Man and Low a certain oppressiveness and a relative disregard for the niceties of pop craft. For one who claims to need tension in his environment, it makes sense that the same element characterizes his favorite works.

The album could hardly have begun on a more dissonant note. Following a Moody Blues-gone-berserk-sci-fi-setting of an intro also known as "Future Legend", Bowie proclaims that 'This ain't Rock 'n' Roll, This is Genocide". It was a rather effective line (it shocked the shit out of people) and serves as a reminder that rock 'n' roll is a product of the same culture that perpetrated the Vietnam war and other atrocities, and that the social, political and economic effects of such a "civilization" are anti-human, anti-life. The fact that Bowie was the only one at that time making such statements emphasizes his objectivity, helped by the fact that he doesn't like rock 'n' roll all that much. It's merely been his vehicle for entering the cultural arena; he later called it "evil" and just as bad as all those Fifties films made it out to be. The song Diamond Dogs, as much as any other on the album, focuses on the milieu that Bowie had inhabited since becoming a rock star, while also chronicling its demise. Side one portrays the rather sudden death of "civilization" while side two looks at the creeping lifelessness left behind. Take your pick of scenarios, in either case destruction just around the corner is the keynote. The peoploids are losing their grasp on humanity and thus their future as well.

Following Bowie's lead into the Diamond Dog's world, it might be worth quoting from "Future Legend", which is printed on the jacket, just to give some sense of setting for what is Bowie's most cinematic effort ever. Beginning with "as the last few corpses lay rotting on the slimy thoroughfare" while "red mutant eyes stared down on Hunger City" the scene is populated by "rats the size of cats", and so on, until we get to "ten thousand peoploids who were split into small tribes coveting the highest of sterile skyscrapers". He then gets into the source of the *Diamond Dog* vision where "packs of dogs" assaulted the "glass fronts of Love Me Avenue", and where minks and emeralds were commonplace and now worthless. There's no food and no electricity. Bowie's sci-fi imagery never fully comes together, but owes a lot to Harlan Ellison, among others, for his story "A Boy And His Dog". Bowie varies his themes from both Orwell and Ellison somewhat by focusing on the world he'd been inhabiting, with characters like "Halloween Jack" ("He's a real cool cat").

Jack makes his entrance in the next song, *Diamond Dogs* which continues the future legend in a Warholian world of survival of the most vampirish. The opening line is "When they pulled you out of the oxygen tent, you asked for the latest parties".

Though it may be grim, life goes on in a rock 'n' roll song, because after all "Diamond Dogs are civilized."

The tale of the Diamond Dogs takes a side-step into *Sweet Thing*, which segues into *Candidate* and then back into *Sweet Thing (Reprise)*. The idea of the candidate wrapped up in a sweet thing is interesting in itself, and the promises made in *Sweet Thing* may as well be the love campaign promises of the cynical Jack, brought to life by Bowie's lower register vocal performance, tenuous sax and sweet thing piano. The voice becomes a growl in *Candidate*, where different sorts of promises are made. Indicating that performance was then a consideration behind his songwriting, Bowie/The Candidate goes into a description of his set. "My set is amazing it even smells like a street, There's a bar at the end where I can meet you and your friends." This line well indicates Bowie's ability to pack a plethora of words to a line and his abandonment of rhyme when there's no reason for it.

Next comes the hit, in the form of *Rebel Rebel*, which like *Diamond Dogs* refers directly to the "young girls", prompting comments that this is the female version of *All The Young Dudes*. Although it's a couple years later and Bowie has changed the world, it's not unusual that "your mother can't tell if you're a boy or a girl". *Rebel* is a guaranteed crowd-pleaser, Bowie's last great rock tune, with a DB *original* gutter line to boot. Bowie has said it's the one song he's not at all tempted to change. It's kind of rough and raunchy in the manner of much of *Aladdin Sane*, and Bowie was quite right in seeing this as the way archetypal rock 'n' roll should sound. His vocal performance is inspired (for once he sounds like he's not acting the part of a rock singer), and for that reason evokes Jagger (or Iggy or even Springsteen); the feel of the track owes a lot to Lou Reed's Velvet Underground.

Side two finds Bowie drawing more directly from Orwell. The source is acknowledged in the way the song titles are printed. Both *Rock 'n' Roll with me* and *We are the dead* are only partially capitalized, against the convention, the reason being that the titles are taken from lines in *19 84*. *Rock 'n' Roll with me* is a rather nice love song (co-written by Warren Peace, alias Geoffrey MacCormack) conveying the happiness of Winston (the main character in *19 84*) when he thinks he can actually participate in a multi-faceted relationship with another human being. Such optimism is quickly quashed in Winston's revelation that "We (Winston and Julia) are the dead". This conveys the ultimate hopelessness in their situation, with the music a perfect match, alternating between the moods of hope and despair which the lyrics describe.

The next song would have been the title track of the aborted theatre piece, and *19 84* also gives a glimpse of where Bowie would go musically in the near future. *19 84* is essentially Bowie's first disco tune, though it draws more from rock than the soul that would preoccupy his next work. Probably one of the first pieces that he'd written for the album, it's also one of the strongest. It is the only song that features someone other than Bowie playing guitar, bringing in Alan Parker to get the sound that Issac Hayes had used on *Shaft*. This was another effective piece of borrowing, and just one of the hints that pointed to Bowie's next set of sounds and images. This song gives the broad picture of Winston Smith's situation in that apocalyptic year and recounts his betrayal.

19 84 leads into *Big Brother*, in which Winston is compelled to recant and give up his mind, not to mention his soul. *Big Brother* segues into the most haunting piece on the album. Continuing the Halloween theme begun with Jack, we get *The Chant Of The Ever Circling Skeletal Family* which sounds just like it should with such a title. The image is of an earth (and ether) inhabited by those so powerless that they're incorporeal. With the forces of repression having won the day on all levels, they are reduced to chanting "Bruh" (half of Brother) in their endless circle. The only relief is provided by an automatic turntable.

With Bowie starting things on the offensive (after all if this was genocide, he was the mass murderer) it's not surprising that the album met with little critical approval. It was considered the child of Bowie's pretentiousness but the album has held up well over time, especially as the world edges closer to the Orwellian nightmare. (Bowie later called television "the most effective fascist", and with all the rock videos that are being dished out, music is now thoroughly in the service of "Big Brother".) In any case, *19 84* might get a little more airplay in '84 than it did in '74.

While there were a few pundits who liked the album at the time, the overwhelming critical reaction was negative although as usual that had little affect on the fans who knew better. In a typical review, Ken Emerson wrote an article for Rolling Stone entitled: "New Bowie: A

Dog". Beginning aggressively enough he said: 'Clearly, David Bowie is not the "homo superior" he once claimed and many believed him to be.' After giving passing praise to Hunky Dory and Ziggy, he puts down all the subsequent work and concludes '..and now comes *Diamond Dogs*, perhaps Bowie's worst album in six years.' He then proposes the rather cynical idea that Bowie, being 'vainglorious' and therefore 'rankled' by his·lack of commercial success in the U.S., took the strategy that if they (the American audience) weren't buying his good stuff then they might 'when he was bad'. While the presumption that he was trying to break into the American market is well founded, it doesn't seem that Bowie's preoccupations and intentions were quite so narrow. Besides, when he put his mind to it the next time around, he succeeded quite handily with a tailor-made record targeted for his audience by name.

Rather than being a merely commercial attempt on Bowie's part, *Diamond Dogs* seems to find Bowie getting in touch with himself as an artist. The record marks a public display of disillusionment which may have been disillusionment with his artistic process as well (thus the sequestered, almost solo approach) and one of his typical reappraisals of what he was doing and why. This rethinking included Bowie's relationship with Tony De Fries, which had degenerated quite a bit after the all out effort to launch Ziggy, and the two rarely saw each other any more. But the problems weren't personal so much as the fact that although De Fries was dependent on Bowie as his "product", De Fries was getting the lion's share of the profits while Bowie did most of the work, at least that which made De Fries' role either possible or necessary. It was Bowie who began the discussions which eventually ended his working/managerial relationship with De Fries.

It has been implied by some writers that Bowie was virtually strong-armed into touring by De Fries and RCA, whose primary considerations were promotional and financial. Yet from the beginning, the *Diamond Dogs* concept was tied up with the idea of a performance, originally as a musical. For as long as Bowie was on the track that he'd begun to explore with Ziggy, he claimed the need to take his theatrical presentation all the way out before abandoning it. Money was, of course, a consideration for Bowie as well, and as it turned out the tour was a financial success. It grossed over five million dollars, though one of its expenses was a 200,000 dollar set by Jules Fisher (of *Hair* and *Pippin* fame). The massive and complex set ended up extracting an even greater toll on the whole tour.

While the set was being constructed and rehearsals were taking place in New York City, Bowie was meeting some musicians and checking out the music, as a result of which a radical revision of the Diamond Dogs tour would be called for and a musical shift provoked that would determine the Bowie (and rock) sound for years to come. It was at this time that David met Carlos Alomar, who has since become his band leader and right hand man. After meeting Alomar on a Lulu session that Bowie was producing, he made the comment to a journalist that 'I've found a really incredible black guy named Carlos. I want a really funky sound.' Alomar helped him get it, and also took over the crucial role of interpreting Bowie's music from his notes, as well as presenting it to the other musicians. This relationship developed gradually as Alomar began by playing essentially rhythm guitar, though his responsibilities grew to major proportions.

At that time ('74) in the U.S., disco was starting to be heard and felt as the natural successor to soul. Considering Bowie's jazz and R&B roots, it's not surprising that this relatively new funk sound would appeal to him. He tuned into this renaissance in black music on the radio (at the upper end of the dial) and while he was in New York he took advantage of the opportunity to hear some of these acts live. On a rather self-congratulatory note Bowie told one reporter:

> Ever since I got to New York I've been going down to the Apollo in Harlem. Most New Yorkers seem scared to go there if they're white but the music's incredible. I saw The Temptations and The Spinners together on the same bill there and next week it's Marvin Gaye. Incredible! I love that kind of thing.

These experiences, along with others that took place in his teens, helped Bowie to prepare for pulling the same trick that Elvis had managed, that is bringing black music to the intimidated, but hungry white audience. Bowie went a step further and became one of the first white performers to be taken to heart at least musically by the black audience, setting the stage for the likes of Hall and Oates and Culture Club, whose soul sound has gone over despite the fact that their images are enough to send a black audience running for cover. In fact when Bowie got to Philly and began recruiting some "funky" musicians, he admits that they approached him rather warily (expecting an asexual alien) until they discovered a common ground in their music.

But before all these seeds came to fruition, there was the spectacular Diamond Dogs tour. It was also called the "Thea Tour" which might be short for "theatre" or the feminine for God, recalling everybody's favorite bad joke. The show generally got rave reviews, contrary to the response that the album received, assisted by the fact that the press was royally flown in for the second show of the tour, which took place in Toronto. With the *Hunger City* set by Jules Fisher and choreography by Toni Basil (who later achieved her own fame for *Mickey*) this was the most lavish and tightest Bowie show yet. With twenty songs packed into ninety minutes, the audience barely had a chance to catch their breath between numbers.

The visual set was the first thing to blow everyone's minds, consisting of three huge lighting towers designed to look like sky-scrapers, along with a moveable catwalk, a blood spurting oversized phallus, plus numerous props which were removed by the back-up singers (Warren Peace and Gui Andrisan) while the rest of the musicians remained largely out of sight and out of the action. It is slightly ironic that all of this effort backed up what was essentially a one-man show, when Bowie might have been expected to take the opposite tack since the idea was first conceived of as a musical. The other musicians didn't much like being hidden away, but at least it looked more like theatre and less like a rock concert. For a description of the Toronto show, we have the words of two of Bowie's biographers, both hinting at Bowie's new role as fashion leader, something that he enjoyed and found challenging up to a point, and found slightly amusing for the reasons given below. Chris Charlesworth mentions that Bowie appeared in light grey pants with a collarless shirt, red suspenders and a jacket apparently without make-up or the wild hairstyle of the Ziggy days. In its place was a neatly parted medium length coif 'leaving little doubt about the masculinity of the performer this time around.' As Miles writes:

> To the horror of all the platform shod, spiky haired fans in the audience, David appeared in flat shoes and wearing a fluffy hairstyle with a parting.

What follows is Miles' rather concise description of the show:

> Each song was linked to the next one and presented with theatrical effects beginning with *19   84*. After *Rebel Rebel* and *Moonage Daydream*, David appeared on the catwalk for the first time while yellow lamp standards gave the set an eerie night time glow and David strolled about in a long trench coat while dancers mimed the lyrics. The whole catwalk swung silently to the ground with David arriving just on the opening beat of *Changes*. *Suffragette City*, *All The Young Dudes* and *Will You Rock And Roll With Me* ended the first act with David taking a theatrical bow as the house lights went up.
> The band stood to the side and were not allowed to intrude visually on what was happening. Earl Slick was on guitar plus Herbie Flowers on bass, Mike Garson on keyboards, and Tony Newman on drums. Dancers Warren Peace (from the Astronettes) and Gui Andrisan also sing back-up and move the props and microphones around the stage to avoid roadies having to appear...
> Act Two opened with *Watch That Man* followed by *Drive-In Saturday*, which was David's only acoustic number of the show. When Earl Slick hit the opening power chord of *Space Oddity*. David appeared to have left the stage then a door at the top of one of the skyscrapers swung open to reveal David sitting on a seat at the end of a long hydraulic pole which extended out so that finally he was seated far above the heads of the front rows of the audience. The attention to detail was such that he sang *Space Oddity* into a radio telephone apparatus instead of a conventional microphone. With multi-coloured lights flashing he assumed completely the identity of Major Tom. [2]

The description goes on (as did the show) but the radio mike recalls some of the smallest, but most typical problems that the tour ran into. Bowie and RCA had planned to do a live album, recording early on so that its release would coincide with the end of the tour. They chose to record the shows at the Philadelphia Tower Theatre, and with David's old friend Tony Visconti supervising the recording, David's radio mike caused a lot of headaches. Other difficulties stemmed from the fact that just before the first show the issue of payment for the musicians arose. Tony De Fries, demonstrating the lack of good judgement and warped priorities that would soon cause a permanent rift between he and David, insisted on not paying the players a penny more than the union scale for live recording dates. When David was informed of this he came up with the additional funds for the musicians out of his own pocket, but this dispute was just one of the reasons postulated for the generally lackluster performances that became vinylized on the *David Live* album.

In spite of the problems, *David Live* served its purpose as an artefact, a souvenir of the tour, and as a palliative for those unable to make the shows. Nevertheless, the proof that David was rather embarrassed by the performance record were his comments about the album:

> *David Live* was the final death of Ziggy. God that album! I've never played it. The tension it must contain must be like vampires teeth coming down on you. And that photo on the cover. My God, it looks like I've just stepped out of the grave. That's actually how I felt. That record should have been called *David Bowie Is Alive And Living Only In Theory*. [3]

Though the tour had better moments than the Philly Tower shows, it finally and quite literally ground to a halt under its own weight. With fifteen roadies required to take care of the stage and equipment, frequent breakdowns and other problems (one time a truck didn't arrive on time and the show went on without the set), everyone was more than ready to jump ship after the July 19th show in Madison Square Garden. There was another leg of the tour planned after a short break, but as it was, the show that would have eaten up Shaftesbury Avenue never made it to England.

So for those that never had the chance to see the Diamond Dogs Revue, here's a little more description of this historic folly:

> The effects came thick and fast. During *Diamond Dogs* he was tied with ropes by the dancers while for *Panic In Detroit*, a boxing ring appeared and David was wearing big red boxing gloves. There was even a big black bodyguard to act as his second and change his gum shield between verses and towel him down.
>
> The last half hour was even more bizarre. David appeared sitting on a platform of mirrors which he climbed inside. The dancers opened the doors and — just like a conjuring trick —

there was no David, just a gigantic sparkling black hand lit by ultraviolet lamps. The hand lowered and became a glittering staircase for David to make an entrance on. The finale was *Jean Genie* and *Rock And Roll Suicide* as a medley with small powerful spots throwing huge shadows of David on the walls of the menacing skyscrapers. Suddenly it was all over and David was gone. The audience cheered for ten minutes but to no avail. No encores, in fact he had already left the theatre. [4]

His exit was in the great Elvis tradition. Not only was it dramatic, but security precautions were always of the utmost importance. In terms of Bowie's future what's interesting here are certain themes that were to resurface, particularly Bowie as boxer/fighter, which image graces the cover of *Let's Dance*. He also continues employing his back-up singers as foils and during his 1983 tour (and in videos) the black hand makes other appearances. While some aspects of this tour have survived, the oppressiveness of the effort has been allowed to rest in peace.

TEN

'Boys keep swinging/Boys always work it out'

'Boys Keep Swinging' — *Lodger*

When the Diamond Dog went on sabbatical, there were a few indications of what the next phase would be, but it was the type of seemingly rapid and radical musical change that has earned Bowie his present reputation as the so-called chameleon of rock, though as always David's exploration in music is a reflection of a personal need to explore facets of himself. Carrying the chameleon analogy a bit further, it demonstrates Bowie's ability to tune into The Next Big Thing, putting his stamp on whatever style or sound is in vogue. A couple of songs on the *Diamond Dogs* album had begun to indicate the direction he was moving in, and what he was listening to as he spent increasing amounts of time in the States. Bowie said about *Young Americans* that '*Diamond Dogs* was the start of this album. Things like *Rock 'n' Roll with me* and *19 84* were embryonic of what I wanted to do.' What he wanted to do seemed to gell with his commercial aspirations, resulting in the crystallization of a singing style that, through all the twists and turns to follow, has come to define Bowie's sound more than any other album (though there were hints of it elsewhere, especially on *Pin-Ups*, where Bowie took his "crooning" o an almost ridiculous extreme). The commercial pressures had a lot to do with the fact that Bowie had yet to score a major hit in the American market. The choice of *Young Americans* for the title indicates a single-minded attack on that audience.

Bowie's strategy for reaching American listeners harks back to one of the oldest tricks in the book written by a segregated music industry. Like Elvis before him, Bowie found a moment when there really wasn't anyone else around better qualified to bring the current black sounds to a white audience, and just like his predecessor twenty years before, he quickly discovered that white soulsters couldn't get hip fast enough. Bowie's plan to do a funk/soul album was realized while he was in Philly for the Tower shows. He dropped by Sigma Studios where Ava Cherry of the Astronettes was recording. Sigma happened to be the home studio of the musicians and engineers creating the Sound of Philadelphia (TSOP), alias Philadelphia International Soul. The feeling of the place was right, so Bowie booked time at the studio during the scheduled tour break, hoping to use mostly resident musicians and singers. Unfortunately, the timing left only drummer Larry Washington available, but after consulting with studio owners Kenny Gamble and Leon Huff,

Bowie was able to round up a kickass funk band. Carlos Alomar was drafted, along with bassist Willie Weeks and drummers Andy Newmark and Dennis Davis (who was to remain with Bowie for some time). From the touring band, Mike Garson, Earl Slick as well as percussionist Pablo Rosario were brought in. Geoff MacCormack (Warren Peace) did more singing and David Sanborne played sax. The cast continued with Ralph McDonald working percussion, with Emir Kassan on bass, and Ava Cherry, Robin Clark (Alomar's wife), Anthony Hinton, Diane Sumler and Luther Vandross all singing backup. There was also another group of contributors involved in some later Electric Ladyland sessions in New York, featuring John Lennon on guitar and vocals, with Jean Millington and Jean Fineburg on backup. For both sessions Tony Visconti once again sat in the producer's chair.

The sessions went extremely well, courtesy of a team of top notch musicians and singers, and a Bowie fairly confident and inspired as song titles like *Somebody Up There Likes Me*, *Win*, *Fame* and *Right* suggest. Everything seemed to fall into place for this one, though not without Bowie's usual attention to detail. Having booked 120 hours at the studio regularly running from early evening to late morning, Bowie spent his days in a suite at the Barclay Hotel working out precise lead sheets and arrangements so that the work in the studio went quickly (though he habitually re-writes lyrics in the control room). Evidently the crew was in fairly high spirits throughout, with stories circulating about their recording a version of the novelty tune *You Can Have Her, I Don't Want Her, She's Too Fat For Me*, which was ceremoniously burned at the end. They also re-recorded *John, I'm Only Dancing*, which has been released in the most confusing configurations of any Bowie tune, and laid down two songs recorded that didn't make the album due to the later impromptu sessions with John Lennon; for posterity's sake (and in case they eventually get released) the cuts were *Who Can I Be This Time* and *It's Gonna Be Me*. Bowie reputedly used the opportunity to tape a couple of Springsteen numbers which have yet to make it onto any release.

As for the result, Bowie was the one to call it "plastic soul", seemingly out of embarrassment that it was so easy and went over so well. Bowie copied the styles of Stevie Wonder, Al Green and even Marvin Gaye, and if everyone else (the white audience anyway) was quite content that it should be plastic if plastic meant graspable, Bowie was conscious of the inherent exploitation in what he was doing. Not that it stopped him. Even as he realized that disco was deadly, he also recognized that disco was what was happening, and largely thanks to Bowie the disco beat is now a solid part of the rock repertoire.

This album had several suggested titles. Mike Garson liked "Somebody Up There Likes Me", and Bowie had considered "Fascination" another song title. The one that almost came to be was "One Damn Song" (one of the best delivered lines on the album) even though he got two damn songs out of these sessions. The hits were *Young Americans* and *Fame*, both of which were quite ironic. *Young Americans* leads off the album, chronicling what has been called *The Great American Post Watergate*

Dilemma. It was written and recorded hot on the heels of Nixon's resignation, which might have touched a sympathetic chord in Bowie, whose birthday is one day before Nixon's. Showing the same concern for history that obsessed Nixon, Bowie asked: "Do you remember/President Nixon/Do you remember the bills you have to pay/For even yesterday". The rest of the lyrics are a nearly indecipherable rant about sordid life in the land of Watergate; if the words had been easier to discern Bowie might well have had to follow Dick on the next helicopter out, but the only thing that comes through is the chorus of "All right/She wants the Young American". Just why he/she wants him/her isn't clear, but it sounds good to be desired. People (especially Americans) lapped it up. Whether or not Bowie had Lennon's blessing at that time, the song has a classic ending with the back-up vocalists intoning "I heard the news today, oh boy" before Bowie the dramatist moans "Ain't there one damn song that can make me break down and cry?", with the emphasis on cry. The reaction to *Young Americans* would have had the Bowie of old crying a few cynic's tears. Maybe it did.

Win is the first of the pithily titled songs and though Sanborne's sax is languid, Bowie sounds sleepy as if he's already won and can't be bothered.

Fascination follows Bowie sharing the spotlight with Luther Vandross who wrote the original music (something for which it took him a while to be recognized) — Bowie knows quality when he sees (and hears) it. Vandross led the backup singers as well as working on the vocal arrangements, and gave Bowie his song, which was originally called *Funky Music Is A Part Of Me*. The funky groove that Luther created makes for an excellent song, although Bowie's *Fascination/Sho' nuff* is almost funny. He may be genuinely funky and a great mimic, but that one blue eye gives the game away. *Right* is a little more on target, with Bowie describing what's right for him. "There's never no turning back."

Throughout the album the focus for once is on the music (and playing) rather than on the lyrics. The musical elements don't vary too much, except in degrees of intensity. The second side has a couple of harder-edged funk numbers, but otherwise the sound (especially the singing) is somewhere between the bedroom breathlessness of Barry White and the punchiness of James Brown. Throughout, the background singers are excellent. The parts are just right and in the right places. The same could be said for Sanborne's sax, the percussion, and the rest of the instruments. All of the songs are ultimately listenable and danceable, but few leave a lasting or distinct impression. A case in point is *Somebody Up There Likes Me*, which remains most memorable as a film title even after Bowie's finished with it. Bowie's cover of *Across The Universe* is better forgotten, and it's unclear just why he included it. It's doubtful that he thought it sounded great. Whatever the reason, it's by far the weakest cut on the album.

The other 'damn' song on the album is *Fame*. The cut was a late entry onto the master tapes, coming about in January of '75 as the result of an impromptu session with John Lennon at the Electric Ladyland Studios.

Bowie and Lennon had been "hanging out" for a few days (Bowie's tour was over and Lennon was free) during which the subject of fame came up more than a few times. Bowie described the background to Tim White for Musician magazine:

> After meeting in some New York club, we'd spent quite a few nights talking and getting to know each other before we'd even gotten into the studio. That period of my life is none too clear, a lot of it is really blurry, but we spent endless hours talking about fame, and what it's like not having a life of your own anymore. How much you want to be known before you are, and then when you are, how much you want the reverse: "I don't want to do these interviews! I don't want to have these photographs taken!" We wondered how that slow change takes place, and why it isn't everything it *should* have been.
>
> I guess it was inevitable that the subject matter of the song would be about the subject matter of those conversations. God, that session was fast. That was an evening's work! While John and Carlos Alomar were sketching out the guitar stuff in the studio, I was starting to work out the lyric in the control room. I was so excited about John, and he loved working with my band because they were playing old soul tracks and Stax things. John was so *up*, had so much energy; it must have been so exciting to always be around him. [1]

The song that came out of it gave Bowie his first Number One single in the U.S. (finally), helped by the fact that it hit on a national obsession as well as one preoccupying Bowie. The song was also the result of a few brilliant decisions. The first was basing the tune on a James Brown riff (Alomar was an ex J.B. sideman, very handy...) Then Alomar added the insistent sound of the telephone ringing, so effective that listeners have gone to answer the phone in the middle of the song. Like *Young Americans*, it's the title phrase that catches the ear, but the insistent "What's your name" sums the whole thing up, and the song reaches its emotional peak when the taped vocals are slowed down for the final intonation of "Fame", dropping three octaves and out. Bowie believes that Lennon's high pitched vocal made the song, claiming that as the reason he shared the songwriting credit, although that certainly wasn't the *only* reason.

Before these sessions came about, Bowie had finished up his Diamond Dogs tour, (renaming it the "Philly Dog" tour) with a new soul-boy image and minus the Fisher set. By the end, things were going more smoothly on the tour, which helped convince Bowie to be strictly his own man from then on. He also credits John Lennon for helping to straighten him out. Lennon was in the process of wresting control of his own business affairs from Allan Klein at the time, and told Bowie that he thought things would be in better order if he handled them himself. This wasn't the first time Bowie had heard such ideas. Marc Bolan had been doing it all along, but after speaking with Lennon, Bowie was to discover just how exploited he'd been, mostly by manager Tony De Fries. One of the main problems was financial. De Fries was taking his percentage off the top, leaving Bowie to pay all the bills at a time when all the limos and the press junkets were becoming unnecessary. Bowie *was* a star by then and didn't have to buy respect. Tours and other aspects of the business were being mismanaged and the "overkill" that had been so effective at one point was now redundant. Bowie claimed to have tired of the entourage and the circusy atmosphere, which he called being "Mainmanned" after De Fries' management company. Bowie analysed how De Fries saw himself, again for Tim White:

I think Tony saw himself as a Svengali type, but I think I would have done okay anyway. Now I look back on it with amusement more than anything else. Everybody was always going to get their *teeth* done or something, brand new people appearing in the office, having changed their appearance completely from the day before and so forth. 2

So Bowie began action against De Fries with the help of lawyer Michael Lippman, who later created problems of his own by deciding he wanted to manage Bowie, who'd have none of it. The litigation progressed slowly, occupying much of the year that Bowie "forgot". He moved to L.A., immersing himself into that city's two major pastimes, spiritualism and drugs; while he rested on his laurels a while. He claims not to recall his Grammy Awards appearance, did recollect wearing a tux but forgot just what the occasion was, and so on. But he was to pull out of the quagmire eventually, guided again by the words of Lennon:

John Lennon had been through it all. John told me, Stick with it. Survive. You'll really go through the grind and they'll rip you off right and left. The key is to come out the other side. 3

ELEVEN

'I could make a transformation as a rock 'n' roll star... I could play the wild mutation as a rock 'n' roll star'

'Star' — The Rise And Fall Of Ziggy Stardust And The Spiders Of Mars

Bowie took on one of his most significant "non rock" projects in the year that he forgot, fulfilling De Fries' prediction that by 1975 he'd have reached his musical peak and would get into other media, most likely film. Bowie fans had been hearing about and hoping for film projects for years but to no avail. There was the unreleased *Ziggy* film. There was *Octobriana* that Bowie was to have produced as a vehicle for Amanda Lear (and because he liked the Russian cartoon heroine) that never came about due to time and financial limitations. Most recently, there had been rumors that Bowie would play the lead in a film based on Robert Heinlein's *Stranger In A Strange Land*. As it turned out, the film he did take on had a similar "alien" lead, though it was a much better story, and ultimately a better film. As events conspired, Bowie was approached by director Nicholas Roeg to play the lead in Walter Tevis' story *The Man Who Fell To Earth*. While Bowie was a second choice to Peter O'Toole, (who probably would have been excellent) it's now hard to imagine anyone else in the role, or for that matter, Bowie not having accepted it.

As is usually the case regarding any significant moment in Bowie's life, there are a few versions of just how the arrangements were made and the decision arrived at. Angie claims that she had to coax David into even reading the script, but when he did he thought it was excellent. Bowie himself says that he wasn't all that impressed with the script, but that after discussion with Roeg he was convinced that Roeg was the director for him and that the role was perfect. As for the story of how they met, Bowie tells about forgetting the appointment that he'd made for Roeg, and when he realized he was an hour late, blew the whole thing off. When he returned home (to his New York townhouse) he found Roeg sitting patiently in the kitchen. While this must have been flattering, Bowie implies that he was nearly shamed into taking the part, but as Roeg has said that he likes actors to be vulnerable, Bowie must have been in just the right state of mind. In fact, Bowie seemed to let his guard down for Roeg to a remarkable degree — if location photos in which David looks like a little boy and Roeg the mother/father are any indication. But Bowie had also studied Roeg's previous films *Performance*, *Walkabout*), was convinced that the man was brilliant and that he would be an excellent mentor in Bowie's long range plans for film directing.

Roeg and Bowie quickly formed another of those "mutual admiration societies" that seem to surround David, with Roeg finding just the right character, look and resonance (based on Ziggy, Aladdin *et al*) for his film, and Bowie finding someone from whom he could learn, calling Roeg a genius, and an old warlock. It also gave Bowie a chance to put his acting where his mouth was, and the entire process (and Roeg's approach) seemed to appeal to him. The six hour make-up sessions were heaven for Bowie, who's always relied on the element of disguise in freeing himself for greater transformations, allowing him to assume another personality more readily.

After the initial decision to make the movie, Bowie had some other career business to take care of. With the film on the horizon, he viewed the mass media with fresh realism, swallowing his abhorrence of talk and variety shows in order instantly and effectively, to reach a mass audience. He also made a breakthrough of sorts by being one of the first white entertainers to appear on the black music program *Soul Train* (which he says he had to get incredibly drunk to be able to do). In this same period he appeared with Cher on one of her TV extravaganzas, making perhaps his most ridiculous appearance ever doing an absurd medley and duet with his host, all bracketed by *Young Americans*. Bowie had finally emerged as that good old "all-round entertainer", and looked almost as silly as he'd originally thought he would. But despite his fears he proved himself a master of the talk-show format; on the Dick Cavett show Bowie was at his coyest and most reptilian, toying incessantly with his walking stick to Cavett's utter distraction. All of this was worth the one reply he made to a comment by Dinah Shore, who remarked that 'Rock 'n' roll has been very good to you.' Bowie then quipped: 'I've been very good for rock 'n' roll.' With that perspective he has little reason to be intimidated by TV.

These exercises in self-promotion behind him, Bowie headed to the wilds of Arizona and New Mexico for the filming of *The Man* with Angie and Zowie on hand for part of the time. His previous experience in film prepared him for all the waiting time and he made the best of it. He worked on his "Autobiography of The Thin White Duke" (of which only one page has ever been published) and talked about several other literary projects which likewise remain unpublished. He was also doing some reading, traveling with a library of some 1500 books (one of the advantages of traveling by train), some of which he'd brought to show Roeg in case the old warlock needed to brush up on his alchemical basics. Bowie also made a trip to Taos, New Mexico to visit a former Buddhist associate, taking along a modified turntable in order to play *Young Americans* backwards, having discovered that it sounded uncannily like a Tibetan chant.

Bowie's interest in all forms of religion and mysticism was undergoing a renaissance. Seeking order in the chaos of all the different teachings, Bowie was at his most confused. It's not clear whether Roeg hurt or helped the process, but along with the new haircut Bowie received for his role as Jerome Thomas Newton, David was given a cross as a piece of costuming which he continued to wear for some time afterwards (and still does occasionally), perhaps thinking that Nick knew what was going on and what he needed.

The movie itself proved nothing if not that Bowie was a box-office draw. While there was some criticism of his performance, often described as wooden (though this may be partially Roeg's responsibility/choice, as he used Bowie like a prop throughout), neither his screen presence nor his aura of vulnerability and capacity for surprise can be denied. While the storyline is quite interesting, the film is episodic, one of moments, most of which belong to a Bowie heavily aided and abetted by the lens, the landscape and his co-stars. The opening and closing scenes alone are enough to leave a strong impression, and though the sex scenes are pure Roeg, some of the segments seem to have been partially inspired by Bowie. Particularly, the choice of TV images that include old Elvis films, clips of Chuck Berry, and a sequence in which Rip Torn runs through a record department looking for Newton's album *The Visitor*, where promo posters from *Young Americans* are hanging every few feet down the aisle.

Bowie was slated to write the music for the film, but due to the pending ligitation between Bowie and De Fries, Bowie lost this opportunity. This is presumed to be one of the reasons why *Station To Station* was completed so hurriedly (and why there are so few songs on it). It also started a guessing game about which of the songs to come out later had been intended for the soundtrack. The absence of Bowie music was the film's loss as well as David's, because the soundtrack was one of its weakest points.

As he moved from the film to the next album, much was happening that Bowie claims since to have forgotten. It's likely that he'd long since begun his flirtation with "fast drugs", contributing to the state of mind given form by the Thin White Duke. At the time, Bowie was living the fast lifestyle of rock star-in-residence in L.A., spending most of his time in a "rent-a-home" with Egyptian decor that came to assume a ritualistic significance in his life. Most of the interviews Bowie granted at this point went to Cameron Crowe, and besides the fact that Bowie would stay awake for days on end (in his impatience always looking for new diversions in the recording studio or by way of rousing friends like Ron Wood with a bottle of champagne), Crowe also describes Bowie on the edge. But even while he was seeing bodies fall from the sky and mumbling incantations to lighted black candles, he maintained a sense of humor. Speaking with Tim White in 1983, Bowie explained:

> I had this more-than-passing interest in Egyptology, mysticism, the cabala (sic), all this stuff that is inherently misleading in life, a hodge-podge whose crux I've forgotten. But at the time it seemed transparently obvious what the answer to life was.
>
> By the end of the week my whole life would be transformed into this bizarre nihilistic fantasy world of oncoming doom, mythological characters and imminent totalitarianism. Quite the worst. 1

110

He began his liberation from the oppressive forces of his own thoughts and fantasies by jumping into the recording of the *Station To Station* album almost immediately after finishing the filming for *The Man Who Fell To Earth*. The personnel comprised the core of Bowie's "band" for the next few years, with Alomar and Slick on guitars, George Murray on bass, Dennis Davis on drums, and with one "guest artist" in the form of Roy Bittan from Bruce Springsteen's E Street Band. In fact, while the musicians were summoned quickly, it seems that the actual production was one of the more difficult processes Bowie went through in his entire career. With much of the material written and rewritten in the studio, it took almost two months, quite a stretch for only five original tunes.

Angie and David were spending less and less time in the same place; she was rarely in L.A. at the time, but after rumors about David's poor health and equally unhealthy state of mind reached her, she flew out to find him dejected, unable to write and strung out from drug use. He managed to pull himself together, and while as usual integrating his state of mind into his music, the cool "techno-Euro-funk" sound that he achieved on the album had wide mainstream appeal. And yet, less than satisfied, ever restless, he began casting about for something fresh even as he was laying down the tracks for *Station*. He realized that he could have repeated the formula he'd arrived at on *Fame* and *Golden Years* more or less infinitely, but sanity and self-respect demanded change. *Station To Station* provided hints of where he might be heading.

Presaging the travel motif of *Lodger*, the title track of *Station To Station* conjures Bowie's mode of travel and the strains of a bi-coastal existence by rail. It's no wonder that he stayed put in L.A. once he got there. The song telescopes the three day journey into ten minutes, beginning with an electronic train chugging from speaker to speaker and continuing in the background for the entire piece. It is on this song that Bowie announces the presence of the Thin White Duke, whose action of "throwing darts in lovers' eyes" encapsulates the mood of the song. The song has several parts, and eventually turns into the kind of all-out rocker which Teri Morris of Rolling Stone had imagined Bowie had forsaken forever if *Young Americans* was taken at face value. As Morris put it: 'He may not be seriously committed to rock, but when the mood strikes it all comes flooding back. Always the actor, David Bowie can assume the role of a rocker and make it work.' While he was rocking he also found time to announce that the 'European man is here' (though not in Europe yet), and in everyone's favorite line, admits: "It's not the side-effects of the cocaine/I'm thinking that it must be love/It's too late to be grateful..."

Golden Years, on the other hand, gave him something to be grateful for. It became the follow-up hit to *Young Americans* and *Fame*, likewise raising its title to a cultural/linguistic catchphrase. The melodic but restrained disco-funk was as powerful as the lyrics, which despite having been called self-indulgent, strikes as rather heartfelt. While Bowie has

111

claimed that his songwriting is his psychiatric couch, this song finds him wresting reassurance from desperation. It hardly matters who he's talking to with lines like "Don't let me hear you say life's taking you nowhere", but the romantic comes through with the call to "Stick with me baby for a thousand years/nothing's going to touch you in these golden years". The fact that the song had some personal significance is indicated by the fact that Bowie offered the song to Elvis (with Angie delivering the tape), although the King never recorded it, probably because by that time it was too late for him to believe it. Bowie may also have forced the feeling, but the effort proved therapeutic for him nonetheless.

Word On A Wing is the next song. It's a "religious" ballad, typical of Bowie's search-that-never-ends (for God) theme, where one is drawn to religion for its solutions, which ultimately must be rejected because they are religious. The crux of the song are the lines "Just because I believe don't mean I don't think as well/Don't have to question everything in heaven or hell." So this time, possibly prompted by Roeg and the character of Newton from *The Man Who Fell To Earth*, refuge is found in the Lord and prayer (also Dylan's preferred foil against the madness).

Even though the sound is heavenly with its choir-of-angels effect, it's not very convincing. The stylization that characterizes the entire album gives the song an unreal and abstract quality. It's this general stateliness and iciness that makes *TVC-15* such an anomoly.

One explanation for *TVC-15* (which says nothing about the song) was given by Harry Maslin, Bowie's co-producer (he was Visconti's second on *Young Americans*), who said that the song was about 'a TV set that ate Bowie's girlfriend'. For what it's worth, *TVC* is somehow related to space travel, a major theme in *The Man Who Fell To Earth*, and certainly evokes a TV set or two, a recurring image from the film. For these reasons the song has been postulated as one of those written for the film's soundtrack, perhaps for Bowie/Newton gearing up for the space shot that never was. It's the liveliest song on the album, and without a lyric sheet (not included this time) the line that kills is the "transmission-transition" refrain, made breathtaking by Bowie's vocal treatment, with the tune carried on Bittan's merrily cavorting piano. It was worth bringing him along for this song alone.

Stay is a great closing number in concert and a smooth effort from the master. Running breathless on a funk groove, it harkens back to the Duke and his line "it's too late..." as Bowie makes another last ditch effort, intoning "Stay, that's what I meant to say...or do something...". The Duke's desperation, alienated and romanticized are almost played out.

The actual closing number of the album is *Wild Is The Wind* about which Charles Shaar Murray noted that Bowie pulled the same "sparse/lush trick" which he'd demonstrated on *Word On A Wing*. He was taking note of the fact that the instrumentation is scant, while the sound is full but delicate; the use of 12-string guitar goes a long way

112

towards achieving the effect. This song was a cover, originally the theme from a 1957 Anthony Quinn-Anna Magnani film with music by Dimitri Tiomkin and sung by Johnny Mathis. Momentarily, Bowie rediscovered the brittle, reedy voice of his younger days. As the last vinyl indication of Bowie's then state of mind, this cut suggested he was blowing away on an uncharted wind, and though there were few who could have known his course, Teri Morris made a good guess, finishing an album review with the line 'While there's little doubt about his skill, one wonders how long he'll continue wrestling with rock at all.' [2]

The answer was, Not long; Bowie probably would have been happy to leave L.A. and rock behind him there and then but there were other considerations. Contrary to his claim after the Diamond/Philly Dog tour that touring killed his art, that 'I will never tour again' and that 'I've rocked my roll', he soon ate his words with the announcement of a thirty-five city Stateside tour. Now at least when he said 'it will make me an obscenely large amount of money', he could expect to keep a good deal of it himself. He also rationalized it by saying that he needed the money to get his production company, Bewlay Brothers, off the ground, which he presumably considered sounded better than needing the money to buy a new watch.

Since Bowie had claimed in a recent interview for Playboy that his main interests were 'Politics, sex and myself', it was appropriate that while he announced his tour plans to England via satellite from L.A., the Spanish government requested the use of the satellite to broadcast Franco's funeral mass. But Bowie flexed his muscles and refused, proving that he was more important than Franco (or Juan Carlos) and that he had as much power as *some* governments. This announcement took place in early December of '75 and though Bowie had already made plans to move Angela and Zowie to Switzerland, his life would soon reach a crisis point, taking him away from L.A. and the lifestyle he'd evolved while living there. While the seeds of change had been planted in Bowie's mind and in his music, he still had to be practically dragged away, having been overtaken by a physical inertia, induced in part by the drugs and in part by the ego inflators, both so available in L.A.

Old friends had been unable to get through to Bowie, but he tells the story of his salvation via such a friend.

> On a winter's day, three days before Christmas, a friend pulled
> me over to the mirror and said, "Look at us both. If you
> continue to be the way you are at this moment, you'll never see
> me again. You are not worth the effort"

Bowie's reaction was to lock 'all my characters away forever', and such has been the word ever since. There has also been some speculation as to who the friend was, and the evidence (since Bowie guards his private life and those of his friends carefully) points to Bowie's personal assistant Corinne 'Coco' Schwab, who has been constantly at Bowie's side for many years. Corinne was one of the few holdovers from the days of Mainman, under whose auspices she first worked for Bowie. Aside from her talents (she is multi-lingual, efficient and likeable, to name a few) her concern for Bowie as a person is near legendary. While Bowie might be worrying about his career, Schwab would be just as likely to be concerning herself with how to put some weight on his bones. The intimacy of her role caused quite a bit of friction between Corinne and Angie — and between Angie and David — who considered Coco invaluable while Angie was becoming less so. Angie attributes the choice of Berlin for Bowie's next residence to Coco's love of that city. Angie preferred their new home in Basle, Switzerland, but couldn't persuade David to stay for any length of time.

Meanwhile, there was a tour to stage, with rehearsals held in Jamaica before moving on to Vancouver for the February 2, 1976 opener, to be followed by visits to thirty-three American cities and finally a long-awaited return to England. It became known as the "White Light Tour", named for Eric Barrett's lighting design composed of fluorescent tubes which both lit and defined the stage. In this setting, Bowie acted out the last of his assumed characters, the Thin White Duke. The entire show was of an expressionist bent, explained Bowie, and the fact that those influences had been gaining ascendence is certainly one of the reasons why Bowie was drawn to Berlin, as well as to painting once again. As it turned out, the tour met with mixed reaction, with most of the complaints stemming from Bowie's extreme coolness, (he'd called himself an "Iceman" back in Ziggy days, but this was the epitomy) bordering on the stiff. He went through his repertoire wearing a cool dress white shirt, black slacks, and a black waistcoat with a pack of Gitanes in the pocket (Bowie reports kicking his drug habit while on tour). By all accounts, the visuals were striking, and while some in the audience were taken by the iciness, others were not; still others, contradictorily, found Bowie to be at his warmest, with the intimate manner of a cabaret performer. Which only proves that a performance is in the eye of the beholder and/or that no two shows are ever quite the same.

The one feature of the tour on which there was general consensus was the high degree of professionalism it reflected, due largely to the fact that Bowie was finally in control. He was working with a small staff composed of *aide-de-camp* Coco Schwab, Pat Gibbons (former tour manager and at that time running Bowie's management/production company), and Barbara De Witt, Bowie's publicist. There were also the usual bodyguards, of whom Tony Zanetta was the other survivor from Mainman days. Shortly after the tour began, Bowie spoke with Chris Charlesworth in Detroit, beginning with a comment about his motivation:

> I'm just doing this tour for the money. I never earned any money before, but this time I'm going to make some. I think I deserve it, don't you?

Of course! The word money appears about forty times in this interview, leaving little doubt as to what was foremost on Bowie's mind at the time. The following relates to the tour and sheds some light on the goings on:

> The other tours were misery, so painful. I had amazing amounts of people on the road with me. I had a management system which had no idea what it was doing and which was totally self-interested and pompous. I was getting all the problems every night. Ten or fifteen people would be coming up to me and laying their problems on me because the management couldn't deal with it. For me touring was no fun at all, so the two major tours I did were horrendous experiences. I hated every minute of them, so I used to say I'd never tour again. Then I would be talked into doing it again to make somebody else some money. 3

Bowie went on to claim that it was the most efficient and pleasant tour that he'd ever made, and that he'd actually had some time to spend with the band and to write some new songs. And of course, he was making a healthy profit. (After all this, he later described the tour as 'hell', though maybe this had as much to do with the efforts of drug withdrawal as the more usual pressures of touring.)

The tour was made manageable by stripping everything down to basics (at least by past Bowie tour standards). The band was composed of those musicians who could pull off the tight rhythmic material from the last two albums. Carlos Alomar was there as right hand man on guitar. Earl Slick was invited along, but made demands for money and exposure which Bowie was unwilling to meet, prompting his last minute replacement with Stacey Haydon. The situation with Slick was a classic showbiz conflict. Slick was represented by Michael Lippman, the lawyer with ambitions to become Bowie's new manager. The animosity between Lippman and Bowie was fueled by Slick's eagerness to make a career with his own band (the effort backfired). Ironically, but testifying to the fact that they still have a good working relationship (and that Slick knows all his songs), Slick was called in at the eleventh hour for the Serious Moonlight tour to fill the gap created by Stevie Ray Vaughn, who was experiencing similar conflicts in 1983 over money, ego and career that Slick went through seven years earlier. (It must be a testament to something that no "core" member of any of Bowie's bands has managed to distinguish himself away from Bowie.) Stalwarts George Murray and Dennis Davis along with Tony Kaye on keyboards completed the line-up. Said Bowie contentedly: 'There are three blacks and three whites, including myself, and that's a good mixture.'

Once the line-up was established, things went smoothly with the staging of the show, which Bowie described as being 'more theatrical than *Diamond Dogs* ever was, but by suggestion rather than over-propping. It relied on modern twentieth century theatre concepts of lighting and I think it comes over as being very theatrical. Whether the audiences are aware of it I don't know.' For these effects, Bowie was going back to Brecht, as well as the early black and white expressionist films he'd been studying recently. He told Rex Reed that he'd stopped going to the movies in the 1930s, stopping at Murnau, Pabst and Lang.

Bowie went on to talk about the origin of his concept for the tour explaining precisely what effect he intended:

> I wanted to use a new kind of staging and I think this staging will become one of the most important ever. It will affect every kind of rock 'n' roll act from now on because it's the most stabilized move that I've seen in rock 'n' roll. I've reverted to pure Brechtian theatre and I've never seen Brechtian theatre used like this since Morrison and the Doors, and even then Morrison never used white light like I do. [4]

Morrison also did a few things that Bowie couldn't touch, and that may partly account for his tone, but Bowie was right about the aesthetics of his '76 shows, which are influencing shows and videos to this day. He was also right to call it a reversion, underscoring his frequent observation that rock is decades behind the other arts, perhaps accounting for his mastery over, and frustration with, such a circumscribed style. His sources and interests go centuries beyond rock music.

There was the usual press coverage of this tour, focusing on reviews and the latest photos, which allowed fans in upcoming cities to get hip to the new image and get their new look together before Bowie arrived. He also got a small bit of negative press (it was *kept* small) when he was arrested in a hotel in Rochester with four others, including Iggy Pop, for possession of marijuana. Bowie's attorney Stan Diamond stated that David wasn't a user and Bowie claimed the same thing in a Playboy interview, where after a lengthy discussion of drugs ('I haven't gotten involved in anything heavy since '68; I had a silly flirtation with smack then, but it was only for the mystery and enigma of trying it... The only kind of drugs I use though are ones that keep me working for longer periods of time.') Bowie commented on his recent bust:

> Rest assured the stuff was not mine. I can't say much more but it did belong to the others in the room that we were busted in. Bloody potheads. What a dreadful irony — me popped for grass. The stuff sickens me. I haven't touched it in a decade. [5]

Bowie paid bail for the group, but continues his anti-drug stance, becoming more vehement all the time in keeping with changing attitudes. In this same interview, Bowie talked about Hitler, hinting at later comments (and some earlier, where he'd predicted that a dictator would take over the U.S.) that were to raise a bit of a stir. The interview described 1976 as Bowie's biggest year yet, and his crusade for world domination. The following are a few of the comments Bowie made which rolled off the backs of most of his followers, thereby proving his point:

Playboy:
You've often said that you believe very strongly in fascism. Yet you also claim you'll one day run for Prime Minister of England. More media manipulation?

Bowie:
Christ, everything is a media manipulation. I'd love to enter politics. I will one day. I'd adore to be Prime Minister. And yes, I believe very strongly in fascism. The only way we can speed up the sort of liberalism that's hanging foul in the air at the moment is to speed up the progress of a right-wing totally dictatorial tyranny and get it over with as fast as possible. People have always responded with greater efficiency under a regimental leadership. A liberal wastes time saying, "Well, now what ideas have you got?" *Show* them what to do for God's sake. If you don't nothing will get done. I can't stand people just hanging about. Television is the most successful fascist, needless to say. Rock stars are fascists, too. Adolf Hitler was one of the first rock stars.

Playboy:
How so?

Bowie:
Think about it. Look at some of his films and see how he moved. I think he was quite as good as Jagger. It's astounding. And, boy, when he hit that stage, he worked an audience. Good God! He was no politician. He was a media artist himself. He used politics and theatrics and created this thing that governed and controlled the show for 12 years. The world will never see his like. He staged a country. [6]

Such thoughts make one think twice about the *Candidate* inside a *Sweet Thing* portrayed on *Diamond Dogs*, not to mention Bowie's later "recanting", which strikes as pragmatism. Bowie's pulled the same trick that Richard Nixon attempted in changing his image so often, and they both succeeded thanks to the same short memories and attention span of their followers/fans.

Following this Playboy interview, Bowie took his tour to England, arriving at Victoria Station wearing a brown shirt, and giving a "Nazi salute" from the back of a convertible. Against a tide of critical reaction, several explanations were offered; it was suggested that the Duke persona had taken over, that Bowie was merely reflecting the prevailing atmosphere, that he was caught in mid-wave and the resulting photograph just looked bad. Even Angie offered that he was working on a film about Goebbels and as usual got carried away by the character. The best thing to come out of all of this was that Bowie inadvertently demonstrated how transitory outrage can be; the negative press was soon replaced by laudatory reviews such as Melody Maker's "David the

Goliath/The Messiah Returns" (maybe he was right, this was what people wanted and needed...). Bowie was nearly above rebuke, and the fans were just glad to have their messiah back. As one biographer reported:

> It was an emotional return for some, and after the final encore of *The Jean Genie* on the first night, there were tears in David's eyes at the reception his English fans gave him after so many years.

Adolf would have been proud.

TWELVE

'I don't wanna go out / I want to stay inside/ And get things done' ..

'Modern Love' — *Let's Dance*

The next stop on the Bowie Odyssey was Berlin, not for world domination but for retreat. He traveled there with Corinne Schwab and Iggy Pop, and later invited Brian Eno along for some collaboration and inspiration. The reason David chose Berlin as a home is not entirely clear, although he claimed it was an "arduous city" and that it was just what he needed after being choked by sycophancy during his years in L.A. and New York. Bowie is a believer in environmental conditioning, and says that he likes to live in a city with tension, which is necessary for his creativity. Berlin was also home to many artists whom Bowie admired in media ranging from film to music and painting. It is a very culturally and politically conscious city, and he hoped he might be able to lead an anonymous life there. Bowie was filled with the images of the city created in his writings by author Christopher Isherwood and by the vivid evocation achieved by Lou Reed in his then recent work *Berlin*, despite the fact that Reed had never visited the place! Bowie migrated to the "real" Berlin in the hope of making art that could conversely originate in Berlin and recreate the rest of the world. (And perhaps himself).

The decision to ask Eno along seems to have been prompted by both musical and personal concerns. The two had known each other as far back as the early days of Ziggy, when Roxy Music, with Eno still in the band, opened for Bowie at the Rainbow. Although that hadn't been the most satisfying experience, Bowie had been following Eno's development since he'd left Bryan Ferry and Roxy, progressing a highly acclaimed career as producer and electronic (cybernetic) wizard. While Eno had done several albums on his own and with guitarist Robert Fripp (founder of King Crimson), he had also worked with Nico and John Cale, suggesting that Bowie and Eno might have crossed paths in the intervening years. Bowie had certainly been listening to Eno's music; Brian reported that both Iggy and Bowie could hum the entire *No Pussyfooting* album when they first met. The story of their first meeting before they decided to work together is typical of the type of encounter that often begins a collaborative relationship with Bowie. Brian and David met backstage at one of Bowie's Wembley concerts (the other typical setting is "some club"), and information was passed from Bowie to Eno that "we may be working together". Whether their meeting was

119

quite the coincidence, and their decision to collaborate quite the happy flash of spontaneity that legend would have one believe, is uncertain.

Eno was sold on joining David in Berlin, where much of the work on what has come to be known as "the trilogy" Low, Heroes and Lodger) was completed. But first they went to the Chateau d'Herouville, where work on Low was begun. Of the three albums, that resulted from their collaboration, Low is the one with the least obvious Eno input, partly because of its transitional nature. Some of the songs on Low were holdovers from the aborted soundtrack album, and the first side is essentially a new facet of Bowie with the old band. But its flip marked a truly dramatic departure for David, one which was to cause more problems with RCA and leave thousands of confused fans in its wake. At the same time, it also won Bowie a whole new wave of followers.

The studio work on Low didn't get off to the most auspicious of starts, although everything was eventually worked through. When Bowie talks about this album being an 'artistic success', the struggles behind it gave it extra significance for him and made it a personal triumph. The project was begun by amassing the band, which consisted of the core of Alomar, Davis and Murray, with the additions of Ricky Gardener on rhythm guitar, Mary (Hopkin) Visconti contributing vocals, Roy Young on keyboards and later Eno on synthesizer and processing, with Eduard Meyer playing the cello. They were brought to the Chateau only to discover that the new owners had allowed the facilities to fall into disrepair, to the extent that the water wasn't drinkable, as a result of which Bowie and Eno suffered the indignity of dysentary. This quaint bout of sickness was followed by a bout of the decline in David's relationship with Angie, which would result in divorce a couple of years later. Just to make life a little more interesting, David spent much of the time involved in a court case. All of these factors conspired to produce what Brian Eno has called an almost perfect collaboration.

Though Eno plays on several of the Low tracks, he is only given writing credit for Warszawa, the piece he describes in the following interview, although it isn't mentioned by name. As a preface he talked about his working relationship with David, and though they later got into more experimental processes so that not all of the work with David was done in the manner he describes, it was the method that produced a significant number of tracks. Says Eno:

> Well, first of all, we both work in very different ways: David works very fast. He's very impulsive and he works like crazy for about two hours or sometimes three quarters of an hour –– and then he takes the rest of the day off. And in that time, he does an incredible amount, very well, very quickly and faultlessly. He just puts on track after track and they're all just right and then he goes away, and that's it for the day. Quite often that's how it works.
>
> Whereas what I do is to –– quite slowly –– build things up over a period, you know. Since I'm using a monophonic

synthesizer, it's incredibly tedious putting on one line at a time, "da-da-da-da..." like that. Very slow. So I got terribly nervous about working with other people around because so little seems to be happening.

Well, as it happened there were two days when we were at the Chateau d'Herouville — being at the Chateau meant that we had it booked all the time, you see — there were two days when David had to go to Paris to attend this court case or something like that — and the studio was still booked and it was still there so I said, "Well, how about if I get on? I'll carry on working and I'll do some things and if you like them, we'll use them, and if you don't I'll use them myself" see, which struck me as an ideal deal. That meant that I could work without any guilty conscience about wasting someone else's time. Because if he hadn't wanted them I would have paid him for the studio time and used them on my own album.

Not only does this prove that Eno is an honorable guy, but shrewd too, because how could Bowie *not* want the tracks if Eno did?

Well, as it happened, I did a couple of things that I thought were very nice and he liked a lot. One of them's a long piece, about six and a half minutes long and it's a very long, grave solemn instrumental thing. David came in and put all the voices on it in about twenty minutes. There's about 110 voices on it. That was the perfect collaboration, you know. [1]

Out of this melting-pot came *Warszawa*, which opens side two of *Low*, setting the mood for that side and also the trend of grouping the less accessible instrumental pieces on the B-sides. Bowie is rather pleased with the second side of *Low* and for good reason — he got the textures he wanted and an almost total contrast to the opening side. If the B-side shows the influences of Eno, Phillip Glass, Steve Reich, Kraftwerk and Eastern Europe, then the A is what punk might have done to pop music, creating short, straightforward, relentlessly rhythmic and European-rooted music.

There's a lot happening on *Low* and as usual the experience begins upfront with the album cover. A lot of people have picked up on the "low profile" visual pun, and the word "Low" in combination with an earthbound heaven-gazing image from *The Man Who Fell To Earth* sets up resonances of its own. (If Bowie had gone along with his original title of "New Music — Night And Day" the visuals would certainly have been different, and the surprise at the contrast between the sides of the album would have been lessened, although people would still probably call "new music", "new music".) The fact that a photograph from *The Man Who Fell* is used again (a still from that film also graces the cover of *Station To Station*) might indicate either that Bowie knew he looked great in the film, that the music was still welling from that source, that he really felt like an alien this time, or that relating the album to film, gives its audience a clue as to how to listen to the music, as well as a reminder of where much of Bowie's head was. It has been suggested that the second side consists of soundtrack music from imaginary films, while the A-side consists of concise sketches, all of which stand without visuals, though they yearn to have that accompaniment.

This "new music" begins with shades of something familiar in the form of *Speed Of Life* which has a few notes in common with *Brown Sugar*, though it doesn't really feel anything like it. The song is over almost as soon as it's begun, totally infectious with a shimmering wave effect that's on the verge of becoming addictive when Bowie drops his voice into *Breaking Glass*. Since Bowie didn't do it himself, someone else had to make a film out of this one, and someone did, making a star out of Hazel O'Connor (though they don't use Bowie's music in the film itself). Out of the general detached isolation of the album, this is the chiller, with the cool psychotic voice calling from down in the cellar, "You're a wonderful person but you've got problems... I'm breaking glass in your room again", with the admonition not to look at the carpet 'cause God only knows what He did there. This cut was one of the first to give prominence to the "smash" drum sound that stops in its tracks, which Bowie later described as 'that depressive gorilla effect that set down the studio drum fad for the next few years.' As *Low* was to spawn as many (maybe more) imitators than any other Bowie album, he went on to say, 'it was something I wish we'd never created, having had to live through four years of it with other English bands, until it started into the "clap" sound we've got now'.

What In The World gets to where Bowie's at, with the world reduced to one room, though it's not Bowie but a girl with grey eyes inside of it. This song is nearly impossible to describe, the sound is seamless and driving (bubbling actually) with Eno, Young, multiple guitars, bass, and those drums filling the tracks. There is some respite in *Sound And Vision*, the album's single, featuring the author in his "blue, blue 'lectric blue" room. (For those that thought *Low* was *the most* alienated offering ever in the world of commercial music, there's Brian Wilson's precedent in songs like *In My Room*; chances are that *Pet Sounds* was one of Bowie's pet records as his production techniques owe a lot to Wilson.) In this song, the melody line is sweet but the vocals are the thing. Bowie pulls all the vocal stops from the Brit Davy Jones to the crooning soulster of *Young Americans* (the music ain't soul but the singing is) and he gets some wild effects blending the high register of his voice with those of Brian Eno and Mary (Hopkin) Visconti. Charles Shaar Murray sees this cut meshing Bowie and Jerome T. Newton to the point that one 'could almost imagine Newton, sprawling smashed on gin in his luxurious prison, crooning *Sound And Vision* to his gigantic video bank.' Too bad it didn't happen.

With accusations flying that Bowie was glorifying a state of psychotic withdrawal (while he would claim to be working through it), Bowie did agree with his detractors when he mentioned that the 'first side of *Low* was all about me: *Always Crashing In The Same Car* and all that self-pitying crap...' Actually, that's the only song that deserves the reproach. While *Be My Wife* might be construed as more of the same, the energy of the music gives it anything but a self-pitying feel. Despair may be where he's coming from ("sometimes I get so lonely"), but the push is towards a solution, though the wife in the song doesn't ring true as an answer. By then things between Angie and David had become nearly impossible. While they had publicly advocated "open marriage", Angie for one was beginning to regret it, especially since David had been flaunting relationships with men, women and lately with transvestite Romy Haig, which finally helped push Angie over the edge. In any case, it doesn't seem likely that David would have been looking for a wife at that point, except perhaps to do his shopping for him.

A New Career In A New Town is something of a continuation of *The Speed Of Life*, this time as a tone poem with a few "events" thrown in. There are no lyrics so it's up to the listener to supply her or his own city, corners and doors. Much the same can be said of side two, which begins with *Warszawa*, essentially an Eno piece, in which Bowie heard and saw reflections of his own concerns. His lyricless vocals strive to convey the struggle for dignity and the need people feel to be recognized as human beings, in the context of a repressive society, or so he says. This may not be exactly what strikes the listener, but living in Eastern Europe, Bowie had taken the opportunity to travel to Poland, and claims that it was his impressions of the country (when confronted with Eno's music) that determined his vocal contributions to the song. The title certainly supports that orientation.

Art Decade defies attempts to explain the title or the sensation of the piece. Although Charles Shaar Murray heard it as soundtrack music for a long tracking shot of the Berlin Wall, it could as easily conjure any place with a surface beauty that snarls its foreboding secrets just below the audible range. There is no writing credit for Eno on this song, but his contribution is strongly felt, along with Eduard Meyer's cello playing.

Weeping Wall is Bowie's spot in the landscape of the art decaden It's a solo piece rumored to have been intended for the *Man Who Fell* and would have been a better choice than the music which accompanies Bowie's introduction to the New Mexican Hillside and planet Earth, or for that matter, several other scenes.

The Subterraneans is minus Eno and another song that was supposed to be for *The Man*. Featuring Peter and Paul on pianos and Arp, the title might well refer to a Kerouac book of the same name, and though the novel is set in an unnamed city, it could have been the same place Bowie was inhabiting and calling Berlin. On the subject of words, Eno makes the comment that, 'it's not lyrics you see, I don't know whether he wants people to think they're lyrics or not'. In spite of this, one phrase sounds a lot like *Caroline* without the "o", and might be a reference to the anti-heroine of Lou Reed's *Berlin* (or the Beach Boys' *Caroline No?*). The influences are conjecture, though Bowie's sax playing again reminds one of Kerouac. Whatever its origins, the piece stands well on its own merits. One RCA exec to whom fell the task of selling the album, was forced to resort to describing it as 'religious'!

Whether or not Bowie intended it to do so, *Low* stirred up some bad blood between himself and his record company. It has to be remembered that David made some much-publicized comments to the effect that he didn't care if the album sold, and in fact almost hoped that it wouldn't. While some saw Eno's "elitist" influence there, the implication was that Bowie would then be free to do what he wanted outside of music, or at least have some leverage with RCA. Even though he must have expected RCA to be taken aback by something so seemingly uncommercial (and apparently totally "different") he didn't expect the reaction to be as bad as it was. The first slap in the face came when the materials were submitted to RCA in time for the Christmas 1976 release deadline and RCA sat on them until early 1977. They did little publicity, not knowing quite how to promote the album they had on their hands, and preferred to rely on the lame rationale that "Bowie records sell themselves". If this was the case, Bowie might have had good reason to question the point of continuing the relationship. He also claims to have been 'hurt' by the company's negative reaction, since *Low* had such personal significance for him.

While Bowie was taking some personal and musical risks and making therapy out of his art, RCA was privately describing the album in terms like 'chamber music for the masses', (which may not have been that far off the mark) and no one, including critics, was willing to go out on a limb to support it. Most kept their mouths shut waiting to see what would happen next. That is one reason that *Heroes* got such raves. They could say what they would have said about *Low* if they weren't so worried about looking foolish. The reaction (or lack of it), might have caused Bowie to doubt what he was doing, but through it all he maintained his belief in *Low's* importance. Speaking about the album several years later he still described it as a 'terribly important album for me personally'. Then he went on to explain why, in terms of the kind of atmosphere he was trying to evoke:

> For me (it created) a world of relief, a world that I would like to be in. It glowed with a pure spirituality that hadn't been present in my music for some time. Mine had in fact almost become darkly obsessed. There was a degree of the Lower Elements that it occured to me had been in recent songs and in the structures of the music.
> There was a cleansing for me in *Low*. I find it has a clean feeling as an album. That album, more than any of the others we did, was responsible for my cleaning up musically and my driving for more positive turns of phrase, if you will, in my music. [2]

The mood of *Low* had more to do with Bowie than with Eno, with

David's efforts towards personal survival and recreation. On *Heroes* and *Lodger*, Eno's experimental influences on the music are more evident. But *Low* was Bowie's struggle set to vinyl.

> Pulling myself back out of that was not quick, it was a good two to three year process. There was a flashback effect. For the first or three years after and while I was living in Berlin, I would have days where things were moving in the room — and this was when I was totally straight. It took the first two years in Berlin to really cleanse my system. Especially psychically and emotionally. I really had to find myself again. [3]

Thus Berlin finds Bowie going through one of his periodic efforts to get back in touch with himself, the same process he goes through almost every time he puts out a record, and one of the prime reasons he's been able to survive and progress. Earlier in 1976 he talked about a similar process, the irony being that he was still in L.A. at the time, in a different situation.

> I set out on a very successful crusade to establish my own identity. I stripped myself down and took myself apart, layer by layer. I used to sit in bed and pick on one thing a week that I either didn't like or couldn't understand. And during the course of the week, I'd try to kill it off.

First he focused on his lack of humor, then his "prissiness". He then asked himself:

> Why did I feel that I was superior to people? I had come to some conclusions. I haven't yet but I dug into myself... I'm still doing it. I seem to know exactly what makes me sad.

The interviewer brushed over the final comment, so perhaps we'll never know what makes him sad, but if Bowie can be believed, we have some indication of what made him happy.

Publicly advocating the simple life (now that he was handling his own P.R.), Bowie proclaimed his love of living anonymously in his apartment above an automobile spare parts shop in the Turkish (Neuikoln) section of Berlin. He took art classes, spent time in museums and had his son Zowie living with him, who since that time has figured as the guiding light and love of Bowie's life. It was well publicized that Bowie was quite happy doing "normal" things like shopping, cooking and laundry, producing much awe among his fans. Bowie also set aside time for painting and woodcuts and began to think more seriously about film. He had Eno in town for work, along with companion Iggy Pop, and while in Berlin they worked on what would be regarded as one of the best albums of Iggy's career.

Iggy was a good partner in crime and exploration, especially of

Berlin's darker side, glimpses of which would show up on the *Heroes* album. But in the meantime the major project was Iggy's *The Idiot*. This wasn't the first musical association between Iggy and Bowie; Bowie had been called in at the last moment to remix Pop's *Raw Power* L.P. back in '72-'73. By that point, it had been too late for Bowie to do much to influence the album, and in the meantime Iggy's fortunes had been slipping. As he got deeper into a drug habit, his musical output had dried up and the Stooges had blown away. He finally ended up admitting himself to a mental institution. At this lowpoint for Iggy the only person who came to see him was David Bowie, prompting Pop to list Bowie as "Savior/Best Friend" in the cast of characters in his auto-biography. David and Iggy started working on some music in L.A., (continued at the Chateau), but the final step in his recuperation was the invitation to join Bowie in Berlin. In a move similar to the one taken to revive Lou Reed's career, Bowie made a deal to produce the album as well as contributing arrangements and co-writing the songs. *The Idiot* came out between *Low* and *Heroes*; arises from a similar environment and probably included most of the same personnel, although there was no credit given to the players.

Besides doing well for Iggy, *The Idiot* served a purpose for Bowie, as it functions as a bridge between *Low* and *Heroes*, providing a foundation for songs like *Joe The Lion*. The album appropriately came out in early 1977 (the year of punk) and despite appearing on a lot of "pick of the year" lists, it too was somewhat overlooked, although it did remind some of the current crop of "punks" of their lineage. There is one song on *The Idiot* that should particularly interest Bowiephiles, since David re-recorded it in 1983. The song is *China Girl* and though it's not clear just who wrote what (Iggy usually gets credit for the lyrics), the major difference lies in the way the lyrics are delivered. Pop's version of the song is sweet menace, bound to confound any China Girl, while Bowie's remake is true to his own style, more subtly ingratiating. While cries were raised that Bowie hadn't achieved what Iggy had with the same song, it was left to Bowie to make a hit out of it.

Bowie's decision to play on Iggy's follow-up tour got Iggy more attention than usual, though Bowie was low-key, playing piano and staying out of Iggy's limelight. The other notable aspect of the tour was that in order to make its start in the U.S., Bowie was compelled to fly, finally forcing him to abandon his pet phobia, which made a whole new lifestyle possible. The ideas behind *Lodger* are almost inconceivable without the aid of jet travel. In retrospect, Bowie described the process of discarding his fear as 'rational', saying that he was ultimately sold by the statistics that air travel was safer than automobile travel. He did confess occasionally to being frightened by American "cowboy" pilots — no doubt the image of Slim Pickens riding that bomb was lodged somewhere in the back of his mind.

Everyone seemed to have a good time on Iggy's tour if photos and radio station jams are any indication, and being a sideman must have been relaxing for Bowie. After refusing to promote *Low* at all, waiting and watching to see what RCA and his fans would do, the tour raised his spirits. Bowie apparently then decided to embark on a tour (and promotion in general) to support the upcoming *Heroes* album. This was done somewhat grudgingly due to the lack of support from his record company, but Bowie typically filed all complaints away in the back of his mind, while waiting for the opportunity to extricate himself.

Due to the fact that *Low*'s release was held up by RCA, Bowie had two album releases in 1977, with *Heroes* coming out in October, following single releases in September. While the tone of *Heroes* was different from *Low*, the players were nearly the same, the major difference being that Robert Fripp was drafted as lead guitarist (an Eno collaborator whom Bowie welcomed). Again they recorded at Hansa (By The Wall) studios, with a similar track listing, making up a song-oriented A-side and a B-side composed mostly of tonal/textual electronic work. *Heroes* features two songs that Bowie must have known would be hits, fulfilling a prediction he'd made to Chris Charlesworth during the *Station To Station* tour. When asked about what would be coming, Bowie replied:

> Albums? I'll make some commercial albums and I'll make some that possibly aren't as commercial. I'll probably keep alternating, providing myself with a hit album to make the money to do the next album which probably won't sell as well. 4

So here was the hit album, mainly by virtue of the title track, along with *Beauty And The Beast*, to quell any doubts that Bowie might have just gotten lucky with *"Heroes"* (by this point writing hit pop songs was almost second nature, and the struggle was to go farther.). In the opinion of many, *"Heroes"* is one of Bowie's best songs ever, a slow building dramatic account of two lovers who meet by the Berlin Wall with the thought of momentary heroism. It's also the only song Bowie's ever written with quotes around it, underscoring the fact that the subjects are not "heroes", but could, or perhaps should be, "'cause though nothing/will keep us together/we could steal time/just for one day." One point that has seldom been raised, but bears consideration in light of the long-running "love-hate" relationship between David and Lou Reed, is that the song bears a deep resemblance to Reed's Heroine. Aside from the fact that the titles are rather similar, Reed's song had always been one of Bowie's favorites, although he doesn't perform it. Friends of Reed have gone so far as to claim that Bowie's desire to "figure out" the piece was his main motivation for befriending Reed, and though this may be going too far, their days of friendship were numbered. This may also account for the title of Bowie's song being in quotes, standard procedure when one is borrowing. Whatever the virtues of the rest of the album, it was mainly due to this track that it was hailed as brilliant while *Low* had been ignored, lacking as it did an instant hit track. *"Heroes"* also highlights Fripp's contribution, as he might well have been brought in to get that *Heroine* guitar line which is deceptive in its seeming simplicity.

As for the album itself, *Beauty And The Beast* opens things on a respectably chilling but confident note. You either love or hate this one for the same reason, because "You can't say no to/The Beauty And The Beast". As with Bowie himself you have to accept the total package, complete with apparent contradictions. Embracing contradiction could be said to have characterized most of David's significant relationships and songs. *Beauty And The Beast* also characterizes the songwriting style emerging from the Bowie pen at the time. While *"Heroes"* was rather typical of the *vignette*, narrative style, the rest of the songs are more surreal constructions. The *sense* of each piece is as unmistakable as the *logic* is elusive. This freed Bowie for some outstanding throwaway lines and a dreamlike quality to match his frequent references to the dream state.

Joe The Lion is probably the best example; a fairly narrative near-epic, conjuring images of a burly "whiskey missionary" (William Burroughs' phrase). The lyrics are amazing, with Bowie evoking the oppressive sameness and deadliness of most lives, ("It's Monday/You slither down the greasy pipe") in which a line like "May you be like your dreams tonight" may be a blessing or a curse. But it's the clarity in the character and the telling of the tale which help recreate Berlin as a state of mind. Says Joe (the lion): "Nail me to my car and I'll tell you who you are". This song is also one of the earliest manifestations of Bowie's new, contemporary set of influences. At points in the song his vocal styling is almost a direct copy of David Byrne's; no coincidence, since Brian Eno was producing Talking Heads at the time. It was a compliment that Byrne would later return.

The same struggle of the individual over the inertial deadweight of his situation characterizes *"Heroes"*. Bowie's vocal performance is unique, with the hopeful and the hopeless almost perfectly blended. The song is emotive and dramatic without the excesses that marred some of the work on *Station To Station* and *Young Americans*. *"Heroes"* was the first album since *Young Americans* to include a lyric sheet, and it's especially appreciated on *Sons Of The Silent Age*, which portrays the mass out of which the faces of the Joes and the young "Heroes" arise. *Silent Age* is as purely poetic as anything Bowie's written. The music is sufficiently oppressive (those gorilla drums) for the subject matter, and features Bowie's sax and boyish accent, with the only glimmer of hope coming from the Beatlesque backing vocals. The last line conveys the song's dominant image: "They never die, just go to sleep one day". "They" are Nixon's silent majority, dulled by proximity to the Wall and draft age.

Blackout is a plea; even in Berlin, Bowie has needed to "get me some protection". The song seems fairly autobiographical, based on an incident in that city when Bowie collapsed with chest pains and was not exactly rushed to the hospital. The delay was apparently more disturbing than the collapse, and the incident seemed to coincide with a personal low point. It followed a crash in his Mercedes in a parking garage a few days earlier — publicly attributed to drunkenness — which his close friends attributed to depression.

While Bowie is usually pictured as having lived a clean, sane life in Berlin, he was known to be subject to bouts of irrational and irresponsible behavior. At that time he was a under a lot of pressure career — and otherwise. Having taken over his own management he felt the particular need of a hit album, he was taking care of his son and his marriage was on the rocks. With all this the album, the oft-stated opinion that *"Heroes"* was more optimistic than *Low* seems to have little basis in fact or feel, with the possible exception of a couple of the lyricless tracks on the second side. *V-2 Schneider* for instance, is an uplifting aerial tribute to Florian Schneider of Kraftwerk, Bowie's favorite member of a band that helped draw him to Germany. In an interview that was given shortly after *"Heroes"* appeared, Bowie described what it was about Schneider that appealed to him (and in passing accounts for the cracked up Mercedes):

> I like them (Kraftwerk) as people very much. Florian in particular. Very dry... When I came over to Europe I got myself a Mercedes to drive around in, cause I still wasn't flying at that time, and Florian saw it. He said "What a wonderful car", and I said, "Yes, it used to belong to some Iranian prince, and he was assassinated and the car went on the market, and I got it for the tour." And Florian said, "Ja, car always lasts longer." With him it all has that edge. His whole cold emotion/warm emotion. I responded to that.' [5]

The response is there in the song, with Bowie doing his bit for Florian with his warm/cool sax playing in an infectious context. Dennis Davis and George Murray were also on for that one.

Sense Of Doubt follows *V-2*, and works as a statement while generating the mood it is named after. There are no lyrics to explain the source of doubt, though it hardly seems to matter since doubt is always of the same ilk. The effect of the piece is achieved initially with the descent on a grand piano aided by the synthesizer and other sounds that are either concrete and/or processed. If Wim Wenders were to use the piece as a soundtrack, it would be at the scene of some crime in a warehouse district in winter by the sea. This foreboding piece moves into and away to *Moss Garden*, echoing Bowie's Japanese influences (now that he was flying, a favorite visiting place.) Earlier in *Blackout* Bowie stated that he was "Under Japanese influence/And my honour's at stake", which is definitely the case with Bowie's koto playing on *Moss Garden*. The sound is great (though relatively few Westerners would recognize "good" koto playing if they heard it) with the koto slipping in to replace the sound of the piano, while the atmospheric sounds from *Sense Of Doubt* carry over. The tone and mood of *Moss Garden* hinge on the koto and the instrument seems to lead the previously turbulent music to a calmer, more contemplative plane where the nightmare of doubt has passed.

The sensation of travel and geography created on this side hints at the organizing principle of *Lodger*, and from the *Moss Garden* it's back to

Bowie's home territory of *Neukoïln*, on which Bowie displays his sax prowess for those who can never get enough of that free jazz. The album's closing piece has an Eno-esque title *The Secret Life Of Arabia*) and a touch of his sense of humor, mainly evidenced by the back-up vocals. Singing duties were discharged by Tony Visconti and Antonia Maass and the piece is upbeat, bouncing its way out of the grooves, and perhaps since this is the last song on the record it explains why people were left with an overall positive impression.

The critics reacted to *"Heroes"* with a vestige of the wariness with which most received the first Bowie-Eno collaboration. This stemmed from a long-standing ambivalence that many felt about both Bowie and Eno on their own, let alone to any product of their joint effort. To compound the half-hearted pundits' reception, those reviewers who favored Eno saw Bowie as an opportunist of pop, while Bowie fans viewed Brian Eno as effete. Bart Testa, writing for Rolling Stone was coming from the Eno camp, but found that *Heroes* quelled most of the doubts that *Low* had raised. He wrote: *"Heroes"* is the second album in what we can now hope will be a series of David Bowie-Brian Eno collaborations.' The reason for the hope is that, 'This album answers the question of whether Bowie can be a real collaborator'. Note was taken of the continuity between the chilling tunes on *"Heroes"* and Iggy's *The Idiot*, but what really delighted Testa were the 'real exchanges, particularly on the B side' between Bowie and Eno. While a lot of Bowie's fans felt left out in the cold, the Eno-Bowie efforts were attracting a lot of converts from both camps, and Testa, like many others was won over and was waiting for the next installment, with only a few reservations held in check for the next installment.

> We'll have to wait and see if Bowie has found in the austere Eno a long-term collaborator who can draw out the substantial works and music that have lurked beneath the surface of Bowie's clever games for so long. But Eno has clearly affected a nearly miraculous change in Bowie already. [6]

There was to be a slight wait however, since for the first time in his career Bowie slowed down his usually gruelling production schedule. There was a tour, a film and personal preoccupations, all of which prompted a longer than usual gestation period for the next album. There were also good artistic reasons for the break; *"Heroes"* sees a few David Byrneisms creeping into Bowie's repertoire, and apparently David was ready to take stock before turning out another record. One of the clear if rarely stated reasons for the positive response to *"Heroes"* was that it marked Bowie's return to the "real world", (one to which his fans could relate) and the fact that their hero had pulled through was a source of joy. Bowie continued his trek from the inside out, seeking new sources of inspiration, surveying the international scene from his new-found aerial perspective. With his advertisements proclaiming: "There's Old Wave, There's New Wave and Then There's David Bowie", the time had come to put some distance between himself and the rest of the pack.

THIRTEEN

'I stumble into town, just like a sacred cow...'

'China Girl' — *The Idiot* 'China Girl' — *Let's Dance*

By mid 1977 the *Heroes* sessions were finished (though the album hadn't yet been released) and Bowie had decided it was time to give the old promo machine a workout. He'd reached the point in his career when he could choose his spots, his ways and means, he was drawn to England for several reasons. He'd been absent almost totally over the previous three years, and in '77 the "explosion" that Bowie had created with Ziggy was finally beginning to rock his home country. In addition to the changing cultural atmosphere, there were certain people in Britain who wielded the power to draw Bowie back. One such person was Marc Bolan, whose career was enjoying a slight resurgence after a bad patch. Bolan was obviously feeling conciliatory towards Bowie, inviting David to appear on his *Marc* television show in September of that year.

Bolan's show that night also featured Generation X, whose lead singer Billy Idol had evidently learned a trick or two from master David Bowie. Bowie's spot was anything but flash, partly thanks to the fact that due to union problems the rehearsal takes were what had to be aired. Instead he was preserved for posterity on video tape in his understated "Berlin" garb of straight jeans, short hair and crucifix while he sang "*Heroes*" and duetted with Bolan, who was sporting his trademark of eye shadow and red nail polish. One of the groups that didn't make the show due to time limits were Eddie and the Hotrods, who reportedly took the train back to London with Bowie; David quite matter-of-factly dropped the bombshell that he'd just filmed a Christmas TV special with Bing Crosby!

He had hardly returned to Berlin when the news arrived that Bolan had died in a car accident, pulling a distraught Bowie back to London. He set up a trust for Bolan's family, and tried to make the best of a gruesome situation. Old debts resurfaced in the form of a bill presented by his former landlord at Haddon Hall for unpaid rent, and when he went to visit his childhood home in Brixton he was too intimidated even to approach the building. But there was also business to take care of, and he set himself up at the Dorchester (former site of his press conferences) to meet the press and give a boost to the just-released "*Heroes*" album. He talked about Berlin and its effect ('Berlin makes me feel very uneasy, very claustrophobic. I work best under these sorts of conditions'), his painting and the portraits he'd done of the Turks in Neuköiln ('shackled in very bad conditions' etc.), but the weight of a stressful situation became too great and Bowie submerged again.

It was shortly after Bolan's funeral that Bing Crosby also died (the airing of their Christmas Special was moved up) and a happy irony turned into a case of strange timing. Bowie and Bing did a duet of *The Little Drummer Boy* which was released as a single for Christmas and sold quite well (though not as well as a previous Crosby Christmas song called... what was it now?). Aside from the initial surprise of the association, which pointed to Bowie's future rather than to his past, the similarities between Bing and Bowie are striking. The greatest living crooner was also an astute businessman, with a TV production company, and other interests which Bowie shared. The timing of Crosby's death just after their appearance together almost seemed to point to his actual successor. With little choice but to go on, Bowie plunged into some new work, though he was to make a poor choice of projects.

David became involved in a film called *Just A Gigolo*, later claiming that he did it as a favor to actor-turned-director David Hemmings. The cast must have also intrigued him, including Marlene Dietrich and Kim Novak, but with a poor story and some untenable production compromises, the film turned out to be a disaster. Bowie was happy to be working in Berlin again, and enjoyed some aspects of the process, hobnobbing with the likes of Maria Schell, who like others who've played opposite David was struck by his abilities as an actor. Her comment was: 'I think he's going to be a very great actor, and you know why? Because he looks at you and he is really feeling it deep inside.' Her actions towards Bowie also emphasize an often overlooked aspect of Bowie's attraction. It's not just his ability to project but the power to draw people in to him. This story emphasizes the point:

> Towards Bowie she (Ms. Schell) seems genuinely maternal, solicitous as many do become who get to know him a little. As filming starts, one day in a gloomy pension in an old stone apartment block, she enters with a vast loaf of bread which Bowie receives with fond indulgence. "Everybody wants to look after my health", he grins. [1]

Unfortunately, David was unable to work his magic with Dietrich, who refused to budge from Paris and did not actually appear in the same frame as Bowie. They *do* appear side by side on the publicity posters and one critic was thrilled by the thought of these two heavenly bodies passing so close to one another.

All this served as part of Bowie's apprenticeship in film, providing as many lessons in what not to do as in anything else. Without going into the details of the film or the reviews (which, as so often in his career, felt the need to be merciful towards David) a couple of Bowie's own comments sum up the situation: '*Just a Gigolo* is all my thirty-two Elvis Presley movies rolled into one.' To emphasize the point, he added that, 'the film was a cack, a real cack. Everybody who was involved in that film, when they meet each other now, they look away. I should have known better.' This may explain why Bowie told Michael Watts during the filming that he now considered himself a "generalist", preferring not to limit himself with the titles of "singer, composer or actor". After calling himself an actor for so many years, rescinding at that point might have been significant. As it turned out, Bowie spent a good deal of time in 1979 promoting the film (attending premieres, film festivals and the like) but aside from bringing him the opportunity to meet Princess Margaret, it was to little avail. Perhaps one of the lessons Bowie learned from the fiasco was the folly of basing a film on a song. The plot was based on a cross between Dietrich's version of *Pretty Gigolo/Poor Gigolo* and a German anthem.

While filming dragged on during the winter of '77-'78, Bowie developed plans for his own music, another world tour, and another film, all of which came to nought. He did manage to get in some travel, this time going to Africa, and he recorded the narration to *Peter And The Wolf* for RCA. Bowie's own reason for doing it (when he heard that RCA was looking for someone) was that the symphony was one of Zowie's favorites. It also happens to be a wonderful version (with Eugene Ormandy and the Philadelphia Orchestra) with Bowie's views on childrearing being met by altering the text so that the guns are "shotguns", not "rifles", and so on.

Peter And The Wolf was an afternoon's work, but in getting ready for the tour, Bowie and the band went into two months of rehearsals, arduous preparation which as usual paid off. Bowie was able to overcome problems that would have overwhelmed a lesser showman. Concentrating on material from *Low* and *"Heroes"*, the lengthy wordless pieces would have put audiences to sleep rendered by any other performer. Accepting this risk, Bowie developed an exciting set, with impeccable timing, relying again on the clean lighting of Eric Barrett, the best band that he could muster and, most importantly, a varied and extensive repertoire.

Beginning the shows with *Warszawa* could have been risky, but it was also Bowie's way of letting the audience know what was coming; as always they were eager to follow his lead, once the game plan was clear *"Heroes"* was a reassuring choice of follow-on (it was a MAJOR hit) and crowd pleasers like *Jean Genie*, *Fame* and a chunk of Ziggy material strung the fans along and helped break up the longer instrumental interludes. Bowie included the Brecht-Weil song *Moon of Alabama (Whiskey Song)* of Doors' fame, but it was sung in German to the delight of all those enchanted by the German/European Bowie. The traditional renditions of *TVC-15* and *Stay* served for encores, with the Bowie standard *Rebel Rebel* to send everyone off in the right state of mind. The shows were an unblighted success. Bowie even tempted and overcame Fate by returning to Earl's Court, somehow managing to coax an atmosphere out of that abysmal hall, to everyone's amazement.

RCA opted for a live tour album, this one called *Stage*, and again it was

134

a double LP. Though rumored to be a soundtrack for a tour documentary due to be shot by David Hemmings, the film never materialized.
(Maybe Bowie saw the rough edit of *Gigolo* and changed his mind.) *Stage*,
like *Live* was more of a business than an artistic venture, as indicated by
some contractual wrangling over the album (would it count for one or
two records?) and the fact that what Bowie did on that tour was to
prove that he could recreate heavily produced, studio-originated work
in a live context. For those possessing the other albums, *Stage* offers little
more than a souvenir of the tour. It lacks any live feel due to the close
placement of the songs with little applause or ambiance. The set was
rearranged so that material from the same studio albums runs
consecutively. Thus one misses the in-performance segues and connections, though the playing and singing are excellent throughout.

Bowie played a portable synthesizer in performance for many of the
pieces, but since he professes to be no "technocrat" on any instrument,
he brought along Roger Powell (the original synthesizer wiz and long-
time associate of Todd Rungren) as well as pianist Sean Mayes, and the
regulars -— Alomar, David and Murray. There was also the customary
second guitarist, this time in the form of Adrian Belew, who has played
with Zappa and others. Like the previous tour, the tight organisation
made allowances for some looser moments and in time-honored
fashion, individual band members were featured at appropriate points.

With a tour break in late summer, Bowie went to Vienna to work on a
film based on a short period in the life of painter Egon Schiele. The film
was to have been called *Wally*, after Schiele's young model/mistress, and
Bowie seemed intrigued with the character of the "nasty little" man,
who also happened to be a great nasty painter. The movie's subjects of
the art world, politics and sex might have been an interesting vehicle for
Bowie, but for reasons unknown ("project cancelled, tumbling down...")
it was not to be.

At least the cancellation freed Bowie for more travel and work on the
Lodger album. Since *Lodger* was the first Bowie album to be supported by
bona-fide music videos, as distinct from the less lavish promos he'd been
doing all along, it's worth noting some of the preoccupations and
influences that colored the project. Mainly due to Eno's influence,
Bowie was attracted to Devo and there was even talk of co-producing a
Devo album with Eno. This plan was abandoned, partly under the
time-pressure of the ongoing tour. What intrigued Bowie about Devo
was their energy and enthusiasm (but not the theory of de-evolution)
and he found them to be 'very interesting people, very much in the same
sort of conversational pattern as Brian and Fripp, but an American
equivalent'. Quick and sarcastic, in other words, as well as having some
beguiling ideas on the use of video. Eno was also working with Talking
Heads at the time, in whose line-up Bowie seems to have found an even
more serious version of himself in David Byrne -— the object of Bowie's
continuing respect and someone from whom he has taken the occasional
stylistic loan. (Tina Weymouth was less than delighted with the trio,
commenting that: 'I can see them when they're 80 years old and all

alone. There'll be David Bowie, David Byrne and Brian Eno, and they'll just talk to each other.') Around this time, Bowie also began to take an interest in The Human League, a British band which has gone on to considerable success with an intelligent brand of synthesized pop. One of their recent hits, *(Feeling) Fascination* sounds like a tribute to Bowie, and they also opened for him on the English leg of his 1983 Serious Moonlight tour.

Work on *Lodger* was proceeding in Montreux, again with Eno and the gang (plus Belew, Mayes and Simon House). When it was finished, Bowie let the PR machine loose, with videos and one major interview in which he explained the album song by song. In this case, Bowie seemed to want to engender a mood of casual creativity pervading the album, though he succeeded only in places.

The album's title, *Lodger*, seems to be an allusion to Roman Polanski's macabre film *The Tenant*, borne out by a gesture that appears in the video to *Boys Keep Swinging*, where Bowie "exposes" himself by removing his make-up (disguise) with a bold back-hand wipe across the face. So from the one room of *Low* to the city (Berlin) of *"Heroes"* we enter the world of the *Lodger*, with postcard-like songs as communiques depicting a world in which nowhere and anywhere are home. A line from *Move On* proclaims: "I'm just a travelling man" and the nagging thing about the travel motif is that Bowie's not travelling out of any inner compulsion necessarily, but because he's able to. It is this same freedom which to some beautifies the album and to others trivialises it. The point is made specifically in contrast to *Low*, which has been called self-indulgent, but which at least faithfully records the fact that Bowie's creative life was hanging in the balance, while *Lodger* comes across as an academic exercise by someone with talent and a recording contract. This is not to say that the subject matter is lightweight or that the music isn't often brilliant — many have thought it Bowie's best work since *Ziggy*. The French Minister of Culture awarded *Lodger* the *Grand Prix du Disque* for best international recording (perhaps recognizing its international theme); the album would have appealed to French sensibilities because it is squeaky clean and for that reason alone benefits from play at high volume.

The album begins with the intro of *Fantastic Voyage*, presumably about our journey on the "spaceship earth". After Bowie talked about variations on four chord changes in this one, he called it a pop song and very old-fashioned romantic, which it is, although the lyrics are strangely uneven. The chorus is brilliant (the beauty of this album is that every song has such a treat) with Bowie's rendition of the famous line, "We're learning to live with somebody's depression." This song is presumed to be about the leaders of nuclear nations, but while its sentiments are admirable, some of its lyrics are trite and condescending. "Dignity is valuable/But our lives are valuable too", he writes/sings. "They wipe out an entire race and I've got to write it down/I'm still getting educated but I've got to write it down". This indicates some humility and perspective on Bowie's part after all.

While Eno was credited with "ambient drone" on *Fantastic Voyage*, he produces the "cricket menace" on *African Night Flight* which proves that Bowie does have a sense of humor. *African Night Flight* arose from Bowie's travels to Africa, and to Kenya in particular, where as he says, there were all these mysterious German pilots who'd been bush hopping in their Cessnas for years. The B movie tableau of long-lost airmen (hanging out drunk in bars in their pilots gear in the middle of Africa) took Bowie all the way back to *Take My Tip* and the rapid fire lyric delivery, this time including some Swahili which Bowie informs means "hello/goodbye" (appropriately enough for a band of flyers who never fly away). The song boasts an intriguing lyric. The key lines are "Gotta get a word through one of these days" and "Seems like another day/I could fly/Into the eye of God on high", with a need to get a word through to "Elizabeth's father." The setting might be from any forgotten outpost of the former Empire.

Move On has been tagged by Bowie as another of his "romantic songs", presumably because of its reference to a girl. With a catalogue of the places he's visited there's a touch of nostalgia about *Cyprus is my island*; all Bowiephiles will recognize the reference to Angie's childhood home. An excellent cut with a full compliment of three "rhythm guitarists", its main interest (aside from a lovely vocal) is the middle section. Bowie explains the origin:

> I was playing through some old tapes of mine on a Revox and I accidentally played one backwards and thought it was beautiful. Without listening to what it was originally, we recorded the whole thing note for note backwards and then I added vocal harmonies with Tony Visconti. If you play it backwards you'll find it's *All The Young Dudes*.

Despite the impression Bowie gives of the wonders of planned accidents, it seems unlikely that he wouldn't have recognized the song, or bothered to check it. The fact that it was *All The Young Dudes* would have been quite gratifying since Bowie hadn't ever released his own studio version of the song. It had been a hugely popular, though Bowie had only released it himself on the *David Live* album.

Bowie also mentioned that he had done the tape playing (which prompted *Move On*) in New York, which he went on to describe as a very enjoyable city.

> (It) is probably having its heyday as far as the arts are concerned. The whole arts thing in New York is extraordinary, much more exciting than London, which is a bit patchy.

True to his habit of being where the artistic action is, Bowie traveled to New York for most of the work on his next album. In the meantime, the essence of *Move On* as well as Bowie's entire collaboration with Eno was PROCESS, the pieces on Lodger being perhaps the most processed

137

work he has recorded. One of Bowie's favorite processes is inversion, a habit that harkens back to his interest in magic and alchemy and the axiom of "As above, so below", which on the two dimensional plane of tape would translate into backwards and forwards. It's also a favorite of Eno's "Oblique Strategies", so named for his inspirational tarot deck.

On *Yassassin*, apparently Turkish for "Long Live", aside from the violin playing of Simon House, Bowie was delighted by the synthesis of the seemingly incompatible styles of Turkish music and reggae which he discovered to be parallel. The guitar and synthesizer form a bridge between those two styles to create' a song in which the best line is the rather tongue-in-cheek, *I'm not a moody guy*, which sounds like Bowie talking rather than the Turks of Neukoïln who are again his subject. *Yassassin* could also have been called *In The Ghetto*; though the music moves, the people are stuck. *Red Sails* follows this tale of stagnation, a song about the joy of movement, purpose be damned. It's all in the insanity (joy) of the last line, "We're gonna sail to the hinterland/And it's far far far... Faa faa da da". It has been said that through *Red Sails*, Bowie beat the pack to pirate chic, and though he claims he doesn't know what the song's really about, its scurvy-ridden subjects are "mercenary-cum-swashbucklers dropped into the China Sea", which makes them sound like the offspring of too many late movies and laughing gas (or more crumbling Empire hysteria).

The second side rests on more familiar (Western) turf, beginning with *D.J.* In his analysis of the record, Bowie has described D.J.s as the real victims of the disco scene, the men under all the pressure and Grandmaster Flash would certainly agree. The D.J. pays the price for a few seconds of gaping silence with the scene set in the opening lines, "I'm home, lost my job/And incurably ill". The next line approaches the heart of the song, uncovering it as a veiled reference to Bowie, alias David Jones alias D.J. So where is Bowie at? He says: "You think this is easy realism", and goes a bit further in the chorus stating that "I am a D.J./I am what I play/I've got believers (Kiss Kiss) Believing me." All this might mean nothing, were it not for the video accompaniment which gives the song perspective. The video shows David acting out the role of a D.J. on the rampage, climaxing in a scene in which he spray paints his initials on a bathroom mirror. Bowie as a graffiti artist reminds us of his frequent efforts to get in touch with himself ("David Jones") and the roots of what he was doing. At that time he said that 'I haven't met David Jones for such a long time that I have to get to know him all over again.' With Bowie's fractured perspective it's no wonder that D.J. would be amazed at the fact that D.B. has believers (Kiss Kiss). This line also recalls Nietzsche, one of the many influences on the young D.J. There's a passage in *Thus Spoke Zarathustra* that's worth quoting just because the language is so similar:

You say you believe in Zarathustra? But what matters
Zarathustra? You are my believers but what matter all
believers? You had not yet sought yourselves and you found

me. Thus do all believers, therefore all faith amounts to so little.

The next step is the hardest one, and Bowie's has yet to take it all the way.

> Now I bid you lose me and find yourselves; and only when you have all denied me will I return to you. [2]

Look Back In Anger is the next and probably worst cut on the album, though for some reason Bowie also made a video out of it which is more embarrassing than the song itself (featuring him as painter). About a "tatty Angel of Death", the song's most striking element is the mock dramatic vocal performance, and its saving grace, the chorus. The hook is "I've been waiting so long". While it's not clear whether the Angel or the Victim is the one speaking, with Bowie's smoking habit it may be significant that the angel coughed and shook its crumpled wings.

Boys Keep Swinging was the third video to be released from the album, and the other single. The effect of the video on the fortunes of the record are instructive and unusual. Video presentations usually help record sales merely by virtue of the extra exposure, but when the video for *Boys* premiered (in the U.K.) the single was doing respectably well, only to plummet into oblivion as a result. If nothing else, this proved that Bowie still had it in him to shock and disturb, as usual sexually and politically. The video featured Bowie performing in a vaguely Fiftyish context, looking so thin and spastic that this alone was disturbing. But when he walked down a runway three times in three different female disguises, only to audaciously expose the deception with one grand gesture, the audience lost it. (While two of his "women" were rather transvestite looking the last aged-Garbo impersonation was excellent, and the blown kiss a killer.) The lyrics and music of *Boys* hardly mattered after the video, although they gave a conceptual, satirical base for the unexpected images that Bowie created for the tape.

As Bowie described the way the song developed it seems feasible that the music may have prompted the lyrics. The musicians were made to switch instruments with the idea of keeping them on their toes (and off the cliche's) and, as Bowie explained, of injecting some freshness into their playing. He put Alomar on drums and Dennis Davis on bass, and Alomar's earnest efforts are a lot of fun. As Bowie saw it, 'They became kids (boys?) discovering rock and roll for the first time.' While the boys keep swinging on the cutting edge of sexual roles, it's appropriate that the next song introduces John, whose only other appearance in Bowie's work was on the side of the dance floor, in *John I'm Only Dancing*.

This time John is the all-male everyman, essentially All American with a heritage going back to Frankie and Johnny. As Bowie forthrightly states, this 'is all about wife-beating —something you are faced with in the American newspapers all the time.' *Repetition* is a song that's really about learning to live with somebody else's depression. Though the scenario is presented matter-of-factly ("I guess the bruises won't show if she wears long sleeves") and while the delusions are presented as plausible, it's all about the one fact that's really relevant, "Well Johnny is a man. And he's bigger than you." That's what the New York Post would like their readers to remember, and the influence of the tabloid is felt even more on Bowie's next album, recorded in NYC.

That piece of socially responsible lyric-writing is followed by *Red Money* which Bowie says, 'I think is about responsibility'. Why? Because 'Red boxes (and sails?) keep cropping up in my paintings and they represent responsibility there.' There is mention of "project cancelled, tumbling down", which recalls the innumerable projects that tumbled down around'Bowie's head, despite which his output has been phenomenal. The nagging social responsibility is still there, but Bowie's got red money (blood money or debts) on his hands. It all started off as a small box delivered by *Reet Petite* (the song that launched Berry Gordy, Jackie Wilson and Motown Records), and focuses on the artistry and business flip side of hard fame. As the song suggests Bowie "didn't know what to do, but couldn't give it away or drop it". This gets back to Zarathustra and the fact that Bowie can't choose to abandon what he's worked so hard to gain. The song's final line of "Such responsibility, it's up to you and me", is essential to the dilemma and hints at the (financial) bond between audience and performer, who is handed the box (cash) on trust that the performer will give his audience back what it needs. It's a heavy responsibility, which Bowie has always recognized and been willing to accept. He may keep moving on, but realizing that his audiences need him, he attempts to meet their needs while never entirely forgetting that they'll take most anything he offers.

Lodger was warmly received and is considered by many to be the best of the Eno-Bowie offerings, containing songs with an experimental flavor producing fresh but accessible sounds. While *Lodger* marked the end of the direct collaboration between the two, experimentation and high tech continued to influence Bowie's next work. While many (including Bowie) have viewed *Scary Monsters* as negative and a backslide, the fact was that a grim and pessimistic view was somewhat in keeping with the times. Bowie was getting back to rock, which had recently fallen under the influence of a punk aesthetic. While Bowie has referred to his spell in Berlin in 1977 as being in 'the wrong place at the right time', his influence has always stemmed from an uncanny instinct for being in the right place either just ahead of the "right time" or just behind it, in the latter case after mistakes have been made by others and he is then able to exploit the potential that they may have recognized. This happened with *Scary Monsters*; Bowie's head was halfway into *Monsters* (both physically in the sense that he was in New York by then, and musically) by the time *Lodger* appeared. Though *Lodger* was considered the last of the Eno-Bowie trilogy, the thread of their association continued into *Scary Monsters* via Robert Fripp and the rest of the session band from the earlier albums.

State-of-the-art technology was again employed, though this time applied to Bowie's own means and ends. His most successful means had always been rock and disco/funk; if they weren't necessarily his personal favorite sounds he was a Seventies artist and they were the prevailing sounds. Bowie has always been, above all, an artist of, if not ahead of the times. With the appearance of *Scary Monsters*, Bowie closed several chapters in his life and career: the Seventies, and his association with RCA, to name but two. At the same time, he used the album to exorcise a few musical and personal demons. And so the artist of the Eighties was born.

FOURTEEN

'Then I came across a monster/Who was
sleeping by a tree/And I looked and
frowned and the monster was me.'

'The Width Of A Circle' -— *The Man Who Sold The World*

Bowie has always been a tightrope walker (now leaning a bit to the left,
now to the right) and as a new decade approached he took care of old
business and prepared to enter the Decade of Divisiveness with a strong
face. He turned his sights to those things generally lurking beneath the
skin of society, the stuff of the collective urban (sub)consciousness.
Bowie has made the remark on several occasions that his records
function like Polaroids, freezing a moment to record where he was at
mentally and physically at the time. While this description is sometimes
mooted to deflect questions about the influence and importance
(historically speaking) of his music, the one thing that *Scary Monsters (And
Super Creeps)* does sound like is New York City, its night time world
which regularly creates stories sensational enough to make the next
morning's headlines. The music is aggressive and angry though coolly
controlled, with the message that *It's No Game*. Shortly after *Scary
Monsters* was released John Lennon was shot, not too far from where
Bowie was performing on stage in *The Elephant Man*, and thus what a lot
of people had been feeling at the time became manifest. In this context a
song like *Teenage Wildlife* takes on added resonance, and this album
becomes another of Bowie's polaroids of shadows on a New York City
winter's night (while the warm inside world lulls itself to oblivion).

The last order of personal business in 1979 had been the finalisation
of David's divorce from Angie. The legal process had dragged on for two
years, but David walked out of court the undisputed winner. He had
custody of their son, not easily managed but made possible in David's
case by Swiss law and his citizenship, and Angie received a lump sum
settlement of fifty thousand dollars. She later wrote a book and tried
hard to escape David's shadow through fashion and theatrical ventures,
though with little success. Meanwhile David emerged from the divorce
relatively unscathed and suddenly ranking as one of the most eligible
bachelors on earth.

David had also spent some time travelling, mainly between New York
and Japan in preparation for the upcoming album, and found opportun-
ities to tip off a few fans as to what might be coming next. Bowie had
shown a video version of *Space Oddity* on the Kenny Everett New Year's
Eve TV show in Britain; it was touted as a 'ritual purification' of the
song with a sparse and restrained arrangement featuring only bass,

drums, piano and Bowie on acoustic guitar. Some had earlier viewed the song in terms of liberation via distance, and it was now being presented with Bowie singing from inside a stylized padded cell (a motif also featured in the later *Ashes To Ashes* video) and the essence of Major Tom's withdrawal was thrown into a new light. *Ashes To Ashes* took both music and image several steps further and stands as the final version of the saga (a song called *Major Tom* came out in 1983, but Bowie will have none of it). With that done and work on Bowie's new album taking longer than usual, RCA also put out a two version single of *John I'm Only Dancing*.

Scary Monsters was scheduled to be his last album for RCA under the existing contract and David was presumably eager for the association to end, because RCA would have extended given the chance. For that reason the album wasn't rushed; every aspect was calculated for maximum effect, especially in the area of promotion, Bowie securing the greatest possible assistance from the company. The folks at RCA were eager to comply, realising that it would be the last Bowie original they'd have a chance to exploit, and they went all out in their sales effort. That the label had never previously treated Bowie product with quite the respect due to a superstar is a reflection of the fact that RCA is not known for being the most far-sighted record company around — with decisions made by boards, boldness was discouraged. But for this last effort money was spent on videos, the best that Bowie had done so far, postage stamps (designed by Bowie) were issued, there were special store displays and any number of other gadgets and gimmicks including the same single with several different sleeves. (This rather novel trick had been used before on *"Heroes"* with great success.) If all this wasn't enough, the release of the album was held up to coincide with Bowie's Broadway debut in *The Elephant Man*, garnering mountains of press, aided by Bowie's own publicists, agents (he was with Philip Morris International) and RCA. The drift of all this PR was to portray this period in Bowie's career as the year he fought back. It was a kind of comeback from Europe (and relative obscurity), and from what might easily have been a major fiasco called *Just A Gigolo* (had it not been for the blindness of fans and critics alike). A challenge always invigorates Bowie, and the lack of critical acclaim for his last few albums (compared to what he was used to) and the blot on his judgment that was *Gigolo*, called for a dramatic statement, musically and as an actor. Bowie had been avoiding journalists rather more than usual, and he felt the time had come to communicate with the press and though the press with his fans, some of whom were tempted to write him off in the same manner that he had scoffed at rock. Brilliantly, and with what seemed a bit of luck (not that much ever really happened around Bowie by chance) he answered all his critics and recaptured his crown. His acting career went legit, stifling the pundits with an acclaimed portrayal of Merrick in *The Elephant Man*, his musicianship produced his most intense rock since *Aladdin Sane* and showed a way out to those who'd been imitating his electronic (Eno assisted) work. That a lot of people missed the point is hardly Bowie's fault.

John Rockwell of the New York Times was one observer who realized what Bowie was up to and up against, and in his review of *Scary Monsters* he touched on several aspects of Bowie's work (and of that album in particular) which are essential to understanding Bowie as a musician. Beginning with the comment that "Above all, David Bowie is really a musician", Rockwell contradicts Bowie's frequent statements to the contrary. He then goes on to qualify the statement, saying that Bowie is neither much of a singer, nor of an instrumentalist. "Yet, over the years, with a variety of collaborators, he has imposed his own musical sensibility." This is a feat in itself, and led to the much repeated comment that by 1980 Bowie was a genre in himself (with himself as the constant subject). Yet for all Bowie's considerable diversity, *Scary Monsters* tended to highlight his consistencies. While Bowie has moved stylistically from jazz through R&B, folk, disco/soul, funk and rock there has been the recognisable strand of his ethos through most of his best (and favorite) work.

Speaking specifically about *Scary Monsters*, Rockwell wrote that "Mr. Bowie's songs thud onward with a glacial insistence, the higher instruments screaming in agony and the whole veritical texture is cluttered up in fascinating ways with electronic 'treatments' and shifting levels of echo". This sound quality benefitted from the affinity with Bowie's material of producer Tony Visconti, who had been back by Bowie's side since *Young Americans*, and the finished result on *Monsters* owes much to Visconti's expertise as both musician and engineer. Rockwell mused on just how Bowie is able (in the studio) to impose a unity on a strong and diverse group of collaborators. While he pointed out the public strength of Bowie's personality, the actual working relationship in the studio allowed for the free flow between Bowie and Visconti of comment, instruction, suggestion, in a manner that reflects an almost perfect partnership. Visconti may have been the one to recommend a change of approach, but Bowie would then be the one to coax the corrected musician, or vice versa. All manner of elements go into a production when this team is in the studio and the way they (especially Bowie) manage to manipulate situations is little short of miraculous considering the multiplicity of relationships, technology and temperaments at work during a recording session.

Pete Townshend showed up on *Scary Monsters*; Bowie must have realized that Townshend's ego wasn't in any danger, and that it'd be fun for him (who else would have the nerve to ask him to play?) to play on one tune. It's slightly ironic that the tune was *Because You're Young*, but if Bowie had a bit of oneupmanship in mind (Townshend as hired gun!) he kept his thoughts to himself. What follows is what he did say:

> He actually does jump up and down in the studio, I mean that floored me... The first time I met Pete was when I took him a record I'd just made called *Space Oddity* (Author: forgetting about the Marquee...). I said, "'Scuse me, Mr. Townshend, would you

play this at your convenience and tell me what you think of it?"
Funnily enough, when he came to the studio to work on this
track, he said, "By the way, I've been meaning to tell you. About
that single — I think it should do all right!" [1]

Robert Fripp was also back again (Adrian Belew had taken his place on
Lodger) and turned in some of his best licks ever for Bowie on this album.
Having worked with Fripp before, Bowie must have figured that a
certain amount of competition would bring out Fripp's aggressive best,
and with four other guitarists, the heat was on. While the subject is
Bowie's working relationship with others some comments from Fripp
are pertinent. After talking about Bowie's multi-facetedness, Fripp said
that basically, 'he's a shrewdie who keeps his ass covered. I think it
would be true to say that the Bowie-Eno-Fripp trio kind of share that in
common.'

The stalwarts of the band were all there with Alomar performing the
duties that make him so valuable. As leader of the band in the studio, in
rehearsal and on stage, Alomar has held a key position which frees
Bowie up immensely. As Alomar described it:

> My responsibility is really to prepare the music from Bowie's
> notes. It's not always an easy process. David feels that the
> musicians in the band should understand his concept of a song
> before they begin to contribute ideas of their own. When he
> explains something to me and I play something which I've been
> given to understand is what he requires, he can, if he wants,
> change it completely. He often does. [2]

As leader during rehearsals Alomar has found himself having
regularly to teach new songs to longer-serving road musicians and old
numbers to new recruits, both due to Bowie's habit of taking the
musicians from the latest album on the following tour if possible.

The core of Bowie's band at any time provides a vital component to
the sound; as the rhythm section it supplies the foundation for the other
textures that "specialists" are brought in to provide. Like Bowie's only
other real band (Ronson, Bolder and Woodmansey) neither Alomar,
Davis nor Murray seem to have any ego problems, saving Bowie's and
Visconti's energy for any touchier visitors.

The use of "guest" musicians on his recordings has long been Bowie's
way of tipping his hat at those he admires. It allows him insight into the
workings of others, a chance to exploit an extant sound, or even to send
a kind of calling card to other rock greats, the likes of Bruce Springsteen,
Todd Rungren, Frank Zappa and Lou Reed. Bowie has never lacked the
ability to turn on the charm when it mattered, though there are some
who have glowed in the warmth of Bowie's presence (and his treatment
of them) but cooled later in the realisation that all of the flattery might
not have been heartfelt. The actor in him has rarely been suppressed for
long.

The guest personnel on *Scary Monsters*, aside from Townshend and Fripp, were Chuck Hammer, then Lou Reed's guitarist, and Roy Bittan who'd played on *Station To Station* and who is a member of Springsteen's E Street Band. Andy Clark played synthesizer and Michi Hirota contributed a Japanese vocal on *It's No Game*, along with back-up singers Lynn Maitland and Chris Porter. Bowie's standing and his reputation for good musical taste would make an invitation to record with him attractive to most; but John Rockwell questioned how someone as physically slight and seemingly vulnerable as Bowie could take command of a group of strong and individualistic personalities for a session. In truth, his aura of vulnerability has always been more of a matter of calculated image, for public consumption, than real. At work in the studio, Bowie has been able to use a combination of clarity of vision, sureness of purpose, a deep understanding of music and the ability to play temperaments off against eachother to good effect. Due to Bowie's frequent self-deprecating remarks, many of his musical associates (from Mott The Hoople to Nile Rodgers) have expressed surprise at just how thorough his knowledge of music is. It shouldn't really be surprising of a man who plays sax, guitar, piano and synthesizer and can tease the requisite four notes from a cello, koto, anvil or whatever's needed.

The *Scary Monsters* experience begins, as so often with a Bowie album on the cover. This one features a composite drawing and photo illustration of Bowie as Pierrot. It is subtly disturbing, an only slightly made up head coming out of an outrageous costume by Natasha Kornilov, but the shadow image with the shrivelled hand and cigarette has a nicely unwholesome and creepy feel to it. The sleeve contains visual references to *Low*, *"Heroes"* and *Lodger*, implying that this is a continuation of the trilogy, while the legs of *Aladdin Sane* serve to suggest that the difference between *Scary Monsters* and its predecessors is the rock orientation (besides, *It's No Game* was allegedly from the *Aladdin* sessions). Grittiness was back in Bowie's style, and the timing was right because one more piece of mood music just might have forced a large number of his fans to write Bowie off.

Scary Monsters has been called "the realist's David Bowie album" and it jumps right into its particular reality. After a few seconds of extraneity --Bowie underwater in the studio --the band grinds into *It's No Game*, (a song which also ends the album), putting everything on the line. The Japanese vocals by Michi Hirota come on like machine-gun fire and Bowie wails/moans his way through, singing some of his most straightforward lyrics on vinyl. "Silhouettes and shadows watch the revolution" while Bowie conjures up images provocative of thought, some aimed at the parochial and politically naive American audiences (the Japanese works as a reminder) by way of lines like "Children 'round the world/Put camel shit on the wall/Making carpets on treadmills/or garbage sorting". *It's No Game* sets the tone for the album; Bowie screams for Fripp to stop playing, and though Fripp complies, the world is less ready to be screamed into submission.

The mood changes somewhat with the vocal entre' on *Up The Hill Backwards*, a song which at one point had the tentative and rather mysterious title of "Cameras In Brooklyn". This song had some unrealized potential and includes Fripp's weakest playing on the album, although it does provide a breather before the title song, which Bowie voices in a Cockney accent through a vocoder (very subtly tuned) to create a sibilant effect that gives the track an icy rather than totally chilling timbre. The song is frequently compared to Joy Division's *She's Lost Control*; not only is the theme similar, but Bowie's treatment mimicks Joy Division's relentless monotone, though it boasts a delicate melody (and an intriguing singing style) which keep it interesting and in Bowie's repertoire. The *Scary Monsters (And Super Creeps)* plaguing this woman are the same ones chasing Bowie, though his get an airing in *Teenage Wildlife*. Dennis Davis got a workout on that tune, but was allowed to sit back for the next number.

Ashes To Ashes (which many mistakenly think is the album title) was THE hit song, the hit to match the one that inspired it *Space Oddity*), though it seems slightly out of place on this album with its bouncing rhythm and piano compliments of Roy Bittan. *Ashes* also inspired a video, the source of the Pierrot costume which defined the image of the album, and the tape deserves a mention in its own right. One of the distinctive gestures of *Ashes* (which appears again in *Fashion*) is the sweeping downward arc of the arm with which Bowie and his female attendants touch the ground. A ritualistic movement, it brings Major Tom down to earth, reinterpreting his story.

With cryptic and loaded lyrics, *Ashes* has been the subject of much analysis, usually because the song relates to *Space Oddity*. In the revised version Major Tom is a junkie and his isolation no longer sublime. Says Tom: "I want an axe to break the ice/I want to come down right now". The track features a wierdly disembodied sound, a throwback to Bowie's predilection for such pure spiritual music the likes of *Word On A Wing* from *Station To Station*. This ethereal sound is largely culled from Chuck Hammer's electronic guitar (guitar synthesizer) producing a sound he'd developed and called "cathedral guitars". While Fripp was always the ace at contributing grittiness, Hammer had the glory sound that Bowie was looking for on this song. *Ashes To Ashes* is so subtle that it needs to be listened to very loud on good hifi on which it can be appreciated that what sound like vocal "oohs" and "ahs" aren't necessarily voices. A writer for Rolling Stone asked: 'Will anyone realize that the curious, ethereal thrumming in the background is actually Chuck Hammer's guitar synthesizer overdubbed four times?' Visconti deserves much of the credit for the technical development of achieving this transcendental sound; the bass player in him keeps the beat prominent, holding the song down, with Murray's bass in particular taking the song from funk to funky.

Aside from the fact that Major Tom was originally asked whose shirts he wore, there seems no other obvious connection between *Ashes To Ashes* and *Fashion* save that they both became runaway hits. Murray and

Davis continue to hold the fort on *Fashion* but the track ends up being Fripp's song. (This is rock, and that means guitar, and while Bowie has described Fripp as rather intellectual, a theorist and co-chinwagger, Fripp has always been one to throw the theorising out the window, march into a studio and lay down some blasting rock solos given half a chance.) To match the guitar playing, Bowie's lyrics are right on target and it was no accident that *Fashion* was so damn danceable since the full irony can only be played out on a disco dance floor, the setting of the promo video which continues Bowie's pro-multi-racial-theme and includes some inspired, funny and absurd dancing. Bowie was one of the first artists to mimic the lip-sync convention of music video-making, featuring a mike stand with no mike and a bass pedal without a bass drum. *Fashion* anticipates Malcolm McLaren's implementation of old-time square dance calls, and its lyrics are a string of metaphors in which the terminology of fashion, dance and politics are interchangeable. Delusion is the message of the whole album and one line from *Fashion*, "They do it there but they don't do it here", sums it up.

Teenage Wildlife, opening the second side, would have been served well by the full funk and screech treatment, but the song doesn't really come alive until the chorus and the final verse. Rather autobiographical, with reference to the "new wave boys", it comes across as Bowie either confronted by himself as a teenager or by some other "teenage millionaire" taking his example from Bowie. The song deserves a lyric reading along with a listen for its fine drawing of a superstar, worshipped, then finally murdered by the ultimate fan whose credo is: "I miss you/he had to go." While Bowie wails that he's not a piece of teenage wildlife, he protects himself from the wildlife always trying to corner him by claiming that he doesn't "Know any hallways", the spots they tend to pick.

Hammer and Fripp both play on *Wildlife* which at one time had the working title of "It Happens Everyday". As it turns out, not all the wildlife surrounding Bowie is teenage; the night Chuck Hammer first met David Bowie was also the same night Lou Reed and David had a big bust-up. After a Reed concert, a large group went to a Chinese restaurant; after much saki had been downed, Lou Reed asked Bowie to produce his next album. Bowie told Reed he'd have to clean up his act; Reed slapped Bowie, and called him a faggot for good measure.

The theme of the next song on the album, *Scream Like A Baby*, is also murder, a throwback to the psychotic *Running Gun Blues* from *The Man Who Sold The World*. The subject is named Sam (as in Son Of...), calling to mind Travis Bickel and other "saviors". The narrator might be Alex of 'A Clockwork Orange', the survivor "learning to be part of society" while Sam can't. *Scream Like A Baby* is wrenching, a good lead into *Kingdom Come*, a Tom Verlaine song which, in the Bowie version, somehow lacks a sense of either defiance or deliverance. The song's point of view must have appealed to Bowie, very much in keeping with a second side that cries "it's all in vain". The song could have been a match for *Ashes To Ashes*, with its similar arrangement, but in place of the *Ashes'* transcendent quality *Kingdom Come* becomes beleagured and oppressive -— "I won't be breaking no rocks when the Kingdom comes", sings Bowie, but with little sense of just when the Kingdom *will* come.

Because You're Young is a scathing, supposedly mature study of young love, but Pete Townshend's usually exhuberant guitar can't pull this song out of its doldrums, with its depressingly two dimensional picture of love ("it's love front to back and no sides").

A reprise *It's No Game* completes the album, though the treatment is a startling contrast to the original. In place of aggression, Bowie is calm and measured, every word of lyric clearly enunciated. Cool and unemotional this time, Bowie leaves the listener with a sharp sense of the sounds and visions of the world, not the flat postcard view of *Lodger*, but a vibrant one, focusing on the rich, teeming life of a big city. It's a world of crime, violence, oppression and alienation; not themes unique to Bowie perhaps, but rarely tackled in such depth by an artist so much part of the mainstream of popular music.

The outsider's view that so fascinates Bowie the songwriter also appealed to Bowie the actor, and thus it was that he came to play the part of John Merrick, The Elephant Man, on Broadway. The role was offered to him at a most opportune moment, as A Broadway play was a useful device for attracting media attention without having to hit the road on tour again (indeed tour plans were cancelled when the role opened up). Bowie's name on the marquee undoubtedly boosted the play's run; his appearances were consistently sold-out, one critic noting that 'There were more than the usual number of people in the audience wearing designer jeans,' which must rank as one of the most low-key forms of dress for Bowie fans.

Bowie got the part thanks as much as anything to his flair for being in the right place at the right time. He met the play's director Jack Hofsiss while he was in New York to do the *Saturday Night Live* show (as usual blowing a few minds by playing with the chroma key) having visited the play (which was already on Broadway in an original cast production). Bowie loved the role, and though it hadn't actually been offered to him he and Hofsiss began to discuss the possibilities. When Bowie was back in NYC recording *Scary Monsters*, Hofsiss got in touch and asked if he'd consider taking over the role at the end of 1980 on Broadway. Being Bowie's first venture in legit theatre (not without some risks to his reputation) it was decided that he'd try out on the West Coast with the touring company and if all went well he would take over on Broadway in the fall.

In the event, things could hardly have gone better; as John Merrick, Bowie enjoyed a success that more than made up for the blot on his credibility as an actor that was *Just A Gigolo*. In a logical progression typical of Bowie's career(s), it was after seeing Bowie in concert and in *The Man Who Fell* that Hofsiss considered Bowie right for the part. Merrick's physical and spiritual isolation from comfortable society had much in common with Bowie's musical characterisations, and, said Hofsiss, 'Bowie's perceptions about the part and his interest were so good that we decided to investigate the possibility of doing it.' Amongst all the accolades there were a few critics who suggested that the role was "actor proof", but one of his co-stars came to the rescue, praising gallantly his immense concentration, a quality he brings to everything he does. There was more than just concentration as Concetta Tomei (Mrs. Kendal in the play) mentioned to Kurt Loder of Rolling Stone:

> First of all, The Elephant Man is a wonderful role, and if you
> really are concentrated about what you're doing, you almost
> can't lose — unless you just can't memorize lines and walk on
> stage. It's a role in which you draw people to you to begin with.
> David apparently has no acting background to speak of, and
> consequently he really has no "technique", as we know Gielgud
> and Olivier as having. *But* Bowie has the technique of
> magnetizing people, and that is something you just can't learn
> in a school or out of books. The guy is an actor, and you can't
> really water it down. He's not a rock performer going into
> acting — he's an actor. [3]

Bowie talked to Rolling Stone himself about his approach to the role — an approach quite typical of his hunger for first-hand experience.

> My immediate reaction was to go to the London Hospital
> Museum, which is still retained in a sort of 1840's brick
> building. And there, among all the other debris of mankind, was
> the plaster cast of the bits and pieces of Merrick, and also the
> church he made (a wooden model of a church visible from his
> room) and his hat and cloak. It made me aware for the first time
> of how grotesque he was — and the plaster sculptures are quite
> stunningly grotesque. And the cap itself is so sad, with this little
> mask down the front. It must have been a dreadful burden. [4]

Bowie took over the role from Philip Anglon, a young unknown, who'd gone through a similar process of initiation (looking at photos rather than going to London), but Hofsiss and Anglon had also already established the outlines of the performance, the method of portraying Merrick's creeping malformation and his attitude towards it. The basic conceit inherent in casting a remarkably handsome young man to portray the disease-ridden and hideous Merrick was designed to avoid alienating the audience, and while Anglon wasn't the box-office name that his successor was, he did have some insights into the portrayal and character that hint at why Bowie was such an excellent choice. About Merrick, Anglon said:

> He had great nobility and dignity and of course, it's very
> important that he's played that way. The secret to playing that
> part is that it must be played in a way that is totally *unsentimental*,
> without a shred of self-pity. As soon as you start asking for pity

you're finished.

He went on to suggest why the part may have been tailor-made for Bowie.

> The role demands the training of a dancer, the voice of an opera singer, and the imagination of an extraordinary painter or of a Fellini.

With all the right qualities, Bowie magnetized and mesmerized audiences, impressed with his acting as well as his charisma. While critics were raving that "Bowie seems to have been sculpted to play the role", the technique of embodying Merrick's contortion (playing the role with no make-up and scant costume) had theatre- and rock concert-goers alike thinking it Bowie's innovation. The fact that Bowie had to visit a chiropractor after each performance was duly reported; as Bowie explained: 'After a show you can't just suddenly lean up out of that position — you'll break your spine or something'. Bowie admitted having become progressively happier and freer over the last few years and, by the end of 1980, things were at a high point. He had made a triumphant Broadway debut, and was enjoying his moment as the toast of New York City, riding high on the raves he was receiving both for the play and for *Scary Monsters*. With the RCA contract fulfilled, he seemed more than ever anxious to further his acting career (to be followed by directing). As 1980 headed towards 1981, the only shadow on David's horizon was John Lennon's death, which occurred while Bowie was in New York. While the world had lost an icon, Bowie had lost a friend in a manner disturbing on several levels. He'd just written a song, *Teenage Wildlife*, that tragically could be applied to Lennon as well as himself. He'd imagined a time "When the fans had killed the man" way back when, and watching the imagined become reality is its own kind of horror. Bowie claimed to have merely gone through the motions in his last few *Elephant Man* performances following Lennon's murder, and once the show closed he removed himself from the public eye for more than two years.

FIFTEEN

'But the film is a saddening bore/'Cause I wrote it ten times before/It's about to be writ again/As I ask you to focus on...'

'Life On Mars' — *Hunky Dory*

There were both practical and personal reasons for Bowie's two year hiatus from the public eye, the practical having much to do with Bowie the businessman. By 1979 he had extricated himself from all managers, opting instead for a small coterie of professionals handling his accountancy, publicity and financial requirements. His own management/production company had been dubbed Bewlay Brothers after the song or its inspiration. Reflecting his seeming ability to switch press attention on and off at his whim, scarcely a public word about Bowie's goings-on made print between 1981 and early 1983. There was talk in the trades that he was record label shopping — those who considered themselves most in the know were convinced that he'd pick Warner Brothers for their extensive film and TV holdings. Bowie surprised almost everyone by eventually signing with EMI, an announcement made at the beginning of '83, in conjunction with news of an album and tour. Bowie had been living in Switzerland for several years now, keeping up the travel schedule that had become the dominant feature of his lifestyle since he'd taken to the air again. Over the years Bowie might have been found in any corner of the globe (and in any setting from the humblest to the most elegant), at one moment descending on a city almost in the manner of a State visit, at another passing unnoticed. His son Zowie (now being called Joey) was attending school in Switzerland, and hardly a public statement in recent years missed attributing a new, more positive and forward-looking outlook to the fact that he is now entirely responsible for his son. Whenever possible, Joey travels with his father. Bowie has taken up skiing, the native sport of his adopted homeland, as well as a martial arts regimen, concentrating on boxing particularly, exercise which helps relax him and develop his reflexes.

While taking a temporary break from the music scene (biding his time in the interest of the best deal presumably), Bowie plunged into film and television work with a number of projects. In keeping with his new role as self-made businessman, Bowie's new image is corporate chic, and lately he has taken to looking like a cross between a Swiss banker and a model for Italian Vogue. Music continued as the Bowie business' bread and butter, with film and television seeming the direction for the future. Bowie had been writing and producing for both mediums for some time (by way of a hobby, if nothing else) and while the acting offers continued to flow, his long-range thoughts were turning more towards directing, until his choice of parts become heavily influenced by what he felt he could learn on any potential project. With his reputation as an actor now fairly well established, Bowie began to talk about himself more and more as a director ('I really am a film director' to which he might have added 'and have been ever since I was David Jones'). Should he become a director, and a successful one, perhaps his next challenge will be painting, with the claim that a painter is "really" what he is and has been all along.

Having developed a hunger to learn about the process of film-making, Bowie took on a variety of projects. He appeared in a BBC production of Bertold Brecht's *Baal*, an early work that probably wouldn't have survived were it not for Brecht's later success; as usual Bowie's task was to portray a rather offbeat character, but, almost more importantly, the assignment gave him the chance to work in video, and with the highly stylized music and writing of Brecht. RCA released a soundtrack album. Bowie also made a cameo in-concert appearance in *Christian F*, though he had no role as such in that film. He did claim that he thought the movie would scare kids away from experimentation with heroin, which may have been his primary reason for doing the film, taking the opportunity as it came to support and participate in the German cinema.

These were relatively small projects, but the other two major film roles that Bowie took on during this period are quite different and indicate the diversity of motivations behind his film work. Bowie was offered a part in a feature called *The Hunger* directed by Tony Scott (brother of Ridley, of *Alien* and *Blade Runner* fame); in this case it seems to have been as much the make-up artist, the female leads and the theme of aging as the role which appealed to him. It was his work with make-up man Dick Smith that Bowie talked about most frequently in interviews for the movie, relishing the chance to work with one of the best in the business in a field (make-up, masks and disguise) that has has long fascinated Bowie. The tremendous job of having Bowie age several hundred years in days allowed him to spend hours under Smith's hands, the resulting physical transformation was nothing short of spectacular. Bowie got to camp with black hair and in seventeenth century garb complete with cello, aside from playing a romantic lead opposite Catherine Deneuve and Susan Sarandon. It was Sarandon's praises that Bowie came away singing, calling her 'pure dynamite' (and later appearing with her on the front page of the New York Post in a cosy photo from a post-concert party together with the ubiquitous Keith Richards). Some people actually liked the movie (most agreed that Bowie was quite good) though the critics panned it. Bowie made his exit less than half an hour into the film, from which point it degenerates into soft-core porn featuring Deneuve and Sarandon as vampire lovers. Reaction to the film was very much a question of taste. It didn't go over too well with serious critics or for that matter with Bowie himself, though he compensated for the frivolity of *The Hunger* by choosing his next film project for the director (cast, location and script helped too) and with an eye to furthering his reputation as well as his education.

Bowie's next role (between filming and release of *The Hunger*, which released just before Bowie's '83 tour was launched) was in Nagisa Oshima's *Merry Christmas Mr. Lawrence*. The "official" account of Bowie's association with Oshima emphasizes coincidence; Oshima went to see Bowie in *The Elephant Man* and 'I knew immediately that he (Bowie) was Celliers. He has an inner spirit that is indestructible, and that is what *Merry Christmas Mr. Lawrence* is all about. The inner human spirit that war cannot touch.' While Oshima did later make those comments, Bowie's story that Oshima then came backstage and 'asked me if I'd be interested in working with him', rather too conveniently fits the standard Bowie mold, and jars somewhat with Oshima's own version of events. According to the director, it was Bowie's appearance in a Japanese saki commercial (the project which prompted the song *Crystal Japan*) that first attracted Oshima's attention after Robert Redford had turned down the role of Celliers. Oshima then sent Bowie a screenplay; the following is Oshima's lengthy account of what then transpired:

> He replied that he was very excited by it and wanted to meet me. When I went to New York to meet him, he was appearing in *The Elephant Man* on Broadway. He sent me tickets and asked me to see the play before we met. I saw it and he was very good, perhaps too good. I don't really like actors who are so exceedingly good. Rather, I prefer actors with abundance of heart and deficiencies of strength...
>
> The next day we met at his office. Now, I had always imagined David Bowie as being heavily made-up and surrounded by bodyguards, and so forth. But he came in wearing a white shirt and white slacks and with just one female assistant. He struck me as being very plain. He was unassuming, unpretentious, straightforward, and down to earth. He spoke candidly. At the end of the meeting I thought we should talk about what he should be paid, but he shrugged it off and said we could talk about that later — he had already decided he wanted to work with me.
>
> I asked him if he wanted to do the music for the film, but I was a little apprehensive because I didn't want people to get the impression that I had cast him in the film in order to get his music. Above all I wanted people to appraise him as an actor. He advised me that the script had to be improved, and I asked if he might recommend a screenwriter to work on it, but he wasn't insistent about exerting any control in that realm. He just wanted to concentrate on his role. I think that the purity of character comes out clearly in the film. [1]

Bowie did concentrate on his character and with his strong sense of what was right for him to do, he ended up changing the way several scenes were played. He did suggest Paul Mayersberg to rewrite the script, the same man who'd tailored the screenplay of *The Man Who Fell To Earth* and though Mayersberg helped bring some things around to a more Western perspective, the reorientation wasn't a complete success. While Bowie was generally pleased (especially with Oshima's working methods and his relationships with cast and crew), he did make the comment that if an English production team had portrayed the Japanese the way the Japanese portrayed the English, it would have been accused of racism. This is slightly ironic coming from Bowie, who's been quoted as saying that one of the things he loves about the Japanese is that the boys are all perfect little queens who suddenly turn into samurai. Indeed this cruel stereotype might be considered the crux of Bowie-as-Cellier's relationship with his Japanese captor in the film. Bowie was excellent at points in the movie (especially in the climactic burial-in-the-sand sequence) though his overall performance suffers somewhat by comparison with a supporting cast which happened to turn in phenomenal performances. Ryuichi Sakamoto, a Japanese rock star, who took a role in the film rather reluctantly as Oshima's price for letting him score the music, was brilliant as Yonio, as was Tom Conti's Lawrence, but one of Oshima's most rewarding casting choices was stand-up comic Beat Takeshi, who played off Conti and brought a powerful element of humanity to the film.

With such competition, critics were still mostly happy to forgive Bowie any and all faults and attribute them to the director, though it was amusing to hear film critics describe Bowie's role as "remote, austere, cold", all the standard words for describing him until their recent replacement by "positive, optimistic, warm" etc. And part of the reason for this shift in association is Bowie's visual image, the P.R. and the music on his most recent album and, as one thing leads to another in Bowie's career, some debt is owed to his experience in the production of *Merry Christmas Mr. Lawrence*.

While it's almost impossible to find a photograph showing a *smiling* David Bowie at any time over the first fifteen years of his career, his exposure to the deceptively dissimilar media of feature film and video had taught him something that few have yet learned: that while smiles rarely work on the big screen, they are precisely what the more intimate video format responds to. Thus armed with a brand new set of caps (installed after *Merry Christmas*), Bowie has taken to the awesome breakthrough of smiling for the video cameras while most other rock stars still think that a James Dean scowl is *de rigueur* for the promo.

When Bowie set off for Rorotonga ('the second most beautiful place in the world') for filming, the record deal with EMI was apparently final, so he was able to combat the isolation of the South Seas and the long hours of waiting around the set by consciously programming his musical environment. He was going through the now familiar process which he once described for Record magazine:

There's always a vacillation in my mind between trying to

experiment with new sounds but also to find the original
earthly enjoyment that I felt for music when I first started
playing it. [2]

To this end, Bowie dug 'way back' through his extensive record
collection, choosing to take with him things that could be listened to
over and over without boredom and which he could enjoy without
becoming inclined to over-analyze. He was as interested in the spirit as
much as the music so his selections included the Alan Freed Rock and
Roll Orchestra, Buddy Guy, Elmore James, Albert King and Stan
Kenton -- 'I took a lot of Stan Kenton'. In the interests of erasing his
footprints, he was coy about mentioning Benny Goodman, from whom
he ended up borrowing a title for his next album and hit song. In sharp
contrast to his past attitudes about his music in general and his vinyl
output in particular -- he always used to discuss a song in terms of a
polaroid, a crystallized moment in time -- with *Let's Dance* Bowie seems
to have been out to create something enduring. After the album
released, Bowie described it as just a sketch and said that with it he 'only
touched the edge' of what he wanted to do, without explaining too
clearly what it was he had set out to achieve. The album takes a familiar
tack of drawing on sounds that are fundamental (in terms of rock
history) but reworked so that they come across as thoroughly modern
-- at least to ears too young to know that Bowie hadn't just invented
jazz and blues yesterday.

Work on *Let's Dance* began right around the New Year of 1983 which
with two scheduled movie releases, the first album in nearly three years
and a world tour, was fast shaping into the Year of David Bowie. He
began the year by turning thirty-six, announcing that he was back in he
studio and that he had signed a recording contract with EMI. The
financial arrangements between Bowie and EMI aroused quite a bit of
curiosity, turning principally on the question of whether he was
receiving seventeen or a paltry ten million for the five record deal;
reports that his fee was to be paid in Swiss Francs may account for the
confusion over the precise figure. Whatever the amount, all the early
indications are that EMI made a shrewd investment; 1983's promotional
blitzkrieg put Bowie on the cover of everything from Time to the
National Enquirer.

Bowie kicked off his formal association with EMI by appearing at
press conferences in both London and New York, spreading the
message that "Bowie is Back", while also presenting himself as the
penultimate music-businessman and clean-living guy; the questions
about music were relatively few, with the massed forces of the press
rather more interested in his lifestyle (factophiles please note: Bowie
wakes up at 6.30 a.m --NO!). Both conferences degenerated into photo
sessions to which Bowie submitted with a slight sense of embarrassment. In the meantime there were a few announcements about what he
was up to, and some interest aroused by his choice of Nile Rodgers of
Chic as his producer. Aside from the fact of David's break with Visconti

(part of a clean break Bowie wanted to make, partly the result of some comments Visconti made about David's and Angie's sexual escapades back in Haddon Hall), the fact that Rodgers was black seemed some kind of statement in itself. Bowie also picked a young white and excellent blues guitarist to play lead, debunking a few stereotypes and stressing one of the intentional undercurrents of the *Let's Dance* project.

While all the talk and interviews helped stir interest, it was the sounds on the album that finally counted for most, producing three hit singles in the process. One of the main reasons that Bowie keeps making music, the reason that he chose it as his artistic starting-point, is that music is the most instantaneous and all-pervasive of the arts. "Pop" hits are nowadays heard almost simultaneously in Rome and Rio, in Glen Falls and Glasgow, for all the arcane shortcomings of the record distribution system; in contrast movies and even exported TV shows like *Kojak* and *Columbo* can take years to make their way around the world. *Let's Dance* was heard all over the globe in '83, on all manner of frequencies (making Bowie almost as omnipresent as Julio Iglesias!). All this testifies to the influences of a man gone from London boy to European man, to international icon. Bowie might be almost as effective on film, but you have to *go* and see films while the music seeks you out.

Over the years Bowie's music has developed an international and across-age accessibility that is rather amazing. While the so-called "art rock" bands have based their music largely on jazz idioms, Bowie took the music that he grew up with, threw in elements (some of the best) of every style that he'd worked in from R&B to funk, bypassing rock to go right back to the blues, placing the jazz feel firmly on the surface (jazz being one of the most international of styles), and he came up with *Let's Dance*. The fusion of American and European styles is what Bowie considers his own contribution; the European influence is a 'specific thematic mastery in terms of motif and melody' which he finds distinctive, while the American is the music itself. Bowie got what he claimed he wanted from *Let's Dance*, 'something that makes a statement in a more universal, international field.'

The 'positive' orientation (sometimes undercut by the lyrics and the mood) of any of Bowie's works testifies to the influence of many younger musicians who've chosen to reaffirm that spirit of rock music. *Let's Dance* features love songs and what by Bowie's standards can only be described as out-and-out pop tunes, perhaps specifically intended for the widest possible commercial impact; a new label, the first new product in ages, and a new Bowie. But the particular musical fusion that Bowie pulls off is perhaps the most unique element of the album, and it seems that one of the first sparks towards what the album became was struck when Bowie saw Stevie Ray Vaughn perform (on a bill with Muddy Waters) in Montreux in the summer of '81. Said Bowie:

> He really bowled me over with his playing; I thought he was one of the most exciting new guitarists I'd seen in years. I tried all out to get him to work with me, which fortunately he did...

Thus Bowie recreated that Buddy Guy Albert King thing that he wanted as the real foundation of the record.

With the blues as a base, the next piece of the *Let's Dance* puzzle fell into place when Bowie returned from the jungles of Rorotonga to the jungle of NYC, where he met Nile Rodgers in a club. When they realized they had much in common musically and in background, the plan of working together evolved naturally. With Rodgers secured as producer (he has an excellent reputation for disco/dance) and with studio time booked, Bowie called Stevie Ray one morning at 4 a.m.; in Vaughn's words: 'it was get up and make sense quick time'. The rest of the crew was brought in by Rodgers, composed largely of people who had worked with Chic. The horn section was borrowed from the Asbury Jukes (whom Rodgers recently produced), and in another racial turnaround, the Simms Brothers (who just happen to be two white guys) were recruited for background vocals. Confounding stereotypes can be a lot of fun, and the Simms do it in style. Carmine Rojas, on bass, was excellent both in the studio and on stage in the subsequent tour, and looks a good bet to be part of the Bowie set-up for some time to come.

With all the Chic sidemen (whose extensive credits also include Propaganda, Weather Report *et al*) more of a Chic sound might have been expected, but instead the common ground that Bowie and Rodgers discovered (highlighted by the mixing mastery of Bob Clearmountain) is what infuses the sound of the album. Both men mention Arthur 'Red' Prysock (also one of Elvis' favorites) as well as several other artists as common influences but it seems that production-wise their meeting point was a focus on arrangements, the horn parts in particular. Rodgers talked to Nelson George about how he got into music in the first place. 'I studied orchestration, big bands, harmony... I mean, I've got a library on orchestration at home that's up to the ceiling.' He went on to describe his approach to the Bowie project: 'I wrote the arrangements based on the demos (three days work for Bowie). When they were played against the tracks, David and I would make some alterations, but nothing very radical. We really heard the music the same way and didn't have a major disagreement over any musical point.' A few more words from Rodgers on working with Bowie echo statements that all of his collaborators have made.

> Unlike some of the groups I've worked with in the past...David has a deep understanding of music. He knows a lot more than he gets credit for. We spent time discussing chords, notes and different approaches to music. At one point, David was so enthusiastic about capturing that rock 'n' roll flavor that he wanted to cut everything live — rhythm, horns and vocals. That's how open he was to doing the unusual.

One thing that Rodgers also found amazing was that from initial discussions to the final mix the whole project took only five weeks, 'the fastest I've ever worked in my life'. A convert, he's realized thus:

> It's just about the most energetic way to make records. The
> musicians were really pumped up because of the fast pace, and
> as a result we got some great performances. [3]

Which is a fact.

The first of the great performances belongs to Bowie himself, this
time in the role of "the singer" (though he has called *Let's Dance* a 'singer's
album,' he also described his role as more of a 'composer than anything
else'). The album opens with a tune called *Modern Love*, and it may as well
be a song for the fans. The accompanying video was made from concert
clips and the faces of the fans say more about modern love (even if the
love on those faces is for Bowie) than the lyrics contribute. The song is a
treat for older fans with the opening, deeply spoken lines of "I don't
want to go out/I want to stay inside/Get things done" -- quintessential
Bowie reminiscent of *Low*. When the drums enter they do so with the
beat that is there for the rest of the album, Stevie Ray adds some special
recipe guitar licks and then piano and horns enter to turn this into a
barrelhouse rocker, though nothing on this album is "pure" anything.
The sound itself is minimal but complex. There are no "depressive
effects" on drums or any other instrument; each part enhances the next
with plenty of space provided by Clearmountain's clean mix. As for the
lyrics and structure, Bowie begins with the statement that "Things
don't really change", and this idea dictates the form of the circular
chorus, with each line advancing from and negating the previous one
simultaneously. It's a great pop song for all of these reasons, though it
had to wait its turn as the third single release.

With the song order reversing the single release order, *China Girl*, the
album's second track, begins with a jokey guitar riff conjuring a
parochial evocation of the Orient, but the tune, written with Iggy Pop,
moves away from the jokes and allows the guitar to take off. The *China
Girl* is the "real woman" of all dreams, and the statements directed to
her are some of the clearest and most straightforward ever on the
colonial relationship of the sexes, with lines (to her) like "I'll give you
television/I'll give you eyes of blue/I'll give you man who wants to rule
the world." Her response is the desired one: "Oh baby, just you shut
your mouth." The lyrics with the vocal inflection make this a standout
line, one that works well in conjunction with the videotape where the
woman's words are given back to her, though they're in Bowie's voice.
The tape provides the most intimate picture yet of a smiling yet coy
Bowie, and the effect is direct enough to be almost embarrassing. The
video offers touches of humor, (so funny that Bowie spits out his
cigarette), the kind of 360 degree pan that cinema buffs die for
(borrowed from some of Bowie's favorite directors) and a final scene of
lovemaking on the beach which evokes a hundred legendary movies,
proving that Bowie knows his film history and realizes the future of
pornography on TV. (There is a "family" edit, and one available to more

risque' TV outlets). *China Girl* was first recorded by Iggy Pop and there are some who prefer his version, but Iggy didn't have the popular base to make the song a hit even with Bowie's help, so perhaps Bowie was doing the song and the Ig a favor.

Let's Dance is one of the slipperiest songs on the album and in some ways a surprising hit. It's surprising because, although some of musical devices are familiar, the structure and arrangement aren't. The instrumental parts play all around the beat, with a dub-like sound that makes the track work like reggae on the body while the ears are taken elsewhere. With the insistent drum intro and the rising vocal pyramid (compliments of the Simms') and a sudden break with the drums sitting back and the bass walking in, Bowie enters to beckon, "Let's dance". With the entry of the horns, the song is transformed and the arrangements that Rodgers and Bowie came up with (plus vocals and breaks) along with some rather tasteful licks by Stevie Ray, make *Let's Dance* as unique as anything that the industry has delivered in a while. It sways and somehow maintains a stateliness that some of Bowie's best known tunes are famous for, but it's much warmer than the likes of *Station To Station*. Sammy Figeroa's percussion deserves special mention, and indeed on the disco version his part is cranked up in a manner that does justice to his contribution.

All this by way of saying that the song is the product of a near perfect synthesis, suggesting a million things musically (Coltrane got credit for some of the horn break sounds) while being uncluttered, danceable and evocative. Its success was helped by being a poetic love song, with lines like "Fall into my arms and tremble like a flower", which Bowie milks for everything it's worth. At the same time the "serious moonlight", beneath which romance unfolds, delivers almost radioactive images, with Bowie wondering just what color "lights up your face". As is often the case with Bowie, the song's promo video adds layers of meaning to the lyrics. The apocalyptic imagery is reinforced by the video's flash of light. Bowie mentioned what the song evokes for him:

> There's a certain angst in the song; it's ostensibly a dance song, but there's a particular type of desperation and poignancy about it, for me, anyway. That comes from devising a lyric that's going for an altruistic love feeling and it just has a slightly evasive quality of desperation about it. [4]

The video has a slightly evasive quality about it. Claiming that videos are like little movies and that 'some movies can have a message', Bowie also talked about getting 'free point time' by dealing with real issues; the "real issue" in this case is racism.

Shooting the tapes for both *China Girl* and *Let's Dance* in Australia (quickly and simultaneously), Bowie explained that his love for the physical beauty of the country is marred by the disturbing treatment of the aborigines. Some of the video's shots and sequences are genuinely innovative, especially the uncommon decision to use real, reaction shots of the Australian drivers watching the aborigine girl scrub an inter-section, while her male counterpart drags a piece of heavy machinery down the street. But when the couple appear afterwards with their American Express card to be treated like any white couple with THE CARD would expect to be treated the comment is disturbingly simplistic. (Was it Bowie's card?)

The song which closes the first side is another love song, the first specifically written with the album in mind. *Without You* sets the tone and the level for the sentiments that find their way into other songs. The lyrics to *Without You*, with lines like "Woman I love you/Without you/What would I do", prompted considerable speculation among those for whom the intricacies of Bowie's personal life are objects of fascination. In discussing the inspiration for *Let's Dance* (and *Without You* presumably), Bowie claimed that he was singing to 'an imaginary person really...I wish I could say...' He went on to talk a bit about the feelings that have him writing in this vein. 'I think at the moment because there's no constant companion in my life or a great love, or whatever, the only great affection that I live with, on a day-to-day basis, is with my son. I think he's been a pivotal reason for why I'm writing about such a two-way relationship thing.' He went on to say that he's 'rather like a sailor' in his romantic relationships, but he nevertheless opted for his own variation on the love song for much of the material on *Let's Dance* because after all love is the foundation of pop music and this was the album on which he was aiming for universality. Being one of the simpler pieces on the album *Without You* served as a good blueprint for the rest of the material. All the tracks feature an instrumental intro, though here it's an almost unnoticed couple of drumbeats. Bowie's vocals are high register throughout, deepening occasionally (without resorting to crooning) but always delicate, and while the effect is slightly artificial it works emotionally -- he sounds vulnerable. *Without You* boasts a simple guitar line perfectly rendered, along with the fine drumming of Tony Thompson, Bernard Edwards' tight bass cameo and Bob Sabino's keyboards doing a delightful organ impression. If there'd been a fourth single this might have been it.

Ricochet is another great cut which does stylistically just what the title claims. The lyrics bring back Bowie as reporter, or at least observer, of the news, through what is more of a message song than anything else on *Let's Dance*. With its vision of mankind laid out in the first line, "Like weeds on a rock face waiting for the scythe", Bowie goes on to make the plight of the common man seem hopeless. Ricochet is the power to bounce back. The song's mood is set by the drum beat and the slightly denser, more monotonous sound from which there is some relief in the chorus. The production techniques (and ideas) make the cut. The most mysterious element sounds like an old recording of a radio broadcast (faintly reminiscent of the ambiance Lennon achieved in parts of *Revolution 9*), snatches of which are mixed in at a low volume. It's not clear whether Bowie is the speaker, but the words sound like his, especially the key and oft-repeated 'And who can bear to be forgotten?", an obsession that Bowie shares with most of mankind.

The next two tunes are covers. *Criminal World* is by the Metros and deals with recurring themes ("criminal world" is a line in *Fantastic Voyage* and the milieu of *Scary Monsters*). While the tune is quite engaging, it must have been the lyrics that prompted Bowie's choice of the song. The contrast between "your heavy reputation" and the discovery of (blackmail) secrets is something with which Bowie would have been able to identify. Discovery and exposure are a disaster; if you can't destroy your enemies, befriend them. Revisiting the world of *Rebel Rebel*, Bowie sings of the criminal world where "The boys are like baby-faced girls" and vice versa. The track boasts some very downbeat "uh oh's", courtesy of Frank and George Simms.

In *Cat People (Putting Out Fire)*, Bowie attempts a reinterpretation of a song for which he wrote the lyrics to Giorgio Moroder's music. Many wondered why he bothered, feeling the original could not be bettered, and blamed laziness (the song being already written). Bowie explained that he had wanted to do his own arrangement in a sparser vein, and there is also some thematic justification for including the song. The clever use of color names in *Let's Dance* ("Put on your red shoes, and dance the blues") might have been an expansion from *Cat People*, with its "eyes so red (green)" and "tears so blue", while the essential Bowie themes of age and time figure in the lyrics.

The moon is a key influence on the album; "serious moonlight" is both a phrase from the lyric of the title song and the name of the tour that followed. The red/green eyes of *Cat People* are described as "colder than the moon". The album's back cover features a reproduction of the painting 'Boxer and The Moon', by Derek Boshier, in which a fighter (the David Bowie of the front cover) is locked in a struggle with the rays of the moon, symbol of mysticism and creativity.

Let's Dance ends on a rather weak note, with *Shake It*, a fairly mediocre dance tune beefed up out of existence by horns, guitar and an overblown vocal arrangement. The song is almost funny, with its cliche'd dance music title reinforced by lines like "I could take you to heaven/I could spin you to hell/But I'll take you to New York/It's the place that I know well", while others are either coarse-romantic ("You're better than money") or echo those of earlier songs on the album. In *Modern Love*, Bowie states that "There's no sign of life/Just the power to charm", a moment of self-awareness similar to the one in *Shake It* when Bowie, talking to a faceless girl and wondering what to say, admits to himself that "my eyes do the talking so well". Hollowness and artifice permeate the feel of the music and, with the exception of *Ricochet*, the second side, while excellent musically, somewhat suggests Bowie was in a hurry to finish the album, and was prepared to lay down a couple of filler tracks.

While Bowie was in Australia working on the videos for *Let's Dance* and *China Girl*, Rolling Stone writer Kurt Loder caught up with him and they talked about several aspects of Bowie's music and attitude. Bowie described the simple and direct approach that he now strives for in the actual recording process as well as in the final sound, partly in response to the 'earnest New Music' (for which he was one of the major inspirations, but which he finds "me oriented", 'cold with its focus on style over content' and lacking in urgency). While some of the same accusations might be leveled at *Let's Dance*, the emphasis was quite different, as the songwriting clearly attests. These are stripped down pop songs –– compare the lyric sheet of *Space Oddity* to *Let's Dance*; there are more words in *Cygnet Committee* than on the whole later album –– Bowie claiming to have taken his cue in part from John Lennon. As Bowie quotes Lennon:

'Look, it's very *simple* –– say what you mean, make it rhyme and put a backbeat to it.' And, says Bowie:

he was right: Instant karma's gonna get you, *boom*. I keep coming back to that these days. He was right man; There is no more than that. There is *no more*.

Bowie then went on to discuss *Let's Dance*:

I've never admitted this before –– because it's never been true before –– but this album is kind of tentative. I mean, I only kind of touched the edge of what I really want to do. I want to go further, much further, with the next one. Rolling Stone: 'And what will that be then?' 'A protest album I suppose.' [5]

Which is just what Bowie said about *Diamond Dogs* prior to its release, so there may be a surprise in the works. It will be interesting to see just what form Bowie's "protesting" takes, though there may be some wait. Now that he can afford to give rein to his multiplicity of interests, there isn't the same urgency for an album every six months that there was in earlier days. Aside from other considerations, his product output will depend somewhat on the terms of his contract with EMI. As this is being written, Bowie is in Japan, on the last leg of a (free) world tour, taking in Western Europe, England, Canada, the U.S. and Japan. During (and even before) his tour, Bowie has been in the news almost constantly, with advance and after show articles, as well as pieces written on *The Hunger* and *Merry Christmas* and a plethora of those that focus on Bowie merely because he's a major celebrity. (These days, being a media figure makes you newsworthy.) His account alone could keep a clipping service in business, but in spite of the millions of words written (and spoken), real criticism is still a relatively rare commodity. By virtue of his talent and his celebrity, his new mantle of warmth and humility, Bowie has achieved the status of loved and living legend, and as such is almost above reproach. But somehow David Bowie has repelled criticism since his early days; it is as though the pundits have always been nervous that a negative word would rebound on them, in part testimony to Bowie's instinct for the surprising and the new. For this reason alone it's worthy of note that the one sour moment of the Serious Moonlight tour took place near the beginning in France; Dexy's Midnight Runners opened for Bowie at an outdoor concert, with soggy and impatient fans calling for Bowie during Dexy's entire set. Leader Kevin Rowland, as blunt as Bowie is tactful, basically told them to fuck off, explaining that Bowie wasn't so great and that if they'd listen they'd discover Dexy's was quite a bit better. While his argument didn't convince the fans, it did convince Bowie to terminate his association with this upstart and ingrate. Rowland's was the kind of unenviable situation that would have frustrated a younger Bowie, though he probably would have suffered in silence, vowing never to get himself into the same mess again. (In fact, his decision to be self-promoted during the Ziggy days was made to avoid just such situations.)

Otherwise the shows went well and smoothly, with Bowie traveling with much of the same band that played on the album. He featured Tony Thompson on drums, Carmine Rojas on bass, and the Simms brothers as back-up singers and as on-stage foils. There is a group of sax and various woodwind players which the program denotes as the "Borneo Horns", comprising Lenny Pickett, Steve Elson and Stan Harrison (the latter two are both on the LP) with Elson doubling on synthesizer. Also included in the touring group on synthesizers and piano was Dave Lebolt who has worked with both Billy Joel and John Cale. The band was rounded out by two regulars of long standing, both on guitar. Carlos Alomar directed the band as usual, and in place of Stevie Ray Vaughn (who couldn't make the tour for reasons neither Bowie nor Vaughn will fully disclose, though it seems Vaughn had other career priorities at the time fostered partly by the exposure given him by his association with Bowie), was Earl Slick whose problems with Bowie in '76, were buried with David welcoming him as someone who 'knows all the songs'.

Slick was finally given the up front exposure he'd been pining for way back when. It was his presence, and costume of jeans, headband and open shirt that helped Serious Moonlight look like a good old-fashioned rock 'n' roll show, complete with the guitar machismo which contrasted so sharply with the 1920's look of Frank and George Simms' striped jackets. Rojas and Alomar contributed an ersatz African feel with batik wraps and with Rojas in sandals, while the horns were off to the side on a Borneo safari. Bowie was liable to wear anything, though suits were favored, sometimes Swiss style, sometimes pin-striped, but somehow the potpourri of styles worked, in a sense creating the shows which were a visual counterpart both of *Let's Dance* and Bowie's career, with apparently disparate elements standing on their own and for their own values, while creating a larger and often unexpected whole.

The Serious Moonlight concerts were virtually unchanged throughout the tour, although they got tighter, and there were some moments of spontaneity in which the band was allowed to stretch out. The most memorable of these was *White Light/White Heat*, the last song of the first set, which Bowie turned over to the crew after some perfunctory stabs at the lyrics, allowing him a few extra moments to freshen up. From the audience's viewpoint the first half of the show flew by; aside from being a tight set it offered a great deal to think about and notice in terms of what was happening, why and how. Eyes that could be coaxed away from Bowie would have witnessed a remarkable lighting show compliments of a well co-ordinated computer, programmed and designed by Alan Branton with production overseen by former designer Eric Barrett. (One of the things that Bowie had most admired about Oshima was that during a five year production stoppage none of his key men had been prepared to work for anyone else. Bowie seems to inspire and desire a similar loyalty.) The colors of the lights were soft pure hues, the manoeuvers so complicated that each light required its own operator. Bowie commented on the set and the lighting, explaining his intentions:

> For this new tour, I felt the need to balance orthodox rock performance qualities against the dignified yet exotic and warm feel of an undefined location. I collaborated with Alan Branton to produce an almost paintbox colour asymmetrical lighting plot, so what we get I think is somewhere between a 50's Soul Show and the second act of "Hong Kong Harry!".

The highlight of the first set was not so much in new interpretations of old music, as an inspired D.J. job by D.B., with carefully, thought-out song programming producing a near revelation. Beginning with *Star*, which established the show's credentials, it followed up with *"Heroes"*, massaging the hopes of the audience. The treatment of *Life On Mars?* was rather like that given *"Heroes"*, reflecting Bowie's awareness that each person in an audience is there to find something particular, something subtlely unique. *Mars?* was bound to be on the shopping list of many of Bowie's older fans, as well as a personal favorite, but it was still shocking to hear Bowie reach all the way back to *Hunky Dory* days and pull that same voice out of the closet. At the same time the song underscored the role of the Simms Brothers, whose ability to match Bowie's voice almost perfectly and cover for him on the higher notes was uncanny.

After the slightly sweet disturbance of *Mars?* came the tension of *Scary Monsters (And Super Creeps)*, which would have been worthwhile for the the roving green lights alone, so that the strong performance was almost a bonus. The mood (and album progression) was continued with *Fashion* which, placed back-to-back with *Let's Dance*, gave as clear a statement on Bowie's current view of things as his fans could ask for. Dancing (and by extrapolation, life) was now perceived as an intimate matter of bodies in relationship rather than mere ego and aggression. Another good match was *Rebel Rebel*, performed out of control, suddenly sounding like a Velvet Underground tune, an impression reinforced when it was followed by *White Light/White Heat*.

The faithful used the break to choose between the seventeen-and the twenty-two dollar T-shirts, only to return to be greeted by the Duke,

Station To Station and a rousing second set "greatest hits" presentation. Bowie pulled out another personal favorite, an excellent rendition of *Sorrow*, following with more crowd pleasers in the way of *TVC-15*, *Fame* and what for many proved the emotional climax of the show, *Space Oddity* back to back with *Ashes To Ashes*. For *Space Oddity* Bowie was isolated (essential Major Tom) and slightly obscured from sight, in one of the shimmering waterfall columns that made up the open back of the stage. This rendition evoked shades of religious ecstacy, transformation and transcendance in some of the more susceptible members of the audience before the song (and the Major) were ritually buried in *Ashes*.

Those just coming to Bowie were rewarded with his most recent material, all performed with consummate style. *China Girl* received the most theatrical treatment of the entire show. The poor Yorick routine during *Cracked Actor* was a throwback all the way to the *Diamond Dogs* tour ('flashback' might be an apter word), but it boomeranged on San Francisco audiences who felt that Bowie's bored demeanor implied that he'd pulled the skull out of the trunk once too often.

The finale showed Bowie as a master craftsman in the performing arena. A review in the New York Times hailed Bowie as a "performance artist", though he is more of a showman than any of the current crop of "performance artists" will probably ever be. He understands that spectacle doesn't necessarily spell entertainment. The key lines of the songs chosen for the lead-out and the encores might have been written precisely for the purpose. Bowie finished off the set with *Stay* ("That's what I meant to say") followed by *Modern Love* ("Never wave bye-bye"), flattering audiences with their power to detain him, though in fact he was being whisked out of theatre and away even as fans were still swooning and clutching their moon balloons.

In cold type, a description of a Bowie concert may read contrived, calculated and stiff. And so it is, if contrived means choreographed, if calculated means calculated to give the fans what they pay for, if stiff means carefully staged. The fact remains that Bowie has no peer in performance; besides, no other rock act has the repertoire to inspire the kind of aural and visual experience that is David Bowie in performance.

While the New York shows were a triumph and the P.R. presented the whole tour as such, the fact is several of the dates weren't sold out. Cities such as San Francisco continue to resist Bowie's magnetism. He nevertheless had fun there, playing D.J. at a local radio station in the middle of the night before the show, and totally revamping his show with the emphasis on Ziggy material (since San Fran had missed that first time around). With all the ballyhoo and the Time covers, it takes a moment to accept that there are still some dark corners of the good ol' rockin' U.S. of A. that haven't succumbed to David Bowie, somewhere the music registers but the name does not, and yet others just beginning to perceive Bowie, but only in terms of his celluloid work.

SIXTEEN

'Future Legend'

'Future Legend' — *Diamond Dogs*

Bowie's former label (RCA) has already made clear that releases and rehashes of the same material (and maybe something "new" occasionally) can and probably will continue indefinitely. The same holds true for those products or productions over which Bowie retains control; were he ever to stop making music, that wouldn't stop the releases. What is now being called *Ziggy Stardust – The Motion Picture* is a case in point. This is the famous "Last Concert" footage shot at the Hammersmith Odeon by D. A. Pennebaker on the occasion of the final Ziggy show. Although the delays surrounding this film (and the soundtrack album, which RCA has already issued) had several causes, the fact that it finally surfaced in early 1984 seems appropriate. Due to the long shelf life of film, its release should maintain the momentum after the hoopla of the *Let's Dance* album, videos, the two feature films and the Serious Moonlight world tour has died down. Without going into the details of the business problems which in part accounted for the Ziggy film's long sojourn on the shelf, Bowie spoke in 1983 about his personal reasons for releasing the film now:

> That's something I couldn't look at for years. I was so fed up with him, it -- all that. But I dragged it out last year and had a look, and I thought, "This is a *funny film!* This boy used to dress like that for a living? My God this is funny! Incredible! Wait till my son sees this!" [1]

Zowie/Joey did, and he liked it, although Bowie explained that his son likes Captain Sensible too and that a lot of the recent British bands 'make Ziggy look like a bank clerk'. According to Bowie, the only other thing holding back the release of the material was that he wanted to remix the sound. 'I don't know what I was on when I mixed it the first time.'

The film had been shown previously by D. A. Pennebaker. It was received with wild applause and ovations, and is a treat for those who missed seeing Ziggy live for one reason or another. At the same time, one can almost read the reviews, before they're written. Correctly attributing major musical influence to Bowie/Ziggy, and the apparent control he exerted at that point, the Ziggy cosmology is lost in what is basically very theatrical rock. While all the elements were there, Bowie is now more subtle and controlled than he was at that early stage. Some reviewers see the movie as quaint, others find something vaguely frightening about the young London audience and breathe a sigh of relief that the past is past.

The archives of unreleased Bowie recordings are fairly extensive, and without predicting which songs might appear when, it seems certain that this horde will be picked through over time. The body of his writing, art and artwork, not originally intended for public consumption, is similarly extensive as is Bowie on video, be it experiment or slick promotional. The best known and most lavish tapes will probably be released commercially; several feature what seem like intentionally repeated motives (the backhand-face-wipe gesture, or the "bring it back down" arm sweep) which would give a compilation a feeling of integration. There are also several promo tapes going all the way back to the clips of *Space Oddity* from the *Love You Till Tuesday* film, on through *Rebel Rebel* and the beautiful black and white *Wild Is The Wind* tape. These items were primarily produced for record company and British television promotional use, but are of an enduring quality that suggests they will be packaged and released in some form or another. All manner of TV appearances by Bowie are immortalized on tape, ranging from talk show interviews to the BBC documentary *Cracked Actor,* and the Midnight Special performances; these may or may not be made commercially available with Bowie's imprimatur. Fear not for images of the idol, they exist and will continue to be manufactured and/or duplicated.

Bowie's immediate future will probably involve work on short videos; he's also indicated that he'll be playing the role of Abraham Lincoln in an *avant-garde* opera by Robert Wilson, to be staged in L.A. during the 1984 Olympics. As Bowie put it, his role will be limited to 'falling out of a balcony, I suspect'. Without time to write the music for the production, Bowie recommended to Wilson that he either get David Byrne or put Iggy Pop and Phillip Glass together 'and see what comes up'. 1984 would seem like a good year to revive the ideas Bowie had originally for a 1984 Diamond Dogs musical theatre piece. Chances are that the bug to stage a musical is still there; in any event, Bowie has some definite ideas on the development of musical theatre, not dissimilar to his opinions on the relationship between rock 'n' roll and film. Referring to the production of the *Catherine Wheel* for which choreographer Twyla Tharp commissioned David Byrne's music, Bowie made the following comments:

> I think there's another format for music onstage. Usually you have a Twyla Tharp who pulls in people like David Byrne. But I think maybe if it started from the rock 'n' roll side, and it pulled in the Twyla Tharps, maybe something interesting could come of it. It's always from the intellectual side first, and I don't think it should be for rock 'n' roll. I think it should come from the meaty bit first, and then try to conceptualise it for the stage. [2]

By 1976 Bowie had already voiced some prophetic views about the relationship between rock music and cinema, saying that 'Some of the most talented actors around are in rock. I think a whole renaissance in film making is gonna come from rock. Not because of it, through it, despite it.' At that time, Bowie was doing some experiments with video (and shooting 16 millimeter film) and in retrospect it seems that his remarks describe quite well the results of the explosion in music video. While Bowie has personally bucked the temptation to make ever more lavish promos, musicians, Bowie aside, are indeed beginning to emerge as this generation's silver screen icons (Sting, Debbie Harry, Lou Reed, Mick Jagger and Bob Geldof have all made serious attempts to move into film acting, perhaps acknowledging that a career in rock 'n' roll can't last forever). More and more videos begin with a non-musical vignette before launching into the featured tune; the barriers between film and music videos are eroding. (With Michael Jackson's *Thriller* they have all but disappeared.) Music videos are not only helping to bring out the actor in a rocker, but providing the next generation of filmmakers with the breeding-ground that used to be the preserve of TV commercials, documentaries or fringe films.

Bowie has been way ahead of the pack in almost every respect. He's been co-directing his own videos (with David Mallet) as well as scripting and acting in them. While he talks about his career as a series of "planned accidents", the plans are what make the accidents possible, and to this end, he's used his exposure to "small-time" and "big-time" filmmaking to learn all aspects of the process from make-up to editing. In many ways it could be said that all that has gone before has been a planned preparation for another career in film. He's said that he 'will be a super filmmaker, and that should be enough to convince most people.

Bowie's choices of acting roles to date suggest a predilection towards serious film projects, with a 'message'. Indeed, his own video work combined the traits of documentary and art film, echoing his abhorance of Hollywood and the priorities of the commercial film industry. Bowie is as much a master of fantasy, costume and elaborate make-up (as well as a certain brand of cutting-edge humor) as the best of them, but he's unlikely ever to want to make a *Star Wars* Mark 2, however much he may envy George Lucas' empire. He may nevertheless become personally responsible for a major renaissance in film: a lot of dedicated Bowie fans are now designers, actors, dancers, editors, and his pervasive influence on the new generation of artists shouldn't be overlooked. His knack for making careers, in the same manner that he's given the likes of Toni Basil and Luther Vandross a chance to show their stuff, is unlikely to fade. High expectancy should insure that his first directorial film project will be shrouded in secrecy and chosen with infinite care.

On the music front, Bowie's current contract with EMI calls for four more albums, perhaps one of which will be a film score. As to the orientation of his next rock 'n' roll set proper, any opinion would be nothing more than a guess. While David Bowie's wide-ranging artistic output has had a profound cultural impact, his greatest talent has always been to demonstrate the capacity for growth and change. The superman who wants to 'make a nuisance in as many mediums as possible' is still at large, and as Nick Roeg once said of Bowie, 'he's just constantly expanding'. About all that can ever be said with certainty about David Bowie's future is that he never has and never will disappoint those who expect the unexpected.

POSTSCRIPT

I just took a Bowie Quiz and had to guess on the question of "How tall is David Bowie?" I answered 6'1" and the test maker claims he's 5'11", so be advised to take two inches off everything I've said about him...

A SURVEY OF COMMENTS ON BOWIE'S SEXUALITY

In an attempt to answer the frequently asked questions of 'Is he...?' or 'What is he?' I've compiled the following quotes on the subject of David Bowie's sexual orientation.

As you will see, the point is not really to answer the questions, but to point out that Bowie has rendered the questions irrelevant. Your reaction is what counts, that's the way it's always been with David Bowie (though his own ambivalence says a lot in itself...).

David Bowie speaking to Michael Watts of Melody Maker, Jan 1972:-

I'm gay, and I always have been, even when I was David Jones.

Mick Rock's thoughts during an interview with D.B., published June, 1972:-

Although he has a wife and child both of whom he loves very much, David is genuinely gay.

Bowie to Cameron Crowe in 1976:-

It's true — I'm a bisexual. But I can't deny that I've used that fact very well. I suppose it's the best thing that ever happened to me. Fun too. We'll talk all about it.

Bowie to Chris Charlesworth in 1976:-

Bisexual? Oh Lord no. Positively not. That was just a lie. They gave me that image so I stuck to it pretty well for a few years.

Bowie speaking with William Burroughs, 1974:-

I'm not sure whether it's me changing my mind or whether I lie a lot. It's somewhere between the two. I don't exactly lie, I change my mind all the time.

A FEW ADJECTIVES (AND NOUNS) THAT HAVE BEEN USED TO DESCRIBE DAVID BOWIE:-

Intelligent
Influential
Innovator
Imitator
In Control
Iceman (Bowie)
Impeccable
Insecure
Ambitious
Actor
Appropriator (Lou Reed)
Arch
Astute
A Liar (Bowie)
A Poet
A Man (Tony DeFries)
A Refugee
A Building
An Industry
Androgynous
AC/DC
Alien
A Generalist (Bowie)
A Genre (Various critics)
Aesthete
Athlete
A Tasteful Thief (Bowie)
Reptilian
Chameleon
Feral
Fey

Fashionable
Fascist
Faultless
Faggot
Philosopher

Creative
Camp
Calculated
Calculating
Casual
Cold
Contradictory
Cagey
Compulsive
Capricorn
Confident
Crooner

Product
Plain (Oshima)
Positive
Negative
Media Manipulator (Bowie)
Manipulated
Musician
Mime
Master Game Player

King
Queen
Prince

Singer
Savior (Iggy Pop)
Star
Superstar
Sincere
Suspect
Shrewd

Light Force (Fan)
Culture Figure
The Greatest

Dad (Zowie)
Director
Directed
Disciplined
Desultory

Genius
Elegant
Expatriot
Tax Exile

Workaholic
Warm
Vulnerable
Vainglorius
Remote

Best Friend (Iggy Po
Beautiful
Bowie-esque
(A critic who shall
remain nameless)

All of the above (Kate Lynch, NYC, 1984.)

173

A BOWIE TIMELINE, INC.
DISCOGRAPHY*

Jan 8, 1947	David Robert Jones was born.
Sept 12, 1947	Haywood Jones and Margaret Mary Burns (David's parents) were married.
1947-1955	David lived at 40, Stansfield Road, Brixton, South London, with his parents and step-brother Terry.
1955-1957	David and Terry Jones lived with a paternal uncle in Doncaster, Yorkshire.
1957	The brothers returned to London and a new home at 4, Plaistow Grove in Bromley.
1959	David got his first instrument, a saxophone, and soon began lessons with Ronnie Ross.
Dec 1962	Sax player David Jones brought the house down in one of his first public appearances, playing with George and the Dragons at the Bromley Tech Christmas Pageant.
1962-1963	Near the time of the Pageant David sustained an injury that caused permanent damage to his left eye. At that time he was also playing with various groups, including The Konrads and The Hooker Brothers.
Spring 1963	David left Bromley Tech with O-levels in art and woodwork, and soon began working as a "junior visualizer" in an ad agency, work which lasted for six months.
1964	David was playing with a band called The King Bees with Leslie Conn as their manager. They were signed to Vocalion-Pop.
June 1964*	*Liza Jane/Louie Louie Go Home* DAVIE JONES WITH THE KING BEES Vocalion-Pop V.9221
Late 1964	Bowie found a new band, The Mannish Boys, and a new manager, Ralph Horton. They were signed to Parlophone.
March 1965*	*I Pity The Fool/Take My Tip* THE MANNISH BOYS Parlophone R. 5250
Spring 1965	Bowie again changed bands; he was then playing with The Lower Third.
August 1965*	*You've Got A Habit Of Leaving/Baby Loves That Way* DAVY JONES AND THE LOWER THIRD Parlophone R. 5315
Late 1965	David Jones became David Bowie.
Jan 1966*	*Can't Help Thinking About Me/And I Say To Myself* DAVID BOWIE AND THE LOWER THIRD Pye 7N 17079

April 1966	Kenneth Pitt became David's new manager, and David went solo while still under contract to Pye Records.
April 1966*	*Do Anything You Say/Good Morning Girl* Pye 7N 17079
·August 1966*	*Dig Everything/I'm Not Losing Sleep* Pye 7N 17157
Summer 1966	David was released from his contract with Pye and signed to a new label called Deram.
Dec 1966*	*Rubber Band/London Boys* Deram DM107
April 1967*	*The Laughing Gnome/The Gospel According To Tony Day* Deram DM.123
June 1967*	*DAVID BOWIE* (LP) Deram DML.1007
July 1967*	*Love You Till Tuesday/Did You Ever Have A Dream* Deram DM.135
1968	David formed his own mime troupe called Feathers, as well as his own "arts lab", and was featured in a film produced by Ken Pitt for which he wrote a song called *Space Oddity*.
1969	David was signed to Philips/Mercury. He also met and began to live with Mary Angela Barnett.
July 11, 1969*	*Space Oddity/Wild Eyed Boy From Freecloud* Philips BFI 801
July 1969	David, Angie and Ken Pitt traveled to the Italian and Maltese Song Festivals.
August 5, 1969	David's father died of lobar pneumonia.
Fall 1969	David took part in a Humble Pie tour to promote his upcoming album.
Nov 1969*	*DAVID BOWIE* (LP) Philips SBL 7912
Late 1969	David and Angie moved to Haddon Hall. During a Christmas separation they decided to marry.
Feb 1970	David announced the formation of a band called Hype.
March 1970*	*The Prettiest Star/Conversation Piece* Mercury MF. 1135
Mar 20, 1970	David and Angie were married.
March 1970*	*THE WORLD OF DAVID BOWIE* (LP) Decca (S)PA.58 (A compilation f David's Deram releases)
Spring 1970	Tony De Fries became David's new manager.
June 1970*	*Memory Of A Free Festival Part 1/Memory Of A Free Festival Part 2* Mercury 6052 026
Jan 1971*	*Holy Holy/Black Country Rock* Mercury 6052 049
April 1971*	*THE MAN WHO SOLD THE WORLD* (LP) Mercury 6338041
Spring 1971	David made his first trip to the U.S., promoting his recent album.

June 1971	Zowie Duncan Heywood Bowie was born to David and Angela Bowie.
Summer 1971	De Fries lands Bowie a recording contract with RCA on the strength of what will be called *Hunky Dory*, and work began on the Ziggy Stardust project.
Dec 1971*	*HUNKY DORY* (LP) RCA SF8244
Jan 1972*	*Changes/Andy Warhol* RCA 2160
Jan 22, 1972	An interview with Bowie appears in Melody Maker in which he "admitted" that he was gay. Ziggy Tour plans and rehearsals were underway while David became England's favorite "outrage".
April, 1972	*Starman/Suffragette City* RCA 2199
April, 1972	The Ziggy Tour previewed in parts of the U.K.
June 1972*	*THE RISE AND FALL OF ZIGGY STARDUST AND THE SPIDERS OF MARS* (LP) RCA SF 8287
Summer 1972	Bowie was busy performing and revamping his own shows, in key London appearances, as well as producing albums for Mott The Hoople and Lou Reed.
June 8, 1972	Following an appearance at a Save The Whale concert Bowie was unanimously declared a "star" by the pop press; this was also the start of a year of almost constant touring, punctuated by the release of *Aladdin Sane* and Bowie's adoption of this new persona.
Sept 1972*	*John, I'm Only Dancing/Hang On To Yourself* RCA 2263
Sept 1972	Bowie began the U.S. Ziggy Tour.
Oct 1972*	*Do Anything You Say, I Dig Everything/Can't Help Thinking About Me, I'm Not Losing Sleep* Pye 7NX8002
Nov 1972*	*THE MAN WHO SOLD THE WORLD* (LP) RCA LSP. 4813 (Re-release of the previous Mercury album)
Nov 1972*	*SPACE ODDITY* (LP) RCA LSP. 4813 (Re-release of the Philips and/or Mercury albums featuring *Space Oddity*)
Nov 1972*	*The Jean Genie/Ziggy Stardust* RCA 2302
Dec 1972	David returned to England to complete the *Aladdin Sane* album and reworked the show before returning to the U.S. and Japan.
April 1973*	*Drive-In Saturday/Around And Around* RCA 2352
April 1973*	*ALADDIN SANE* (LP) RCA RS 1001
June 1973*	*Life On Mars/The Man Who Sold The World* RCA 2316
June 3, 1973	Following a concert at the Hammersmith Odeon Bowie announced that the show was his "last".
June 1973	Bowie and part of his band traveled to France for work on *Pin-Ups* and *Diamond Dogs*.

Sept 1973*	*Sorrow/Amsterdam* RCA 2424
Sept 1973*	*The Laughing Gnome/The Gospel According To Tony Day* Deram DM123
Oct 1973*	*PIN-UPS* (LP) RCA RS 1003
April 1974*	*DIAMOND DOGS* (LP) RCA APL1.0576
April 1974*	*Rock 'n' Roll Suicide/Quicksand* RCA LPBO 5021
June 1974*	*Diamond Dogs/Holy Holy* RCA APB0 0923
Summer 1974	The Diamond Dogs Tour got underway in Canada and traveled through the U.S, breaking temporarily in NYC for work on new album. *David Live* was recorded during some of the early dates.
Sept 1974*	*Knock On Wood/Panic In Detroit* RCA 2466
Oct 1974*	*DAVID LIVE* (LP) RCA APL2. 0771
1975	This was the year Bowie later claimed he "forgot".
Jan 1975	An impromptu recording session with John Lennon resulted in the song *Fame* and called for a remastering of the *Young Americans* LP.
Feb 1975*	*Young Americans/Suffragette City* RCA 2523
March 1975*	*YOUNG AMERICANS* (LP) RCA RS.1006
Spring 1975	Bowie was on location in New Mexico and Arizona for the filming of *The Man Who Fell To Earth*, while otherwise calling L.A. home.
May 1975*	*London Boys/Love You Till Tuesday* Decca F. 13579
May 1975*	*IMAGES* (LP) Deram DPA 3017/3018
August 1975*	*Fame/Right* RCA 2579
Sept 1975*	*Space Oddity/Changes* RCA 2593
Nov 1975*	*Golden Years/Can You Hear Me* RCA 2640
Jan 1976	Bowie left L.A. for his "White Light Tour" and he settled in Berlin shortly after the tour ended.
Jan 1976*	*STATION TO STATION* (LP) RCA APLI-1327
April 1976*	*TVC-15/We Are The Dead* RCA 2682
May 1976*	*CHANGES ONE BOWIE* (LP) RCA RS. 1055
July 1976	*Suffragette City/Stay* RCA 2726
Summer 1976	Bowie was living in the Neukoïln section of Berlin, traveling in Eastern Europe and enjoying the companionship and collaboration of Brian Eno and Iggy Pop.
Jan 1977*	*LOW* (LP) RCA PL. 12030
Feb 1977*	*Sound And Vision/A New Career In A New Town* RCA PB. 0905

Spring 1977	Bowie played piano on Iggy Pop's follow-up tour to *The Idiot*. For this occasion he resumed flying.
June 1977*	*Be My Wife/Speed Of Life* RCA PB. 1017
Sept 1977*	*"Heroes"/V-2 Schneider* RCA PB. 1121
Oct 1977*	*"HEROES"* (LP) RCA PL. 12522
Winter '77-'78	Bowie was on location for the filming of *Just A Gigolo*.
Jan 1978*	*Beauty And The Beast/Sense Of Doubt* RCA PB. 1190
March 1978	Bowie embarked on another tour of the US and Europe, with a break in May during which *Peter And The Wolf* was recorded. Another live recording was done and released as *Stage*.
May 1978*	*PETER AND THE WOLF* (LP) DAVID BOWIE WITH EUGENE ORMANDY AND THE PHILADELPHIA ORCHESTRA RCA Red Seal RL-12743
Sept 1978*	*Liza Jane/Louie Louie Go Home* DAVIE JONES WITH THE KING BEES Decca F. 13807
Sept 1978*	*STAGE* (LP) RCA PL. 02913/(2)
Nov 1978*	*Breaking Glass/Art Decade* RCA BOW1
1979	Now living and working in Switzerland, Bowie also took time to travel to Africa and Asia. From this time on there would always be work on at least two video tapes to accompany each LP release.
March 1979*	*I Pity The Fool, Take My Tip/You've Got A Habit Of Leaving, Baby Loves That Way* THE MANNISH BOYS/DAVY JONES & THE LOWER THIRD EMI Nut EP EMI.2925
April 1979*	*Boys Kept Swinging/Fantastic Voyage* RCA BOW 2
May 1979*	*LODGER* (LP) RCA BOW LP.1
June 1979*	*D.J./Repetition* RCA BOW.3
Late 1979	David's divorce from Angie became final; another recording session was under way and discussion began about Bowie performing in *The Elephant Man*.
Dec 1979*	*John I'm Only Dancing (Again) (1975)/John I'm Only Dancing (1972)* RCA BOW.4
Feb 1980*	*Alabama Song/Space Oddity* RCA BOW.5
Spring 1980	Bowie started rehearsals for the part of the Elephant Man.
Aug 1980	*Ashes To Ashes/Move On* RCA BOW.6
Sept 1980	Bowie opened in *The Elephant Man* on Broadway, to rave reviews.
Sept 1980*	*SCARY MONSTERS (AND SUPER CREEPS)* (LP) RCA BOW LP2

Oct 1980*	*Fashion/Scream Like A Baby* RCA BOW T.7
Dec 1980*	*THE BEST OF BOWIE* (LP) K-Tel NE.1111
Jan 1981*	*Scary Monsters (And Super Creeps)/Because You're Young* RCA BOW 8
1981	While keeping out of the public eye, Bowie was consistently involved in film and video projects. He appeared as himself (in performance) in the film *Christine F*, and was featured in a BBC production of Bertold Brecht's *Baal*.
May 1982	*BAAL* (Soundtrack) (LP) RCA CPLI 4346
1982	Bowie's major projects in '82 were all film related, including writing lyrics and singing the theme song to *Cat People*, playing the male lead in *The Hunger*, and playing the role of Celliers in Nagisa Oshima's *Merry Christmas Mr. Lawrence*. *The Hunger* and *Merry Christmas* were both released in 1983.
Oct 1982*	*CHANGES TWO BOWIE* (LP) RCA AFLI 4202
Fall 1982	Bowie was in the process of negotiating a recording contract with EMI.
Jan 1983	Bowie was "officially" signed to EMI, with the simultaneous announcement of an upcoming LP and world tour.
March 1983*	*Let's Dance/Cat People (Putting Out Fire)* EMI B8158
April 1983*	*LET'S DANCE* (LP) EMI S-17093
May 1983*	Bowie commenced his "Serious Moonlight Tour" which lasted six months moving through Europe, Canada, the U.S., Japan and Australia.
June 1983*	*China Girl/Shake It* EMI B8165
June 1983*	*GOLDEN YEARS* (LP) RCA AFL.1 4792
August 1983*	*Modern Love/Modern Love (Live Version)* EMI B8177
Oct 1983*	*ZIGGY STARDUST, THE MOTION PICTURE* (LP) RCA CPL2 4862
Nov 1983	RCA releases a single from the "Ziggy" soundtrack LP of Lou Reed's *White Light/White Heat* as performed by Ziggy and The Spiders during their last show.
Jan 1984	The Ziggy Stardust movie is finally released.
May 1984	RCA releases a compilation album, *FAME AND FASHION*.

SOURCE NOTES

Chapter 1

1 **The (London) Times Of London,**
January 8, 1947
2 **Rolling Stone** (Mick Rock), June 8,
1972; p.14
3 **David Bowie Black Book**, Miles, p.1
London: Omnibus Press, 1980
4 **Musician** (Timothy White), May,
1983 (No.55); p.57
5 **The David Bowie Story**, George
Tremlett, p.17 New York: Warner
Paperback Library, 1975
6 **Face** (David Thomas), Spring, 1983,
p.18
7 **The David Bowie Story**, George
Tremlett.
8 **Musician**, May 1983, p.9
9 **Playboy** (Cameron Crowe), Vol.23,
No.9, 1976; p.58

Chapter 2

1 **Musician**, May 1983, p.58
2 **Bowie, An Illustrated Record**, Roy
Carr and Charles Shaar Murray,
p.120 New York: Avon Books, 1981
3 **David Bowie Black Book**, p.10
4 **The David Bowie Story** p.30
5 **Ibid.**, p.23

Chapter 3

1 **The David Bowie Story**, p.28
2 **Ibid.**, p.29
3 **David Bowie Profile**, Chris
Charlesworth, p.11 London:
Proteus Books, 1981
4 **Melody Maker**, February 26, 1966
5 **Ibid** 6 **Musician**, May 1983, p.59
7 **Ibid.**, p.59

Chapter 4

1 **Melody Maker**, October 11, 1965
2 **Melody Maker**, October 11, 1965
3 **Playboy**, Vol.23, No.9, p.68
4 **David Bowie Black Book**, p.27
5 **Musician**, May 1983, p.59

Chapter 5

1 **The David Bowie Story**, p.94
2 **Melody Maker**, March 28, 1970
3 **Melody Maker**, (article entitled
'Mainman') Date Unknown
4 **David Bowie Black Book**, p.38
5 **The David Bowie Story**, p.105
6 **Ibid.**, p.107
7 **David Bowie Black Book**, p.54
8 **Rolling Stone**, (John Mendelsohn),
April 1, 1971, p.18

Chapter 6

1 **Melody Maker** ('Mainman' article)
2 **Rolling Stone**, June 8, 1972, p.14
3 **Ibid.**, p.14

Chapter 7

1 **Melody Maker**, January 22, 1972,
p.19
2 **Ibid.**, p.19
3 **Elvis**, Albert Goldman, p.93 New
York: Avon Books, 1981
4 **Ibid.**, p.98
5 **Bowie, An Illustrated Record**, p.45
6 **Ibid.**, p.48
7 **The David Bowie Story**, p.131
8 **Rolling Stone**, June 8, 1972, p.14
9 **Rolling Stone**, (Tim Ferris),
November 9, 1972 (No.121), p.42
10 **David Bowie Black Book**, p.63
11 **Ibid.**, p.63

Chapter 8

1 **David Bowie Black Book**, p.68
2 **Bowie, An Illustrated Record**, p.61

Chapter 9

1 **David Bowie Black Book**, p.77
2 **Ibid.**, p.80
3 **Bowie, An Illustrated Record**, p.66
4 **David Bowie Black Book**, p.80

Chapter 10

1 **Musician**, May 1983, p.122
2 **Ibid.**, p.60
3 **Playboy**, Vol.23 No.9, p.74

Chapter 11

1 **Musician**, May 1983, p.60
2 **Rolling Stone**, (Teri Morris), March 25, 1976, p.60
3 **David Bowie Profile**, p.50
4 **David Bowie Black Rock**, p.93
5 **Playboy**, Vol.23 No.9, p.64
6 **Ibid.**, p.68

Chapter 12

1 **David Bowie Black Book**, p.103
2 **Musician**, May 1983, p.64
3 **Ibid.**, p.62
4 **David Bowie Profile**, p.51
5 **Melody Maker**, February 18, 1978, p.38
6 **Rolling Stones** (Bart Testa), January 12, 1978, p.38

Chapter 13

1 **Melody Maker**, February 18, 1976
2 **The Portable Nietzsche**, Walter Kaufman, ed., p.190 New York: The Viking Press, 1968

Chapter 14

1 **Rolling Stone**, November 13, 1980, p.11
2 **A-Z Of Rock Guitarists**, Chris Charlesworth, p.6 London: Proteus Books, 1982
3 **Rolling Stone**, November 13, 1980, p.11
4 **Ibid.**, p.11

Chapter 15

1 **American Film** (Tadao Sato), September 1983, p.32
2 **Record** (J. D. Considine), May 1983, p.12
3 **Musician**, May 1983, p.64
4 **Record**, May 1983, p.12
5 **Rolling Stone**, (Kurt Loder), No.395 May 12, 1983, p.28

Chapter 16

1 **Rolling Stone**, No. 395 May 12, 1983, p.25
2 **Ibid.**, p.28

THE BEST IN ROCK 'N' ROLL READING
Bestselling rock references

A-Z OF ROCK SINGERS
by John Tobler

The third volume in the highly acclaimed A-Z of Rock reference series, this book turns the spotlight onto the greatest singers in the first 25 years of rock 'n' roll. Over 250 singers whose distinctive styles, songs and personalities stand out as landmarks of rock history are profiled. Presented in encyclopedic form, each entry contains career background, an assessment of the singer's best work and selected discographies.

128 pages: 60 black/white photos. 8 pages of colour. Selected discographies.
ISBN: 0 86276 139 5 p/b

A-Z OF ROCK GUITARISTS
by Chris Charlesworth

A companion in the A-Z of Rock reference series, this book brings together the techniques and styles, personalities, classic cuts and performances of over 200 of the world's greatest rock guitarists and bass players.

128 pages: 120 black/white photos. 8 pages of colour. Index and select discographies.
ISBN: 0 86276 080 1 p/b

A-Z OF ROCK DRUMMERS
by Harry Shapiro

Part of the popular A-Z of Rock reference series, this book focuses on the over 200 drummers who have given the beat to rock 'n' roll from the sixties to the present, from the legendary Ginger Baker to Stewart Copeland of the Police.

128 pages: 120 black/white photos and 8 pages of colour. Index and select discographies.
ISBN: 0 86276 084 4 p/b

ROCK HERITAGE: THE SIXTIES
by Chris Charlesworth

The first volume in a trilogy on the history of rock 'n' roll, this book features a 20,000-word commentary on international developments of the most tumultuous decade in pop music, portraits of the musicians, songwriters and industry personalities in the vanguard of the rock revolution, a ten-year chronology, and a comprehensive survey of the charts, concerts, festivals and songs that were the sixties.

160 pages: 70 black/white photos. 16 pages colour. Select discography.
ISBN: 0 86276 131 X p/b

THE PERFECT COLLECTION
Edited by Tom Hibbert

The ultimate rock list book – 200 albums to have on a desert island.

96 pages: 100 black/white photos.
ISBN: 0 86276 105 0 p/b

RARE RECORDS
by Tom Hibbert

In-depth information on little known masterpieces and the record collecting trade. A must for all collectors.

128 pages: 50 colour and black/white photos.
ISBN: 0 86276 047 X p/b

THE BEST IN ROCK 'N' ROLL READING
Definitive career studies

DAVID BOWIE: A ROCK 'N' ROLL ODYSSEY
by Kate Lynch

The world has seen many faces of David Bowie – Ziggy Stardust and Aladin Sane, musician and actor, husband, playboy, and single parent. The man who claims he is the real David Bowie released LET'S DANCE in 1983, an album that went platinum with two gold singles and a sold-out world tour to support it. Kate Lynch's biography traces the intricate paths of David Bowie, and could not be better timed to coincide with peak interest in the man and the mystique.

160 pages: 24 pages of black/white and colour photos. Complete discography, filmography and theatre career details.
ISBN: 0 86276 221 9 p/b

PETE TOWNSHEND
by Chris Charlesworth

The first full-length biography of the leader of the Who offers a unique behind-the-scenes look at the music of one of the most talented, flamboyant and influential characters in popular music. It includes previously unpublished information about Townshend's family background, the early days of The Who, and a synopsis of his solo career. Much is being written on this band, who have just completed their farewell tour and album, and Chris Charlesworth's biography will take an important place as an honest and insightful portrait of this legendary rock star.

160 pages: 24 pages of rare photographs. Full group and solo discographies.
ISBN: 0 96276 245 6 p/b

BLOOD ON THE TRACKS: THE STORY OF BOB DYLAN
by Chris Rowley

The rock poet of the sixties is still singing to us in the eighties – his newest release, INFIDELS, has drawn the now-standard controversial reaction. He spoke for an entire generation as he sang for peace – to whom does he speak as he sings for salvation? This detailed study traces the complicated paths of this important singer/songwriter.

160 pages: 50 black/white photos. 8 pages colour. Complete discography.
ISBN: 0 86276 127 1 p/b

THE BEST IN ROCK 'N' ROLL READING
Definitive career studies

SLOWHAND: THE STORY OF ERIC CLAPTON
by Harry Shapiro

In many ways the story of Eric Clapton is the story of rock since the early sixties. Dubbed Slowhand during his stint with John Mayall's Bluesbreakers, he has drifted through many careers over two decades – fronting supergroups, playing session work, turning up as a backing musician for an old friend. Always he has carried the reputation of being the world's greatest blue/rock guitarist uneasily. His recent solo release, MONEY AND CIGARETTES, won great acclaim. This is the first full-length biography on this enigmatic rock star.

160 pages: includes 24 pages of black/white photos. Complete discography.
ISBN 0 86276 148 4 p/b

MARVIN GAYE
by Sharon Davis

The roster of Marvin Gaye hits over 20 years reads like the soul music Hall of Fame. Songs like CAN I GET A WITNESS, HOW SWEET IT IS, AIN'T THAT PECULIAR have all become soul standards; duets like YOU'RE ALL I NEED TO GET BY and AIN'T NO MOUNTAIN HIGH ENOUGH are classics. Marvin Gaye has made a dramatic comeback with SEXUAL HEALING, a single that went gold, and the platinum album MIDNIGHT LOVE. He is still the master of moody, midnight soul.

128 pages: 40 black/white photos. 8 pages of colour. Complete discography.
ISBN: 0 86276 193 X p/b

NEIL YOUNG
by Johnny Rogan

Johnny Rogan's bestselling biography of one of rock's most enigmatic and most popular performer/songwriters traces Neil Young's long and varied career from his days with Buffalo Springfield and his early solo work to mature classics like the albums AFTER THE GOLDRUSH and RUST NEVER SLEEPS, his brief collaboration with Crosby, Stills and Nash, and his continually adventurous music of the late seventies and eighties.

170 pages: 16 page black/white section. Complete discography.
ISBN: 0 86276 012 7 p/b